The EVERYTHING® Homebuilding Book

Dear Reader:

I grew up in a log cabin that my father built. It was perfectly situated in a wooded area, giving my outdoorsy parents the opportunity every day to enjoy the essence of nature. My sisters and I spent our days traipsing through the woods and running through the pastures. Our evenings were spent in the comfortable and cozy cabin, our castle. My parents had a dream for their home and their family. It took a lot of courage, planning, sweat, and frustration, but they made that dream come true. And I wouldn't have wanted it any other way.

You, too, can make your dreams for your home and family come true. It will require a lot of time, thought, and hard work, but it can be done. As in any other great adventure, the first step in your homebuilding endeavor is to acquire knowledge. Are you ready to take that first step? Then read on.

Happy homebuilding!

Lesley Bolton

Mark Schmidt

The EVERYTHING® Series

Editorial

Publishing Director	Gary M. Krebs
Managing Editor	Kate McBride
Copy Chief	Laura MacLaughlin
Acquisitions Editor	Eric M. Hall
Production Editor	Jamie Wielgus

Production

Production Director	Susan Beale
Production Manager	Michelle Roy Kelly
Series Designers	Daria Perreault
	Colleen Cunningham
Cover Design	Paul Beatrice
	Frank Rivera
Layout and Graphics	Colleen Cunningham
	Rachael Eiben
	Michelle Roy Kelly
	John Paulhus
	Daria Perreault
	Erin Ring
Series Cover Artist	Barry Littmann
Interior Illustrator	Argosy Publishing

Visit the entire Everything® Series at everything.com

THE

EVERYTHING®

HOMEBUILDING
BOOK

Build your dream home

Lesley Bolton with Mark Schmitt

Adams Media
Avon, Massachusetts

An Everything® Series Book.
Everything® and everything.com® are registered trademarks of F+W Publications, Inc.

Published by Adams Media, an F+W Publications Company
57 Littlefield Street, Avon, MA 02322 U.S.A.
www.adamsmedia.com

ISBN: 1-59337-037-7
Printed in the United States of America.

J I H G F E D C B

Library of Congress Cataloging-in-Publication Data
Bolton, Lesley.
The everything homebuilding book / Lesley Bolton with Mark Schmitt.
p.   cm.
(An everything series book)
ISBN 1-59337-037-7
1. House construction. I. Schmitt, Mark. II. Title. III. Series:
Everything series.

TH4811.B623 2004
690'.837–dc22

2003021800

This publication is designed to provide accurate and authoritative information with regard to the subject matter covered. It is sold with the understanding that the publisher is not engaged in rendering legal, accounting, or other professional advice. If legal advice or other expert assistance is required, the services of a competent professional person should be sought.
—From a *Declaration of Principles* jointly adopted by a Committee of the American Bar Association and a Committee of Publishers and Associations

Readers are urged to take all appropriate precautions when undertaking any homebuilding task. Always read and follow instructions and safety warnings for all tools and materials, and call in a professional if necessary. Although every effort has been made to provide the best possible information in this book, neither the publisher nor the author are responsible for accidents, injuries, or damage incurred as a result of actions undertaken by readers. This book is not a substitute for professional services.

Many of the designations used by manufacturers and sellers to distinguish their products are claimed as trademarks. Where those designations appear in this book and Adams Media was aware of a trademark claim, the designations have been printed with initial capital letters.

Please note that, while for consistency reasons, the pronoun *he* is used throughout this book, we fully recognize that homebuilding is an activity in which both women and men can participate.

This book is available at quantity discounts for bulk purchases.
For information, call 1-800-872-5627.

Contents

Acknowledgments

I'd like to thank Mark Schmitt for sharing his knowledge and expertise throughout the writing of this book. Special thanks also go to Eric Tamewitz, house designer extraordinaire and good friend, whose contributions made this book possible.

Top Ten Benefits
of Building Your Own Home

1. You will save money.

2. The home will be tailored to your own personal wants and needs.

3. You can build a home as unconventional and unique as you'd like.

4. You can take advantage of the latest technology to make your home more energy efficient than houses built just a few years ago.

5. You get to choose the exact location of your home.

6. You maintain control of the entire project and get to set standards of quality.

7. You will derive great personal satisfaction from completing such an important project.

8. You can build your home to be more structurally sound than the minimal requirements called for in building codes.

9. You will gain invaluable experience for any future building projects.

10. You can build your house with an eye toward increasing its future resale value and turning a profit.

Introduction

▶SO YOU'RE THINKING of building your own home. Congratulate yourself on working up the courage to take the first steps in making your dream a reality. Such an endeavor can be extremely intimidating and overwhelming. But it can also be one of the most rewarding projects you will ever take on. You and your family will derive years of pleasure from a home that is individually tailored to your needs and wants—well worth the sweat, emotion, time, and money you will invest. Well, for most people it is. Of course, that is a decision you will have to make for yourself.

You aren't alone out there. Every year, more than 100,000 people build their own new homes. That means that more than 100,000 individuals just like you made a conscious decision to put their doubts and excuses aside to step up to the challenge of homebuilding. Those who are most successful put a lot of time into planning and educating themselves for the project before beginning work. That's where this book comes in.

The Everything® Homebuilding Book is designed to give you a real-world look at the advantages, challenges, joys, and frustrations of building your own home. As you will soon learn, there are several aspects and phases of homebuilding. This book will walk you through each step, including financing the project, deciding on a style of house and the location, designing the house to accommodate the needs of your family, getting the proper permits, and actually building the house—everything it takes to turn your house into your *home*.

This book will also show you how to participate in the building of your home—even if you have never picked up a hammer in your life. For instance, you can save money by acting as your own general contractor, which basically requires an ability to communicate with and manage others and balance a checkbook. If you have no formal construction experience but you'd still like to take a more active role in the building process, you can still strap on the tool belt. Most people have the common sense and basic skills needed to do some of the construction work. Whether you want to do the work yourself or hire it out, you will find the information you need regarding the phases of construction.

You must have three things to be a successful homebuilder: courage, determination, and knowledge. Courage will enable you to step up and begin your endeavor. Determination will get you through the rough spots and help you to keep your goal in mind throughout the process. Knowledge is your source of power. It will allow you to properly design and build the house that is best suited for you and your family. With these three things on your side, you *can* build your own home.

Deciding to build your own home is one of the biggest commitments you will ever make. It requires a lot of time, thought, and planning on your part. It is recommended that you read this book cover to cover before beginning your homebuilding endeavor so that you are well-informed and armed with the knowledge needed to make wise and realistic decisions. After weighing all the pros and cons, it's quite likely that you will come to see that your dream can and should be a reality. Let *The Everything® Homebuilding Book* be your guide to the intimidating but rewarding and conquerable world of homebuilding.

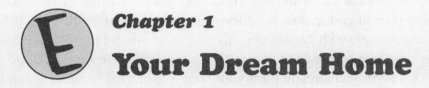

Chapter 1

Your Dream Home

Building a home isn't a project you should take lightly. Before you decide to make the leap, you'll need to first consider several things. This chapter will help you get started on the extensive thought process that is necessary for getting ready to build a home.

Reasons to Build Your Own Home

For most people, making the decision to build a house is a difficult one. It certainly requires a lot of thought and preparation. To help you get started in making that decision, the first thing you must do is explore your reasons for wanting to build a house. This might sound trite, but your reasons are actually very important. Not only will they help you make your final decision, but they will also help you get through the whole process with confidence. Your reasons will be there to fall back on any time you start asking yourself, "What have I gotten myself into?"

It's likely you already have your own reasons for wanting to build your own home. Perhaps you've been studying the real estate ads for years, with an entire community of real estate agents at your beck and call, but still you simply cannot find anything close to that picture in your head of the perfect house. Maybe your reason for wanting to build is simply that you can. Maybe you're still searching for the validation you need to convince yourself (and others) that your dream is not only possible but also a good idea. If so, take a look at some of the common reasons people have for building their own homes.

To Save Money

One of the top reasons many people build their own homes is to save money. You can find any number of books and articles claiming that you can save 25 percent or more by building your own home. While it is quite possible that you will save money this way, the amount you save depends on how much work you do yourself and the amount of planning and preparation you put into the job. This can be anything from conducting extensive research to picking up a hammer and pounding nails. Of course, the total cost of your home will vary widely according to the kind of home, the number and type of extra features, and the location you choose.

FACT

You'll find many homebuilding articles and books that say the best way to save money is to be your own general contractor. Chapter 2 discusses the role of a general contractor and helps you explore whether this is a route you would like to take.

The amount of money you save is in direct relation to the amount of work you do. Your time and efforts aren't free. Therefore, some people would argue that you really aren't saving anything since you will be putting in a lot of time and work yourself. On the flip side of that, you may enjoy doing some of the work yourself, and, therefore, the money you save will be a result of a pleasurable experience instead of a chore. This book is full of money-saving tips and strategies. For right now, just know that it is possible to save some money by building compared to buying.

To Make a Profit

Some people choose to build their first home in anticipation of being able to build a second dream home. These people plan to build a house that will thrive in the future real estate market. They have done extensive research and found an area that will be a prime location and plan to include features—such as designing for energy efficiency or including a Jacuzzi bathtub—that will make the home a hot item and increase its resale value.

These people are employing money-saving techniques to get more out of their homes. In addition, they are gaining the experience and know-how needed to make the process easier during their second, and more important, project. This isn't to say that your first home will not turn out the way you want it to, but let's face it: The more experience you have, the better off you are.

To Suit Your Home to Its Owners

Not everyone is looking for exactly the same thing in a house. If that were the case, the world's streets would be lined with cookie-cutter homes. Remember, variety is the spice of life! A feature you think you absolutely cannot live without may be extraneous to someone else. Many people build so they can design the home that best suits their needs and wants.

By building your own home, you will no longer have to "put up with" the small closets or low ceilings of a home that's already built. You have the power to personalize your home—even create that dream home you've always longed for.

Your lifestyle, needs, and personal taste are all factors in the decisions you make when building a home. A family with seven children would likely build a different home than a retired couple. A couple that entertains with regular dinner parties may care a lot about their dining room, while a couple that despises cooking and eats out on a regular basis may forgo the dining room altogether in favor of a simple eat-in kitchen.

Personal Satisfaction

Building your own home takes a lot of work. This is true regardless of whether you choose to dirty your own hands with the construction work or to hire someone to do it for you. This labor comes with its own perks, though—according to some people, the biggest is the personal satisfaction that comes from completing such a project. As you begin to learn more about the process of building a home, you will likely come to have a greater respect for the people who do this work every day. To take on such an endeavor yourself will make your heart swell with pride—not to mention the way you'll feel when you actually complete it. Making the decisions and designs that slowly manifest themselves into an actual dwelling, one where your family creates precious memories, certainly entitles you to bragging rights. For most people this will not just be a house, it will be their *home*.

Types of Houses

Once you are convinced that building a home is the right path for you, it's time to think about what type of home you want. There are many questions for you to consider. Do you want a single-story or a two-story home? What kind of materials do you want to use in construction? Do you want a more modern look, or would you prefer to copy a style from another time period? Do you want your home to have an urban or rustic look? As you ponder these questions, let's take a look at some of your options.

Onsite or Offsite Building

When most people think of homebuilding, they think of the actual building of a house on a piece of land, complete with sweaty construction workers. However, this isn't your only option. You can, of course, build your house at the site, but you can also have it built elsewhere and brought in. Surely you've seen those "wide load" trucks on the highway, hauling a part of a house. That part is brought in along with many others, and the house is put together at the site. Other types of offsite buildings are available in kits that are assembled at the site. The kits range widely in what they include, so be sure to do your homework if this idea appeals to you!

If you choose to go with a home that is built offsite, make sure you do your homework. Thoroughly research any company you are considering purchasing from. If possible, speak with people who have been customers. And make sure the home meets the specifications of local codes.

ALERT!

The type of lot you purchase will affect the style and design of your home, so it's a good idea to first purchase or locate your building site before deciding on a type of house. For instance, you wouldn't be able to build a 70-foot ranch-style house on a 60-foot lot.

Both the onsite and offsite options have their own sets of advantages and disadvantages. Onsite building allows you to monitor all aspects of construction as well as make changes (though costly) throughout the building process. However, it takes a lot of work and time to construct such a home. Offsite building is usually a cheaper and faster alternative. However, as these are factory-built homes, you are limited in the designs you can choose from. Be sure to explore all your options before settling on a construction type.

Materials

Straw, sticks, or brick? Learn from the three little pigs, and thoroughly research your building materials. These days, you have a wide variety to choose from. You can build a home using logs, laminated timber, brick, adobe, stucco, vinyl siding, or even straw bales. As you do your research, you will probably find more building material possibilities. You can certainly choose to be as creative as you like and to use an innovative solution—such as solar paneling, for instance—but remember that your choice involves the cost of your materials as well as what you think is aesthetically pleasing.

Styles

You have a plethora of house styles available to you. Take a long drive, and note all the different styles you come across. Does any one jump out at you in particular? Perhaps you find something similar to what you had in mind except for a few things you'd change here and there. This is where your creativity comes into play. In Chapter 5, you will learn the basics of designing your home; still, to keep those creative juices flowing, it's a good idea to have a few styles in mind before you reach that point.

You may want to consider the specific features of your home site when choosing a style for your house. For instance, if you are building in a wooded and secluded area, you may want to go with a more rustic style home. Or if you are building in or near a historic district, you may want your home's style to reflect a certain time period.

There are simply too many styles of homes to mention here, but you can always visit the Internet or take a look through architecture magazines and books to get more ideas. Looking beyond what you can see all around you, remember that you don't have to settle on an already established style—you can always create your own! (Just as long as you also keep resale value in mind for the style of home you choose.) For right now, think of whether you want a modern home, a rustic home, or a home in a style that is copied from a different time period. Narrowing it down that way will help you start thinking in the right direction.

Be Realistic

If your idea of a dream home is a castle, complete with a moat, set on a large estate in the middle of a large city (convenience, after all, is important to you), then it might be time for you to get your head out of the clouds and take a course in Real World Living 101. The point is that you need to be realistic. If you have only one child and do not plan to have any more, it's a little over the top to plan on an eight-bedroom home. While you definitely want your house to reflect your personal taste, you just as certainly want to build a house that will function well as your home.

Money Matters

Many people begin their homebuilding endeavor with grandiose designs and schemes in mind. They want their homes to stand out and be impressive. Some people can afford an extravagant mansion, but most of us cannot. Money does matter, and it will play an important role in your final plans. It's best to get this in your head now. If you begin to discuss financial matters later and find that you must tear down your dreams only to rebuild them on a smaller scale, you may become unnecessarily frustrated and discouraged.

Later in the book, you will learn how to do cost estimates and how to find financing for your home. For right now, all you need is a realistic idea of your finances. You already know your income. Probably, you have a pretty good idea of where you want to build, and you should have a basic idea of the style and size of home you want. With that information, start searching out the prices of homes similar to yours in your same general location. Talk with lenders and real estate agents to get an idea of the monthly payments for these homes.

ALERT!

Keep in mind that this initial research is meant simply to give you a broad idea of the type of home you can afford. (We'll cover financial matters in detail in Chapter 3.) If you plan to add more features, such as a pool, be sure to pad that price a bit.

If you find that homes like your ideal, in the same area, are all way out of your price range, you will want to consider either building somewhere less expensive or scaling down your dreams to fit your budget. On the other hand, you might find that you have more than enough cash to build what you want. In that case, you have the freedom to consider adding even more features to your design plans.

Fulfilling Your Needs

Before you begin to ponder what extra accents you can afford, pay close attention to the features you need to actually fulfill your family's needs. You want your home to be functional, not just a trophy house. For instance, the first concern of many homebuilders is how many bedrooms the house should have. If you have (or plan to have) children, you definitely want more than just a master bedroom. If you frequently entertain out-of-town guests, a guest room is almost a necessity.

The importance of features will vary from house to house. Discuss your plans with your family. You may find that your initial plan for a single bathroom doesn't go over so well with your four daughters. Spend a couple of days paying attention to your family's living patterns. In what rooms do you spend the most time? Are you a bunch of pack rats? If so, you may want to consider additional closet or storage space. Maybe you have pets, and you want to add a mudroom or utility area leading to the outdoors so they don't track in mud and dirt all over the new carpet.

FACT

The length of time you plan to live in a house has a direct impact on the needs the home must fulfill. If you plan to live there for the rest of your life, you may not want an enormous amount of extra space that will be difficult to manage in your elder years. If you are planning to build and then sell, you will want to create a home that will satisfy the needs of an average family.

You know your living needs better than anyone else. Use these needs as the basis of your house plans. From there, you can move on to the extra things your family might want. Be realistic in deciding both your wants and needs, and you will be able to build a home that is ideal for you and your family. If you allow your general contractor to have a hand in designing your home, you will have that extra assistance in staying realistic. Your general contractor can also show you how to get the most house for your money, eliminating complexities and excessive costs.

Deciding What You Want

When you have figured out what your family needs, you get to move on to the fun part—the added features that will make your home your own. You've probably already got a mental (if not physical) list of features you would like for your home. If not, take another drive around to look at the houses that appeal to you. What makes them stand out? You may decide it's the bay windows that will make the perfect addition to your house. Or maybe you can justify a second-story balcony as both a functional and aesthetic addition.

Visit friends and family and examine their houses. Ask them about the features they think they wouldn't be able to live without. Talk to others who have built their own homes, and discuss their experiences and opinions on additional features. Brainstorm with everyone who will be living in the house. (You never know, that five-year-old of yours might come up with the idea of the century!)

Write Down Your Ideas

A brainstorming session won't do much good unless you remember all your great ideas. It's important to keep track of all your fantastic ideas by writing them down. Designate a member of the family to be the note-taker for family discussions. You may also want to keep this master list in a central location so it is easy for people to jot down an idea or two as they think of them.

Nothing is set in stone at this point, so have fun with the idea process. Be practical but also creative during brainstorming sessions. This is a great way to get the whole family involved and excited about the project.

This list won't necessarily reflect all that will become part of the house, but it will be a sounding board for the habitants to voice their thoughts. The thought process is a very important part of the prebuilding phase. Without it, your project could easily turn into a disaster. The more minds that collaborate on a project, the more input you have at your fingertips when making final decisions.

Create Three Lists

Once you have exhausted your mind, it's time to buckle down and truly decide what you want. To do this, start with your extensive list of ideas, and break it down into three separate lists. The first list is for those features that you can realistically add to the home you are to build. The second list is for any features that are probably not feasible now but that are still good ideas—maybe you can use them later on. The third list is the catch-all for those outrageous ideas (such as the secret passageways your ten-year-old wants) that may have been fun but are not likely to ever actually exist in your home.

For some features, you will probably have to do a little feasibility and pricing research before you know whether they belong on the first or the second list. For instance, let's say you really like the look of bay windows, but you have no idea how much more it costs to install them (if anything) than it does to put in ordinary windows. On the other hand, some items will automatically make that first list—such as the two-car garage that you know will make your home an easy seller in the future real estate market. Keep in mind that these lists may change once you get into the designing phase. Still, it's always good to have a jump start on the thought process.

Get Organized Now

You've got a lot of work ahead of you, so it's best to get organized now. As you progress further along in the building process, you are going to notice a rising sea of papers around you. You don't want to be stuck in an endless paperwork search, like for those financial forms that "were just here" to take with you when meeting with a prospective lender.

You will be handling contracts, and you should be able to pull those out and consult them at a moment's notice. Needless to even mention, you certainly don't want to lose the house plans right before breaking ground!

The best way to take care of your important papers is to create an organizational system. For some people, a job like this is a piece of cake; for others, it seems like an impossible task. If you don't already have an organizational system established, you may want to begin by getting yourself some manila folders and labels. A simple three-ring binder with divider tabs can also work just as well. There's no reason why your organizational system should be complicated. As long as everything is clearly labeled and easy to find, any system you devise for storing important documents and plans will work just fine.

ALERT!

Beginning an organizational system is not enough. You must also stick with it. Resist the temptation to set important house papers on the kitchen table "just for a minute." Put them in their proper place right away. Once you get used to using your system, you will find that it's easy to maintain.

Since you have already created a list of the features you want for your home—and, hopefully, a list of the features you need as well—use these as the beginning of your organizational system. Label this first folder "Ideas," or give it some other name that may seem appropriate. This is where you will store not only your lists, but also any notes you take as you go through the initial thought-process phase. Jot down the types of houses that appeal to you, your reasons for building, and any other ideas that come to mind.

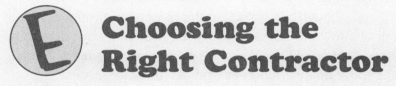

Chapter 2

Choosing the Right Contractor

One of the first steps you'll need to take on your homebuilding endeavor is to choose a general contractor. You can either hire a general contractor or do the job yourself. In this chapter, we discuss what a general contractor does, with the goal of helping you decide who will be best for this important job—the general contractor, or you.

The Contractor's Job

Many people make the assumption that a general contractor is the homebuilding jack-of-all-trades. While the contractor is certainly knowledgeable in all areas of homebuilding, he doesn't build; he manages. (Not all general contractors are men; as you've probably seen on those televised building shows, a lot of women are just as good at the job. In this book, though, we'll stick to the masculine pronoun for the purposes of clarity.) You aren't likely to see the contractor driving nails or installing electrical wiring. He is the person responsible for hiring and overseeing the manual laborers who do the actual work.

In no way should this distinction undermine the importance you place on the general contractor. In fact, he probably has the most important job in the homebuilding endeavor. As you will soon learn, being a contractor is not easy. This person must possess several skills, all of which are necessary to enable the building project to progress efficiently and effectively.

Specified Tasks

A general contractor manages the homebuilding project, but what exactly does the management job entail? If you hire a general contractor, you will probably have a contractor's agreement that spells out all the responsibilities and duties of the contractor. You are always free to claim some of these jobs for yourself. Here is a list of the responsibilities that most agreements assign to the contractor:

- Estimate cost.
- Create a labor schedule.
- Hire and pay subcontractors.
- Supervise and inspect the work of the subcontractors.
- Purchase materials and schedule their delivery.
- Coordinate all required inspections.
- Secure needed permits.
- Keep the building site safe and make certain all insurance concerns, such as worker's comp, are covered.

These are some of the most common duties of a general contractor. It's up to you to decide how much or how little the general contractor does. You're the one in charge. He may be the boss of the job site, but you're the boss of the project.

Some general contractors help the owners through the financing stage by recommending lenders or talking with the bank or lender about the project. If you are nervous about approaching a lender, you may want to hire the contractor to help out with this. A good general contractor knows his stuff and should be able to answer questions the lender may have.

Most general contractors are organizational geniuses. While it's always a good idea to keep copies of records yourself, you can also ask your general contractor to keep records of all purchase orders, invoices, receipts, plans, permits, inspections, and so on. It's likely that he will do this anyway, but you should never work on an assumption.

Human Relations Superstar

In addition to the ability to take on all the specified tasks, the general contractor must also command some truly excellent human relations skills. If you have ever held a management position or been in charge of a group of people, you know how important it is to be able to communicate effectively to others. In a project the size of a house (literally), communication is critical. It can make or break the success of the project.

As you know, the general contractor hires the subcontractors to do the actual work. It becomes his responsibility to relate orders and information to the workers, to schedule tasks, and to ensure that the work is done in a timely and productive manner. Problems will definitely arise, and it is also his responsibility to handle them. In order to do all this, the contractor must have excellent people and management skills.

FACT

If you want the work on your house to be done well, and you want the subcontractors to show up when scheduled, then the general contractor needs to have an authoritative presence and the ability to command respect. A contractor's job performance is dependent upon his ability to manage people.

The general contractor also orders materials from suppliers. To do this job effectively, he should be able to communicate his needs in a professional manner and to establish a relationship that stresses quality and cost maintenance. He must be able to ask the appropriate questions of suppliers in order to find the best in town and negotiate for discounts. He will also have to coordinate material delivery schedules with the supplier. If the contractor is a good communicator, all of this will be done with the least problems possible.

Licensing Considerations

Licensing requirements vary by state. You may be surprised to learn that not all general contractors need to be licensed. For instance, in Indiana, a general contractor does not need to hold a license to operate. Anyone in that state can call himself a general contractor, regardless of education, knowledge, or experience. Then again, there are states—such as Massachusetts—that require licensing for general contractors and for anyone supervising a construction site.

It's important to check with your state licensing board and review the requirements (if any) before you hire a general contractor. You can visit *www.contractors-license.org* to get a list of licensing requirements by state. This site will also give you the addresses and phone numbers of state licensing boards so you can check out a particular contractor.

In some cases, specific contractors—such as plumbing contractors or electrical contractors, generally hired as subcontractors—need to be licensed. Again, individual state licensing boards can give you this information.

ALERT!

Always check the requirements of your state's licensing board before hiring a contractor or choosing to act as general contractor yourself. The licensing board will also give you information on the insurance coverage that is required for workers.

For the most part, if you choose to act as general contractor for your own home, you don't need to hold a license. This is because you are building for yourself, not someone else. (Of course, you will still have to abide by local building codes and secure the needed permits.) However, this exemption may come with certain stipulations. For instance, you may not be able to sell your home for a certain period of time.

Hiring a Contractor

A lot of people choose to hire a general contractor to build their homes. If this is the route you choose, you should be comfortable with and confident in the person you are entrusting with this important project. So how do you go about finding such a superman (or woman!)? It's a good idea to begin your search with referrals.

Talk to people who have built their own homes recently. Ask them to describe their experiences with their contractor. Did they have any problems with the work? Was the contractor easy to get along with? Did he do the best job possible? If these people were going to build another house, would they hire the same contractor? Unless the contractor is a family member or close friend, you are likely to get an unbiased recommendation from those who have been through the process.

You may also want to talk with local building suppliers or others in the building industry. Track down some reputable subcontractors and find out the contractors they've have good experiences with. Word of mouth is a powerful tool, but be sure you note the source of information. Some suppliers have established relationships with contractors and know they will get business by recommending them. The same goes for subcontractors. Regardless, it's good to create a sound list of candidates. You will know more once you begin interviewing.

The Interview

Once you have a good list of candidates, get on the phone and start scheduling interviews. You may find that some of the contractors will not be available for the dates during which you wish to build. If a particular contractor has come highly recommended and you can be flexible, you may want to consider rescheduling your building project. Of course, doing this will probably mean taking a chance on cutting out other possible candidates. Keep your options open. Gather as much information as you can before you make any final decisions.

ALERT!

Keep good notes of your interviews. Don't rely on your memory to record everything that was said. Jot down your feelings about the candidate and whether you think you'd be able to work well with him. Notes like these will come in handy when you start narrowing down the list.

You will have your own interview questions that are specific to your individual project. However, it's also a good idea to include most, if not all, of the following. During the interview, the one subject you must cover thoroughly is the contractor's experience. Ask about his experience as a general contractor, including work on the actual construction of homes and with suppliers, subcontractors, and lenders. Request references—in all likelihood, the contractor will already have a list in hand. (Remember that requesting references is not enough; you must also check them out.) Ask the candidates about the type of license they hold, and request the number. You must check this out as well. Ask each candidate to describe his working relationships and the way he handles problems. Finally, ask him what specifications he needs in order to create an accurate bid.

The Bids

When all the interviews are over, it's time to start narrowing down your list. It's likely that you've already picked out a few possibilities of contractors you feel would do an excellent job on your home. If not, review your interview notes, and start comparing candidates. Contact the lucky finalists. Give them each a copy of the specifications—make sure each contractor receives the exact same specs—and ask for a bid. If the contractor is experienced, he will know what you are looking for, but just to be sure, include any specific requests you may have. For instance, you want to know the proposed time frame for the project. Make sure the bid states exactly what is included in the price and who is responsible for what. You'll want the bids to be as specific as possible so they will be easy to compare.

If the bids come in and you aren't happy with what you see, you can always negotiate. You can discuss ways to cut costs without cutting quality with the contractor. Or you can just tell the contractor what you're looking for and go from there. It's not unusual for homebuilders to make a few changes to the specs and request a rebid. Remember, building a house isn't cheap. If you want quality, you're going to have to pay for it.

Working with the Contractor

You are confident in your choice of contractor, but that confidence is not enough. It's imperative that you sign an agreement with the contractor outlining the terms of the job in writing. Never assume that verbal understanding and a handshake are enough. A contractor's agreement protects both you and the contractor.

The general contractor will probably have his own contract already drawn up. Be sure to read it thoroughly and to get all your questions answered before signing. You may even want to have a lawyer review your contract before you put your name on the dotted line. Never sign something you are uncomfortable with.

Your relationship with your general contractor must be based in trust. You should be able to trust him to do the best job he possibly can, and he should be able to trust you to let him do his job.

The amount of time you spend with the contractor depends upon how involved you are in the project. If you hire the contractor to handle just about everything, you won't need to be at the site every day during construction. On the other hand, you may choose to take a more active role in the building and share some of the responsibilities with the contractor. In that case, the contractor shouldn't be surprised to see you at the site pretty often.

FACT

A good general contractor can be a powerful ally in your home-building endeavor. If you listen to his advice and suggestions—most of which will be based upon his experience—you may find that you can save money while building a more efficient home.

Let the contractor know how to reach you and when the best time is to contact you and vice versa. Discuss with the contractor how problems will be handled and to what extent you want to be involved. You don't need to know that Johnny Construction was three minutes late to the site today, but you do need to know that extensive backordering has put you three weeks behind schedule. If you keep the lines of communication open, your relationship with the contractor will be productive.

Be Your Own Contractor

Lots of people choose to be their own general contractors, taking on all the responsibilities that go with the job. Some do this so that they can be in complete control of the project—after all, no one knows your mind better than you do. Some simply want the experience and view the project as an exciting challenge. But most people decide to be their own general contractors to save money. A general contractor's fee is usually around 20 percent of the total value of the project. If you can do without him, that means big savings for you. But before you get too excited, think about all the factors involved in being your own contractor.

Time Involved

First of all, you must realistically consider the amount of time involved in taking on the contractor's responsibilities. Building a house is no easy task. Even if you have a great crew of subcontractors, you will have to devote a lot of time to the project if you want it to be completed anything near on time. If you had a few years to play with, you could keep your full-time job and just work on the weekends. But that would mean paying more in interest on your construction loan, and in the end you probably wouldn't save anything by doing the work yourself.

The amount of time you decide to spend at the work site depends on how confident you are in the subcontractors, how much of the work you want to do yourself, and the coordination of your delivery and inspection schedules. While it is quite possible to do some of the general contractor's job over the phone, you will need to make visits to the site regularly.

ALERT!

As general contractor, you will be responsible for hiring and paying subcontractors. If you pay subcontractors by the hour, they will be considered your employees. That means you must fill out the necessary tax forms with the IRS. If you hire on a contract basis for a total amount, you needn't worry about payroll paperwork and withholding taxes.

Figure out how much time your current job, relationships, and lifestyle will allow you to spend on such a project. Maybe you can work out a schedule at your current job that gives you more time to devote to the project. Your family and friends will probably understand that you won't have as much time for them during this big project, but you should make sure that taking this time away from them won't damage those relationships. Also take into consideration any commitments you currently have in your life. If you serve on several committees, for example, you need to notify them that you may not be able to devote as much time to them as you had before.

Dealing with Difficulties

Keep in mind that as general contractor, you are the one who has to handle all the problems that come up. You also have to be prepared to answer any questions your subcontractors, suppliers, inspectors, and lenders may have. This is a tremendous responsibility. You've got to know your stuff. This is in no way meant to discourage you from becoming the contractor for your new home. You can do it. The information you will gain from this book and from talking to others will arm you with the knowledge you need to succeed in a homebuilding endeavor.

Maybe all this sounds like a little too much for you to handle, but you still can't let go of the money you'll save by forgoing the aid of a general contractor. All is not lost; you can always hire a knowledgeable subcontractor to be your right-hand man. You can arrange to have the chosen subcontractor at the work site when you cannot be there. This person can act as your consultant, taking on responsibilities and handling any particular problems that may arise, according to whatever agreement the two of you devise. This will also help to free up some of your time.

Hiring Subcontractors

If you choose to take on the role of general contractor, you will be in charge of hiring subcontractors. As you know, subcontractors are the expert tradesmen who will be doing the housebuilding work for you. These people are your team. They will work with you and with each other to build your ideal home. Obviously, it is important that you find subcontractors who are reputable and experienced. The better the subcontractor, the easier your job.

Who's Who

So you know you need subcontractors, but what kind? There are many different types of subcontractors that you can hire to help build your home, each one specializing in a particular area. The kind of subcontractor you hire depends on how much of the work you're going to do yourself and on the design of the house. (For instance, if you're planning to hang, tape, and float your own drywall—or if you're not planning use drywall—you wouldn't plan to hire a drywall contractor.) Here's a list of the common kinds of subcontractors, along with a brief description of their jobs:

- **Concrete subcontractor:** Pours concrete (for instance, for foundation, patio, garage).
- **Drywall subcontractor:** Hangs, tapes, floats drywall throughout the house.
- **Electrical subcontractor:** Installs the electrical system, outlets, and switches.
- **Flooring subcontractor:** Installs the flooring materials.
- **Foundation subcontractor:** Installs the foundation.

- **Framing subcontractor:** Builds and erects the house's frame.
- **Grading subcontractor:** Prepares the site for the foundation.
- **HVAC subcontractor:** Installs the heat, ventilation, and air conditioning systems.
- **Insulation subcontractor:** Installs the house's insulation.
- **Landscape subcontractor:** Implements the landscape design.
- **Painting subcontractor:** Paints the house.
- **Plumbing subcontractor:** Installs the plumbing system, fixtures, and hardware.
- **Roofing subcontractor:** Installs the roof.

Where to Look

The best place to begin your search for subcontractors is, again, through referrals. Talk to other people who have built their own homes. Hunt down some general contractors and suppliers and get their opinions. Also be sure to talk to other subcontractors—usually, one subcontractor will have a good working relationship with another and can serve as a good reference.

If referrals aren't getting you anywhere, you can always check the ads. You'll find these through various sources: online, for instance, or in the Yellow Pages. Sometimes you can even find subcontractors in the classified section of the local newspaper.

Another way to find subcontractors is to visit a building site. Here, you can talk to the general contractor or to the subcontractors themselves. Just keep in mind that this is a job site, and they are there to work. Don't try to conduct interviews on the spot; you'll just disrupt their work schedule.

In hiring subcontractors, you should plan to go through the same interview and bidding process as for a general contractor. Be sure to get licensing certification and references, and check this information out. Your building project will go much more smoothly if you hire subcontractors who are trustworthy and hardworking. However, trust alone is not enough. Be sure to have written contracts with all subcontractors you hire.

You're the Boss

Being the overseer for your building project also makes you the boss. You are responsible for paying the subcontractors according to the payment terms stipulated in their contracts. Never agree to pay for a job in advance. You should only pay for work that is completed and that is done correctly. Most subcontractors work on a payment plan that calls for some money to be paid before the entire project is finished. This partial payment should reflect the amount of work done. For instance, if the framing contractor has completed 30 percent of the work, you could make a partial payment not to exceed 30 percent of the total amount you've agreed on. You should also make sure all relevant inspections are done before making either partial or full payment to any of your subcontractors.

ALERT!

If you choose to be your own general contractor, keep in mind that subcontractors will generally have technical questions for the general contractor. You'll need to be around to field these questions and to find the answers quickly so your workers can stick to the construction schedule.

In the ideal subcontracting situation, there will be respect and trust on both sides. The subcontractors will trust you to be there when problems occur and to promptly pay them for work done properly. You will trust the subcontractors to show up on schedule and do their jobs well. While you are in charge of the job site, try to let them do their work. You went the extra mile to find the best workers, so let them do what they do best. It's difficult for anybody to take pride in his work and do his best with someone standing over his shoulder scrutinizing every little thing. On the flip side, don't be afraid to do inspections and ask questions. Find a middle ground that is comfortable for both sides. Ⓔ

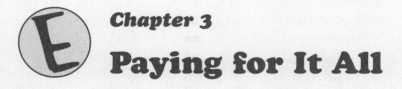

Chapter 3

Paying for It All

Y ou dream of building your own per-fect home. There's only one thing standing between your dream and reality: money. Unless you have money to burn, you need to find a way to finance your home. This chapter will show you how.

Estimating Costs

The only way to find out how much money you need to beg, borrow, or scrape together is to estimate the cost of building your house. In Chapter 1, we discussed why it was a good idea to drive around and find price ranges for comparable homes. Based on that research, you already have a pretty good idea of the kind of house you can afford. Now it's time to go into the details. To do this, you need to estimate construction costs.

FACT

There will be two types of loans you can apply for: a construction loan and a home mortgage. The construction loan is a short-term loan that pays to have the house built. The home mortgage is a long-term loan that is usually put together so that it pays off the construction loan when the building project is complete.

One-Stop Shopping

Your choice of house design can affect the way you go about getting cost estimates. If you decide to go with a stock house plan or to build your house from a kit, you'll get a prepared list of materials, making your cost estimate a lot easier. The same principle applies if you choose to hire an architect to design your home. However, keep in mind that the lists may not always include everything required. Go over these lists with diligence before assuming you have all the information you need.

Purchasing manufactured or modular homes will also make your cost estimating experience less of a headache. But don't assume that the price of the home is all you'll need to figure on. You'll also have to consider costs for excavating and laying the foundation. The contractors or companies you choose to hire to do the work can also put an estimate together for you. If you're going to do it yourself, then you'll need to go through the work step by step and determine the costs associated with each phase.

Materials and Labor

Cost estimating can get a little more complicated if you plan on doing any of the building work yourself—it's hard to budget the cost of your own labor, especially if you've never done a particular job before. Even if you know you won't be hiring people to do certain jobs, you can still get their help by asking for bids, the more specific the better.

With house plans in hand, contact local general contractors, specialty subcontractors, and suppliers, and request bids for construction costs and materials. Their expertise and experience allows them to make accurate bids, which will give you a pretty accurate cost estimate to work from. This doesn't mean you have to hire them to do the work or supply the materials. You are simply finding out what the jobs will cost you.

Make sure you cover every aspect of building your home in the cost estimate. You don't want to show up to a meeting with a lender only to discover you forgot to account for framing costs. While the list will certainly change from project to project, you will need to account for both labor and materials in several basic categories. Your individual plans may call for more or different costs, so be sure you go through the following list with your particular project in mind. Here are some basic costs to keep in mind:

- Excavation
- Foundation
- Framing
- Concrete
- Windows and doors
- Roofing
- Siding
- Electrical
- Plumbing
- Heating, ventilation, and air conditioning
- Insulation
- Floor coverings
- Drywall
- Cabinets
- Interior trim
- Painting
- Lighting

- Water
- Sewer
- Utilities
- Permits and fees

Other Considerations

Depending on your individual project, you may want to add other items to your cost estimate. For instance, let's say you wanted to landscape your home site. You would get bids from landscaping contractors and add this cost estimate to your list. Perhaps you want all-new appliances to go along with your brand-new home. If that's the case, make sure you account for this expense as well.

It's a good idea to cushion your cost estimates by 5 to 10 percent to take care of unexpected expenses, things you forgot about, or other problems that may occur. It's a lot easier to ask the bank for a little more of a loan than you think you need. If you ask for too little, you'll have to go through all that paperwork again if you need more down the road.

Take a look at your plans. Any features you plan to add on while building have to be added to the cost estimate. Consider everything from a garage to a deck, from a central vacuum system to a fireplace, and from wallpaper to laundry chutes.

Finding a Lender

Whew! As if just figuring the costs weren't enough trouble, now you have to go on the hunt for someone to lend you the money to pay for it all. Most people visit banks, mortgage companies, or credit unions to apply for house loans. If you hire a general contractor, ask him to recommend some lenders. If you have checking or savings accounts, you might want to apply for a loan through your financial institution. Sometimes knowing the lender can help. If none of these scenarios applies, you can research institutions that specialize in home construction loans. Don't pick just one lender. Apply to a few different institutions.

Before Visiting the Lender

You want to walk into the lender's office with confidence and show you know what you're doing and what you're getting yourself into. The best way to do this is to be prepared with everything the lender will want to see. Here's a list of the materials you need to bring with you to the lender:

- Current employer information, including name, address, and current pay stub for all those who will be signing the loan
- Bank and credit card statements
- Information on pension plans, life insurance policies, and investments
- Social security numbers
- Tax returns and W-2s for the last two years
- A catch-all financial statement listing both your assets and liabilities

In addition to these materials, you will also be asked to fill out an application. Drop by the financial institution ahead of time and pick up the form so you have it filled out and ready to go when you visit the lender. It's also a good idea to call ahead and make sure you have all the information the lender needs.

Before you visit a lender, make sure you get a copy of your credit report. Mistakes do happen. It's possible that your report shows items that could hurt your chances of securing a loan. It's better to be in the process of fixing these problems than to be surprised when the lender points them out to you.

The Lender's Job

It is the lender's job to lend money to people who will pay the loan back. Sounds easy enough, but figuring out what loans will actually be repaid isn't easy at all. Lenders have to take something of a risk when they loan out their cash. The less of a risk you are, the better you look to most lenders. So how is the risk level determined? All lenders have their own set of guidelines they use when considering an application. However, there are three formulas almost all lenders use:

1. **Mortgage-payment-to-income ratio (MR).** The principle, interest, taxes, and insurance of your monthly mortgage payment should be between 28 and 30 percent of your gross monthly income.
2. **Total debt-to-income ratio (DR).** The total of your monthly debt payments should be between 36 and 41 percent of your gross monthly income.
3. **Loan-to-value ratio (LV).** This is the ratio of the total value of the house and land to the loan amount. Most loans will not go higher than 90 percent of appraised value of the house.

The lender will calculate the MR to determine your maximum monthly house payment. Then, DR is calculated in order to figure in your debt. Once all this is done, the lender will figure out the highest monthly payment you can afford and calculate a loan amount. This loan amount must usually have an LV of 90 percent or less in order to be eligible.

It's a good idea to apply to more than one lender. The more loan approvals you get, the more options you have to choose from. Multiple offers also give you some negotiating power, which you can use to try to eliminate or reduce some of the fees that come with taking out a loan.

Ways to Improve Your Chances

There are a few ways you can improve your chances of getting a loan to fund your homebuilding project. First of all, you might want to reconsider being your own general contractor. Even though this plan is likely to save you money in the long run, most lenders hesitate to give out loans to those who plan on running the show without any previous experience.

This isn't to say that it's impossible to be your own general contractor and still get a loan; it's just a little more difficult. If you really want to do the job, you will probably have to prove to the lender that you know what you're doing. Accurate and complete cost estimates will help, and so will arming yourself with the information in this book. Another option is to hire a general contractor on a consultant basis. You can still do the work yourself, but this shows the lender that somebody with experience is there to back you up.

Managing Debt

Your debt is going to work against you. Pay off as much credit card debt as you can before you approach the lender. If you can't pay them off, consider consolidating your debts onto a single low-interest card, thus reducing your number of payments and most likely the payment itself. If you have any other outstanding debts that you can pay off, certainly do so. The less debt you have, the greater your chances of receiving a loan.

Check out your credit report and make sure there aren't any mistakes on it. If there are, contact the company and work to rectify the problem. Even if the problem isn't solved before you visit the lender, there will be a record of your call, showing that you are indeed working on it.

Current Assets

If you currently own your home, you might consider selling. Most financial institutions aren't interested in offering loans to borrowers who already have a mortgage payment to make. Many people sell their homes and live in rentals or mobile homes during the construction process.

FACT

One thing a lender loves to see is a big down payment. The bigger the down payment you can make, the better your chances of getting approved for a loan. The down payment shows the lender that you are able and willing to participate as an investor in your house project. That makes you less likely to default on the mortgage and a better loan prospect.

You should also try to purchase your future home site before applying for the house construction loan. You don't necessarily need to have it paid off, but it's best if you have made several payments to build up equity.

The Construction Loan

A construction loan is a short-term loan that is used to finance the building of your home. It is probably a little different from the loans you're used to. The construction loan is not disbursed up front, in one lump sum. Instead, it is paid out in installments over the course of the building. The interest rates for a construction loan are most likely going to be higher than those for a home mortgage. This is the lender's way of gently pushing you to get the construction done faster.

How a Construction Loan Works

A construction loan is paid out in installments, according to the amount of work that has already been done on your house. Many loans will stipulate a draw schedule that defines certain milestones that must be achieved before they can be paid for. On some loans, you can request a draw for the amount of work that has been done. In other words, after 10 percent of the house has been completed, you can then take a draw of 10 percent of the loan.

Of course, the lender isn't going to just take your word for it. If you request a draw, or if you are working under a draw schedule, the lender will send out an inspector to make sure the work has been completed. If the inspector is satisfied, you are then allowed to receive the draw.

QUESTION?

What is a draw?
A draw is an amount of money that is paid to you from the construction account. The amount of the draw will vary according to the amount of work that has been done. You can think of a draw as an installment payment made to you from the lender.

As you've probably guessed, you're going to need a chunk of start-up cash before you can secure a construction loan. Since the loan money won't be given out until *after* the work is done, you'll need some funds of your own to get things started. Be sure you can afford all closing costs, permits, and site preparation before you apply for a loan.

It's in your best interest to try to get both the construction loan and home mortgage from the same lender. Look into getting a convertible loan (otherwise known as a construction permanent loan). This type of loan covers both the construction loan and home mortgage. The construction loan is made first. Then, when the project is finished, the construction loan rolls over into a permanent loan, or home mortgage. This not only makes the borrowing process easier, but it also saves you additional closing costs.

Getting a Construction Loan

When applying for a construction loan, you will need the same information as for a regular loan (such as proof of employment and social security numbers) and a few other things besides. Namely, you need to have a set of house plans, your cost estimates, names of contractors and subcontractors, and a survey of the proposed building site.

The lender wants to know that the home you plan to build is worth more than the construction loan amount. Therefore, your home will be appraised. Some lenders will look over your house plans and compare your proposed home to others in the neighborhood. It's a good idea to build a home that is comparable to those in the same neighborhood. But try to keep it from being more extravagant. Higher-priced homes surrounding yours will raise the property value of your home. But if yours is the higher-priced home, it will only serve to raise the property value of those around it. If your loan is approved you will likely receive around 75 percent of the home's appraised value.

The Home Mortgage

As you know, the construction loan is a short-term loan meant to provide you with the means to build your home. While you are building, you pay interest on this loan but no principal. In other words, you don't have to start paying the loan off until construction is complete, and you only pay interest on the amount of money you have already been paid out in cash. So what happens to the rest of the money you borrowed once the house is complete? When you are given an occupancy permit, the construction loan is paid off by a home mortgage.

How a Mortgage Works

If you own a home now, you are probably already familiar with mortgages. The home mortgage is a long-term loan—whose rate is usually lower than a construction loan—that is paid off over the course of fifteen or thirty years. A home mortgage can only come into effect after the house is finished because the house itself is the collateral used to secure the loan.

FACT

Some of the mortgage loan agencies you may want to check out for more information are the Federal National Mortgage Association (FNMA, or Fannie Mae), the Government National Mortgage Association (GNMA, or Ginnie Mae), and the Federal Home Loan Mortgage Corporation (FHLMC, or Freddie Mac).

Several different kinds of loan costs and fees associated with home mortgages will be added to your down payment at closing. Each lender has its own set of fees, but some of the most common are loan origination fees, credit report fees, loan processing fees, escrow fees, appraisal fees, title insurance fees, title search fees, notary fees, and city or county taxes.

Types of Mortgages

There are three general types of home mortgages available. The most sought-after is the fixed-rate mortgage. The monthly payments for fixed-rate mortgages are often slightly higher than the other loan types, but the interest rate and monthly payment stay the same for the life of the loan.

Therefore, if you can secure a low interest rate, you'll be pretty well set for the next fifteen or thirty years.

Next is the adjustable-rate mortgage. As the name implies, the interest rate for this type of loan changes periodically according to a standardized index. The initial monthly payments for this type of mortgage are usually lower, as are the interest rates. The institution can afford this since they can raise the rates and thus the monthly payments over time. Even so, there is generally a cap on how much an interest rate can increase.

Third is the graduated-payment mortgage. This is the least desirable type because you end up owing a lot more than you would with the other two types of mortgages. Basically, loan payments start small over the first few years and then gradually increase. This allows the borrowers time and money to get settled into the home. The problem with this loan is that during that first low-payment period, the principal of the loan actually increases, making the overall loan amount larger than it has to be.

Money-Saving Tips

This book offers plenty of money-saving tips for the various stages of building; however, there are some ways you can save money before you even start construction. First and foremost, be a smart consumer and shop around. Hunt down the best suppliers, general contractors, subcontractors, house plans, and loans. Your goal should be to get the best possible house for the least possible amount of money. This doesn't mean you should cut corners where quality is concerned, but you should be sure to get the biggest bang for your buck.

Smart shoppers do extensive research. In all your excitement, you may want to get started on the house as soon as possible. But instant gratification does not apply here, so you might as well resign yourself to the fact that this project is going to take several months. So how could a few extra weeks of research hurt? If anything, as you will probably discover right away, it can only help.

Another great way to save money is to reconsider certain features. Examine your cost estimates for any extras that you can add later. This isn't to say you can't have it; just not right now. For instance, do you really need a pool right away in order to live comfortably in your new home? Does the landscaping really have to copy Queen Victoria's courtyard? Can you survive without that fancy intercom system? Is it necessary to get all brand-new appliances, or can you use your year-old washer/dryer a little longer? These are examples of things that are easy to add on later, one by one, when you have a little extra money to spend. If you pay for them now, through these loans, they're going to cost you a lot more just in interest alone.

Chapter 4

Legal Details

Before you can start construction, and even during construction, you're going to find yourself swimming in a sea of paperwork. From building permits to contracts, you should be familiar with the documents and legal details that are meant to protect you and your home. The information in this chapter will help keep you from drowning.

Building Permits

Some of your first steps will be taken in the direction of your local building department/building inspector's office. That's where you'll apply for a building permit. This office will also supply you with complete information about building codes. The purpose of these codes is to ensure that buildings meet appropriate health and safety standards for their various purposes. Your house plans must comply with your local building codes before you can get a building permit.

You might choose to hire a professional to design your house. An architect will know the building codes inside and out—or certainly should. However, if you draw your plans up yourself, you must get a copy of the local building codes to ensure that your house fulfills their safety requirements. Because there is a lot to learn, and because you won't be permitted to take occupancy of your home unless it passes inspection, it's not a bad idea to hire an architect to review your house plans. If you purchase stock plans, be sure they comply with building codes or can be modified to do so.

FACT

Just recently the International Code Council (ICC) consolidated the building codes of the three main building code organizations: the International Conference of Building Officials (ICBO), Building Officials and Code Administrators International (BOCA), and Southern Building Code Congress International (SBCCI). There is now one set of model codes to be used throughout the nation. You can visit the ICC Web site at *www.iccsafe.org*.

To apply for a building permit, you must visit your local building inspector's office and request a building permit application. This will be turned in along with other specified materials such as floor plans, plot plans, and any other information your local building department wishes to review. You will be charged a fee and then asked to sit back and wait while your application is being considered (this can take a few months, so practice your patience).

The department may return your plans to you and ask that you make some changes. Make the changes, and resubmit your plans. When your plans fulfill the building requirements and the department is happy, you will be given a piece of paper that you will be required to display at the building site. You've just obtained your building permit!

Zoning Laws

If you're planning to live a life of convenience and have your eye on a spot nicely situated next to a grocery store, a bank, and a strip mall featuring all your favorite stores, think again. You won't be able to build your home there. Why not? Because zoning laws won't allow it.

Zoning laws restrict the use of particular areas of land and can also regulate the kinds of buildings that are constructed there. Zoning laws are meant to protect the value of the land; your local government's planning board has thought them out carefully. Whether you have already found your future home site—you hope—or are still looking, it's a good idea to visit the planning office to get a copy of the county or city zoning map.

Types of Zones

Since zoning restrictions are created on a local level, zones may differ from one town to its neighbor. However, most zoning defines appropriate areas for commercial and industrial building and land use, as well as agricultural, environmental, and your favorite, residential.

Commercial and industrial zones are where you will find local businesses, stores, and industrial parks. If you have major industrial plants in the area, these are also a part of this zone. Agricultural zones are usually large plots of land on the outskirts of the town. Often you will see this land used as farmland. Environmental zoning protects land from being developed and is what would wreck your plans to build a cabin in the middle of your state park. You are interested in land zoned for residential use.

Residential Zoning

Residential zoning outlines plots of land that can be used to build dwellings. However, there's more to it than just that. As you conduct your research, you will come across specifications within the residential zones that your home must meet in order to be approved by the planning board. Ignoring these specifications can result in some pretty big fines.

If you have your heart set on building on a plot of land that is zoned other than residential, or if you simply must build outside the specifications set for a particular residential zoning area, you will probably have to take your case before the local planning board. This isn't to say you'll get what you want, but it's worth a try.

Specifications to zoning laws specify where on a plot of land you can build your home. For instance, some residential zones specify that you must build your home a certain distance from neighboring homes. Others are so detailed they set baselines for your yard area. If you are planning to build within a subdivision, pay close attention to the specifications set out in the zoning laws. These communities are often planned to look nice, neat, and uniform. When looking for a piece of property, consider whether or not you are permitted to have detached garages or storage buildings. Some neighborhoods and subdivisions do not allow such structures to be built on the property. Some subdivisions even limit the type and size of pets a homeowner can possess. Always check with the local planning board before building.

Contracts

You will be dealing with several contracts during your homebuilding endeavor, or at least you should be. Don't try to weasel out of any paperwork by doing without contracts. It's unlikely that your workers would be happy without contracts—if you find some who are, you'll probably find out pretty quickly that you don't want their services, anyway.

Contracts are legally binding documents that secure a promise made from one person or company to another. The agreement made is deemed binding once both parties show their consent by signing the document. As contracts are meant to protect both parties and will stand up in court, it is imperative that you understand what you are signing.

Who Signs Contracts?

If you have chosen to hire a general contractor, then you will need to have a contract with that person stipulating what his job entails and what he is responsible for. Additional details regarding payment will also be included. If you have chosen to act as general contractor yourself, then you will want contracts with each individual subcontractor. Again, you will need to stipulate the work that is to be done and include payment details. "What if" clauses should be included in all contracts with those you hire. For instance, you need to spell out what happens if the work is not done or the project falls through.

When you secure a loan through a financial institution, you will be asked to sign a contract. This contract is your promise to repay the amount of money borrowed, plus interest. Payment schedules will also be included. Just as you included "what if" clauses in your contracts with contractors, the financial institution will incorporate these as well within the loan papers. Be sure you understand all terms and conditions.

You will undoubtedly come across more and different contracts you need to go ahead with construction, such as contracts with suppliers, surveyors, architects, and even attorneys. The important thing to remember is that you always have the choice of whether to sign. If you don't agree with the terms, don't put your name on the thing. But keep in mind that the other party has that same choice. You may not *like* everything stipulated in a contract; what's important is whether you *accept* it.

ALERT!

If you decide to go with a contract a contractor has already prepared, go over that document word by word. It's not a bad idea to have an attorney look it over as well. If you don't understand something, ask. Never sign your name without understanding exactly what you're signing.

Where to Get a Contract

You use a contract the contractor has already drawn up, write one yourself, or hire an attorney to create one for you. Pick the method you are most comfortable with. However, if you decide to write your own contract, it's a good idea to have an attorney or other experienced person take a look at it to make sure it's complete and also that it's legal.

Change Order

You will work hard to make sure you design and prepare for the exact house you want to build. You may think your plans are perfect and that you won't even have to consider any alterations. However, as you begin building, you just might decide you want (or need) to make a change or two—or several. Your general contractor or one of your subcontractors might also recommend a change that would improve the structure or save money in the long run.

It's unlikely you are going to tell your crew to do whatever they want and make any necessary changes as they see fit. Nor do you want just anyone ordering your crew to make an alteration here or there. You want to be in charge of the situation and give or refuse your approval for any proposed changes. So how can you make sure this happens?

ALERT!

Make sure that your contract with a general contractor or sub-contractors stipulates that you (or your designated representative) are the only person authorized to approve changes and that a change order must be prepared and signed before the change is made.

When you want to make a change to the building plans, you will need to create a change order, a legal document detailing the change to be made. The change order is signed both by you and by the contractor making the change. Information on the change order should include the following:

- Your and the contractor's contact information
- Date of the change order, along with the job number and location
- A detailed account of the change to be made
- The effect of the change on the building schedule, including the new completion date
- Cost of the change
- A statement of acceptance
- Signatures, with dates, of all those authorized to make the change

Inspections

Once you have the money and a building permit, you're finally free to build, build, build until you finally finish that dream house of yours, right? Wrong. Throughout the course of your building project, you will get regular visits from inspectors who will be checking up on your progress and the quality of your work. Don't feel like you're being singled out—this is standard procedure. Typically, inspectors come from two sources: the financial institution that lent you the money to build, and your local building department.

The Financial Institution

As you know, when you get a construction loan, a draw schedule is usually set up to regulate how money from the loan is used. Usually the schedule is based on the completion of certain projects. For instance, in order for you to get the money to pay the framing contractor, the financial institution must be satisfied that the framing was in fact completed. It would be bad business for them to simply take your word on the matter, so they send out inspectors instead.

This method not only regulates how borrowed money is used, it also ensures that the money is being well spent. The financial institution has an investment in your building project, and they want to know they've made a healthy and worthwhile investment.

Local Officials

When you get your building permit, make sure you find out the inspection schedule. Most building departments use a standard schedule that follows the project through certain milestones. For instance, it's likely you will need an inspection following the laying of the foundation, after the framing is done, once the electrical and plumbing are installed, and so on. These officials are there to see that you are indeed following the building codes and building a safe home for all occupants. The building department will advise you on how to set up the inspections. Keep in mind that they usually require some advance notice.

It's in your best interest to be nice to the inspectors. While they are professionals, they are also human and can be influenced by the attitudes and moods of others. Don't argue when they tell you to change something or offer their advice. Remember, these people know what they're talking about.

Inspection Tips

Inspections are essential to the progress of your building project. Therefore, it's wise to do all you can to make them go as smoothly as possible. First of all, when scheduling inspections, always give appropriate advance notice. Don't call the building department and demand that an inspector show up the same day. This will give you a bad reputation that may not easily be forgotten.

Always make sure that the work to be inspected is in fact ready to be inspected. It isn't going to make a good impression to bring the inspector all the way out to the site only to hear him tell you what you already know: The work is incomplete and therefore can't possibly pass inspection. If you have already scheduled an inspection and the work is not ready, call the inspector's office and reschedule.

Finally, schedule the inspection for a time when you can be present at the site. It is a big help to hear about any problems straight from the inspector while he or she is there to show you what he's talking about. The inspector may have questions for you as well.

Liens

Anyone planning on building their own home needs to be familiar with liens. A lien is a document that gives contractors and subcontractors the right to a portion of your property until their services have been paid for. Anyone you hire to work on your house can file a lien on your property, which can create problems at closing if not taken care of. While this may not seem fair, try to see it from their point of view.

Let's say the electrical contractor puts in a lot of time and hard labor to fulfill his service agreement with you. He's done his job, and your house is all wired for electricity. When he holds out his hand for the check, you turn away. For one reason or another, you do not pay him. Because he has not yet been paid, he owns the electrical part of your house. Filing a lien gives him the right to demand payment, out of the proceeds from the sale of the house if necessary. This gives him quite a bit of power, as the house cannot be mortgaged if there are liens against it.

FACT

General contractors and subcontractors aren't the only people who can file a lien on your property. Anyone who is involved in the building of your home, including the supplier and lender, can make a legal claim against your property.

The contractor has secured his rights to payment, but once he is paid, he needs to give up those rights. If you will be working with a financial institution to pay your workers, it's likely that the lender will require the contractor to sign a lien release, which waives the contractor's rights to the lien once he has been issued a check. While this is standard practice, it doesn't hurt to double-check with your lender that this is done. If you are paying your contractors out of pocket for their work, then you will want to create an affidavit for the contractor to sign once he is paid. This document should state that the contractor relinquishes all rights for legal claim against your home.

Insurance

Accidents happen, and natural disasters strike. There's not much you can do to stop them, but you can protect yourself from a huge financial loss if some calamity does happen. We're talking about insurance. There are at least two types of insurance you'll be dealing with when building a home: builder's risk insurance, and worker's compensation insurance.

Builder's Risk Insurance

Builder's risk insurance protects your homebuilding project from natural acts that could damage your property, such as tornadoes, hail storms, or hurricanes. It also often covers the losses from theft, fire, and injury on your property. Most financial institutions will require you to have this type of insurance policy before they turn your project into an investment.

Check with your current insurance agent to see what he has to offer. Be sure to read the fine print—not all of these policies are created equal. For instance, you may find that in order to be covered against theft, the building must be locked; therefore, you aren't covered against theft before you have a building that *can* be locked. If you aren't satisfied with what one policy offers, ask for amendments or shop around for another.

Worker's Compensation Insurance

State laws require that every employee must be covered by worker's compensation insurance in case an accident were to result in a job-related injury. As construction is typically considered a high-risk job, the premiums can be a bit pricey. However, this is not an area where you want to try to cut costs. If a worker got hurt, and you did not have the insurance to cover him, he could sue you for close to everything you've got!

ALERT!

Even if your general contractor and subcontractors have their own insurance policies, check with your state statutes to see what is required. Sometimes the builder must have a separate policy to cover anyone working on the site.

If you have chosen to hire a general contractor, he will probably already have a worker's compensation policy for the workers he hires. However, it's not enough to take his word for it. Request a copy of his certificate of insurance and keep it filed away. Often, subcontractors also have worker's compensation insurance for their employees. Again, put your mind at ease and get a copy of the certificate.

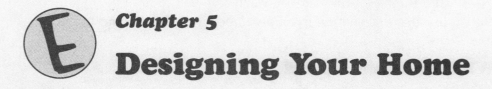

Chapter 5

Designing Your Home

Designing your home is one of the most important—and most fun—phases of the homebuilding process. The house design will affect the cost and schedule of your project, as well as how much fun it is. It's important that you take your time with this phase and carefully think about and prepare your house's design.

Putting Your Ideas to Work

In Chapter 1, you were asked to create files that included your ideas and dreams for the house you want to build. Hopefully, you have been adding to these files as you've continued along the thought process. If you haven't already begun to create lists of features, cost predictions, and the type of house you want, now is the time to do so. You will use this information to help you begin designing your home.

What You Can Afford

Cost considerations will play a major role in the type of house you design. You should already have an idea of what you can afford to spend to build a house. As a general rule, the bigger the house, the more money you'll have to spend. Keep this in mind as you daydream about that mansion, complete with ballroom and indoor swimming pool. Your local real estate agents should be able to give you an approximate cost per square foot of homes in your area. Use this as a general guideline when deciding on the size of your place.

You'll want to design first for those things that are necessary to your family's basic comfort, before you spend money to add on extraneous features. So, how many bedrooms and bathrooms will you need? How much storage space is required? Must *all* bedrooms have walk-in closets? Do you need a mudroom or a utility room? Think about the living areas. Consider how much time your family spends in different parts of your house, like the living room, dining room, study, and game room. Is a formal dining room necessary to your lifestyle? Does anyone work from home, and will they require an office? Think about your family's habits, patterns, and lifestyle. What features in a home are necessary to your comfort and standard of living?

Once you determine the needs the house must fulfill, then you can start considering your wish list of features you simply *want* to have. You may not be able to afford all items on that list, so pick out those that are most important to you and include those first in your house plans.

To the Drawing Board!

Now it's time to make use of all those fabulous ideas. Whether you are going to purchase stock plans, hire an architect, or do it all yourself, it's a good idea to sketch out your ideas before you get to the actual process of creating the house plans. Don't worry, there's no need for an architecture degree—or even good art skills, for that matter—to take your ideas to the drawing board. You should consider the floor plan before the exterior design, because once a floor plan is achieved, most exteriors can be adapted to fit the floor plan.

Sketching out your ideas will help you to visualize the layout and flow of the house you want to build. It will also help you determine if your layout ideas will realistically work. You will be able to study the traffic patterns and privacy of rooms. You will also be able to tell if you are granting too much or too little space to particular rooms. For instance, you may have originally sketched a small kitchen to leave more room for the dining room, only to later find that the kitchen doesn't give you enough space to fit all your appliances. The best part about sketching out your ideas, however, is that you can make changes easily and for free!

Sketching out your own rough house plans will save you time as you search for or create the actual house plans. You can hunt for stock plans that are similar to your sketches, instead of browsing randomly, or you can take your ideas to an architect and easily convey a clear idea of what you want.

To sketch out your ideas, grab some graph paper and a pencil and clear off the dining room table. You might need a tape measure as well. Assign a set dimension to each square on the graph paper. (For instance, one square might equal a space 3 feet high and wide, or 9 square feet.) You don't have to so exact as to include measurements for wall width—unless you want to—but try to be as accurate as you can. Remember, this isn't the final plan, only a rough draft.

Make the outline of the house first, and then start plotting rooms. Be sure to add all essential elements, like where doors are to each room, and to add hallways, stairs (if your house is more than one story), and fixed appliances to make sure you have enough room for it all. Have some fun with this, and play around with the layout until you find one that suits your needs. It costs you nothing to make changes at this stage, so try out every possibility.

Thinking Ahead

As you are designing your home, look to the future. Your house will probably be sold some day, whether by you or your heirs or your heirs' heirs. It's a good idea to do what you can to make sure that your house is marketable when the time comes. Think about things that the average person looks for when buying a home. Number of bedrooms and bathrooms, a two-car garage, energy efficiency, traffic patterns, and a well-organized layout should all be taken into consideration. Your local real estate agents and even architects and designers will be able to tell you what features buyers look for.

While you certainly want to design a home that is best suited to your family's needs and lifestyle, it might be a good idea to cut back on unique customizing as much as possible. This isn't to say that you shouldn't build the house you want. But if resale value is a priority, you want to build a house with appeal to a wide market. Unique homes are typically more difficult to sell and may bring in less than their expected value.

ALERT!

If there are certain features you really want, can't afford, and plan to add on later, take them into consideration as you design your house and allow for the expansion.

Even if you are determined that you will never move from your dream house, you still need to look to the future—the future needs of your family. For instance, if you are a newlywed, perhaps children are a part of the future picture. Will you have enough bedrooms to accommodate the five children you plan to have? Perhaps someone in your family has a physical condition that will eventually make stairs difficult to manage. Should you plan a first-floor bedroom or design a one-story house? Do you plan to put in an in-ground pool? If so, you'll need to consider where gas and electric lines run so that when the pool is dug, you don't have to reroute all the utilities. Of course, you can't always predict the future, but if you plan for all you can now, you can save yourself some time, money, and hassle later.

How to Make Your Home Energy Efficient

No one likes paying those monthly energy bills, so why would you want to pay more every month than you have to? When designing your home, it's a smart move to make it energy efficient. This decision might cost you a little more up front, but the savings you will enjoy over the long run are definitely worth it. Your goal here is to explore your options in keeping your house warm in cold weather and cool in hot weather without expending exorbitant amounts of energy to do so.

Designing for Energy Efficiency

While you're still in the design stages, there are a few things you should consider in terms of making your home more energy efficient. Windows and doors don't provide the insulation that walls do; they allow air to leak out of your home or get in from outside. So, to maintain better insulation, you might limit the number of windows or doors, or you might choose to install smaller windows. If you just can't give up any windows, then try to put as many windows as possible on the south-facing wall, and to keep the wall with the fewest windows facing north. The southern wall gets the most sun exposure and thus brings in more solar heat.

You may want to install ceiling fans throughout the house to improve air circulation and use the air you have trapped in the house. Finally, reconsider any fireplaces you might have planned. True, fireplaces add a cozy touch to any room, but they are also very inefficient sources of heat. If you absolutely must have a fireplace, visit your local supplier and discuss which model would be the most efficient within your price range.

Choosing Materials for Energy Efficiency

Your choice of building materials also affects the energy efficiency of your home. Talk to your supplier, general contractor, architect, or subcontractors to get their advice. They work on new homes all the time and will be up on the latest in energy-efficient materials.

Calculate the payback period for energy-efficient products. For instance, if you pay $2,000 extra for an energy-efficient appliance in order to see a savings of $50 per year, you won't see a payback in energy-saving costs for forty years. With a little comparative shopping, you can find energy-efficient products that will both help the environment and save you money.

As you know, windows can account for significant energy loss, so be sure to get the highest grade of window you can afford. (Wooden frames typically offer better insulation than metal, and double-glazing is usually a smart buy.) Shop around for the best insulation you can afford on your budget. The better the insulation, the better your home's heating and cooling systems will perform for you. (Different types of insulation are discussed in detail in Chapter 15.)

Landscaping for Energy Efficiency

You can also use carefully planned landscaping to increase the energy efficiency of your home. A few well-placed deciduous (or leafy) trees will block the sun's rays from your home in the summer and let light through in winter, when the leaves fall. You can plant trees and shrubs to create wind barriers during the winter to keep some of that cold air from hitting your home. Believe it or not, you can effectively use landscaping to reduce your heating and cooling costs by up to 20 percent! If you hadn't already considered landscaping, you might want to think about it now. Make a visit your local landscaping companies or garden centers for ideas specific to your region.

Hiring an Architect

Most people use the services of an architect in one way or another when building their homes. You might design the house yourself and create your own plans and then have an architect review them for compliance with local building codes and for general completeness. You might purchase stock plans that were designed by an architect, thus using the architect's services indirectly. You can purchase stock plans and hire an architect to make changes to the design that better suit your needs. Or you might hire your own individual architect to design the house of your dreams.

If you are planning to customize your home from standard house plans or to build a house that's truly one-of-a-kind, then it's a good idea to hire an architect. As you will soon see, house plans are very detailed and must be precise. It takes an experienced hand to perfect them, which is why the architects get paid the big bucks. Some architects will charge by the hour, others will be paid a percentage of the home's value (usually between 5 and 15 percent). How much you pay depends upon the kind of services you contract for. You will pay more to have the architect design your home and draw the plans, while you'll save a little cash if you design the house yourself and have the architect draw up the plans.

Finding an Architect

To find a qualified architect in your area, talk to other people who have built homes. You can also ask suppliers, contractors, and the building department for recommendations. Of course, you shouldn't hire based solely on someone else's opinion; you'll need to interview the architect to make sure he will be able to provide what you want for the price you are willing to pay. Find out whether the architect you choose is licensed in your state, and check up on the information you are given.

FACT

The American Institute of Architects (AIA) is the national trade association for architects. You can visit their Web site, *www.aia.org*, to find member architects in your area and to get advice on selecting an architect.

You want an architect with experience building homes and not just museums or shopping malls, so ask your candidates to describe their experience with homebuilding as well as how long they have been in the business. Request sample house plans and references. Always take the time to check references.

Discuss what services you will require from the architect, and find out the charge for those services. Also find out how the fees are calculated—will you be charged by the hour or a percentage of the home's value? Will the architect be able to offer money-saving options during the designing phase? Will there be any additional fees not already mentioned? Of course, you will also have a list of questions specific to your homebuilding project and your service needs.

Working with an Architect

An architect is an excellent source of information and can be a great asset to your homebuilding project. Architects know the local building codes, understand the effects of different materials, can offer money-saving tips and options, and may even help during the construction phase. Keep in mind that the more specific you can be about your needs and wants, the easier it is for the architect to deliver the services you require.

When you meet with the architect, be sure to bring along your rough sketches of your house plan. These are a great starting point. Also be sure to give the architect your budget requirements. He or she should be able to work within that budget while getting you the most for your money in both quality and quantity. In addition, your architect can tell you when you are going over budget or where cutting corners can save you money.

Purchasing Stock Plans

Many people choose to purchase stock plans for their designing needs. You can find stock plans online, in books, magazines, and catalogs, and directly from house plan services companies. While these plans won't be as unique or customized as those an architect would draw up for you, there are thousands of designs you can sort through and choose from, allowing for a wide variety of styles and designs. In other words, just because you choose to purchase stock plans doesn't mean you'll be building a cookie-cutter home.

The main advantage of purchasing stock plans is the price. It'll cost you a pretty hefty sum to have an architect draw and design your home. For just a fraction of that sum, you can purchase several copies of house plans that include everything you need. However, you'll have to be sure that the stock plans will comply with your local building codes. Sometimes a stock plan service can provide you with plans that are specific to your local standards, but some can't, so it's a good idea to get a professional to review the plans for compliance.

Today, there are computer programs that will help you design your own home. These programs are a lot of fun, and you can indeed use them to create professional-style house plans. Still, you should always have your creations reviewed by an architect or builder to ensure they are accurate and correct and that they comply with local building codes.

For those of you who like the idea of saving money with stock plans but who still want a customized home, don't despair; there's a solution. All you need to do is find a stock plan that is close to what you want, decide what changes you want, and then hire an architect or draftsman to alter the stock plans. This way you get a custom home that will best suit the needs of you and your family without having to pay an architect's fee for designing an entire house.

Most people can design their homes with the help of a general contractor and draftsman, without needing to hire an architect. A draftsman will work for a flat fee totaling some hundreds of dollars, as opposed to an architect, who will probably work for a percentage cost— maybe in the thousands of dollars. Some lumber companies will furnish a draftsman's services in exchange for buying materials from their company.

Understanding House Plans

Regardless of how you acquire your house plans, you have to know what you're looking at once they're in front of you. Most house plans are comprised of several sets of plans, each specific to a particular building phase or aspect of the house. For instance, the house plans will include floor plans, which you are already familiar with from our discussion of drafting floor plans earlier in the chapter. These plans will show the dimensions of the house and each room and where everything (including windows and doors) will be located throughout the house. Other plans include plot, or site, plans, which will show the lot with the house positioned; elevation plans, which show all sides of the house as it will look when finished; foundation and framing plans, which will each show the plans for those particular building phases; and HVAC, electrical, and plumbing plans, each of which will show the layout for the particular work to be done.

Saving Money with Design

There are several ways you can save money through conscientious designing. One of the first things anyone in the business will tell you is to build up, not out. It costs less to build a two-story home than a one-story home with the same square footage. Think about it. For conversation purposes, let's say that you want a 2,000-square-foot home, and you choose to build a single story. From there, you know that the foundation must be at least 2,000 square feet and the roof will have to cover the entire 2,000 square feet. That's a lot of material costs right there. Now, if you had chosen to build a two-story home of the same size, each story would be 1,000 square feet, along with a similar reduction for the foundation and roof. Do you see how you're saving quite a bit of money here? The material costs of the foundation and roof have essentially been cut in half.

Another piece of advice you're likely to hear is to keep walls to a minimum. This isn't to say that you should use plastic beads to divide rooms, but if it is possible to combine two rooms, then do so.

▲ **Sample floor plan**

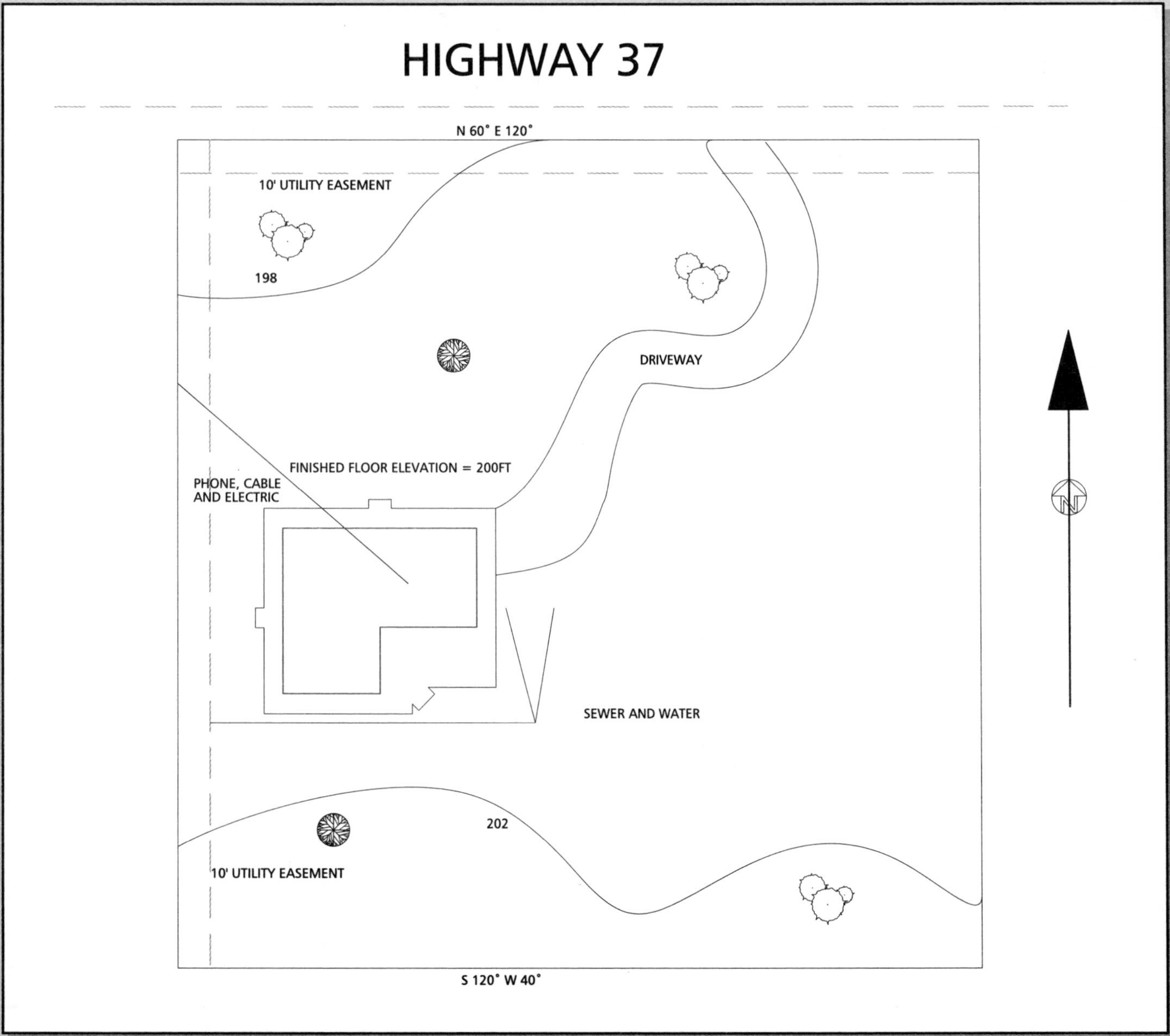

HIGHWAY 37

N 60° E 120°

10' UTILITY EASEMENT

198

DRIVEWAY

FINISHED FLOOR ELEVATION = 200FT

PHONE, CABLE
AND ELECTRIC

SEWER AND WATER

202

10' UTILITY EASEMENT

S 120° W 40°

▲ Sample plot plan

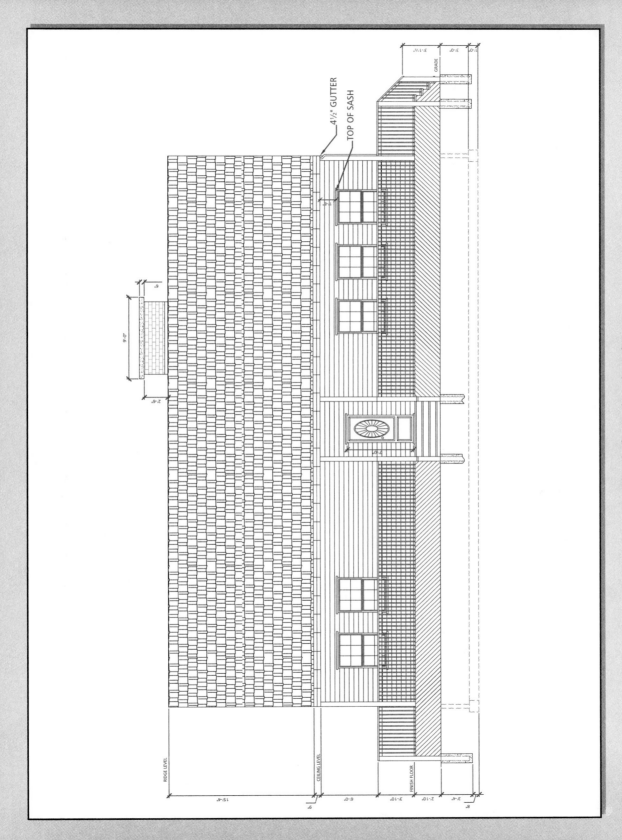

▲ Sample front elevation plan

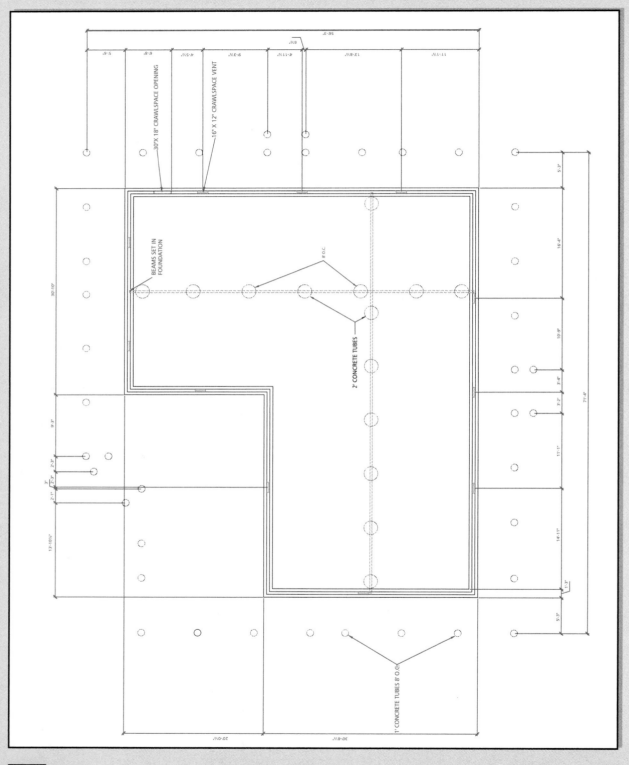

▲ Sample foundation plan

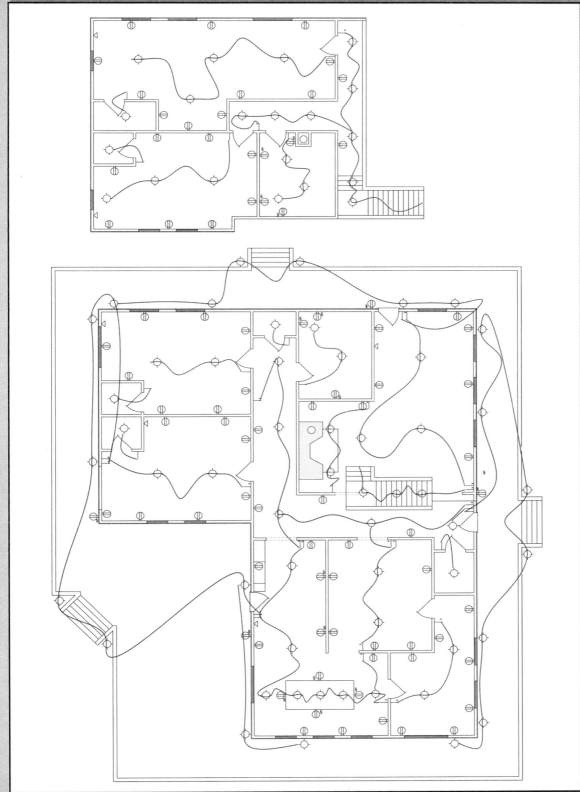

▲ Sample electrical plan

For instance, you could combine the dining and living rooms into one big, spacious room. This will save you the cost of materials to build those walls. Also try to keep hallways to a minimum. Hallways can eat up a lot of your building materials, and they also require more energy for heating and cooling. With a little careful designing, you can keep the number of and length of hallways to a minimum, thus saving yourself money now and in the long run.

ALERT!

Be wary of fancy designs. A rectangular design is more cost efficient than any other. You can always use all that money you saved in building a home with just four outside walls to add on some of those extra features and make it look even fancier than that hexagonal home you wanted so badly at first.

Of course, you can always save money by building a smaller home, but who wants to do that? If you don't like the idea of a smaller home, perhaps you'll go for fewer features. Do you really need that top-of-the-line turbo deluxe super dishwasher right now, or will your older one hold out for a bit longer? How about the stained glass windows handcrafted by faraway monks—can you live with plain glass for a while? You can save yourself money by doing without certain features now and adding them later when you can pay for them out-of-pocket. Keep in mind that if you include them now, their cost becomes part of the loan you will have to pay back plus interest.

Finally, designing is itself is a money-saver—careful designing and planning, that is. The better you design right now, the fewer the changes that will be needed during construction. Making changes during construction can be expensive, so it's a good idea to make as few of them as possible. By being very meticulous and thorough with the design and house plans, you will do a lot to reduce the number of significant changes you'll have to make. Ⓔ

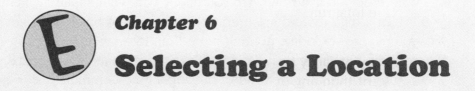

Chapter 6

Selecting a Location

Y ou've been making decisions on the style, size, and type of home you want to build. But you cannot make this dream a reality until you have somewhere to put it. The land you build on is just as important as the home itself, so it's essential that you take your time and make informed decisions regarding your home site.

City? Country? Or Somewhere in Between?

The first big decision you have to make regarding your lot location is whether you want to live in the city, in the country, or in a suburb. Each has advantages and disadvantages that you must weigh carefully before making a final decision.

Where do you live now? Are you happy with your situation? Perhaps you live in a big city and are tired of the hustle and bustle of everyday life—you're sure you'd like nothing more than to move to the country where everything is peaceful and you have more space. Or perhaps you live in the country and are tired of making a long commute just to get groceries—you're convinced you'd love the convenience of city living. Even so, keep in mind that the grass is always greener on the other side. That's why it's important to look at the pros and cons of each situation.

The Urban Zone

The city has many conveniences that the country and suburbs cannot offer. For instance, if you live in a city, you are probably close to shopping, entertainment, restaurants, employers, and so on. Having all these amenities within a short commute (possibly even walking distance) is a huge advantage that many people enjoy. Cities also offer public transportation, making the commute that much easier.

While convenience is often a main attraction for city living, some people enjoy the city for the diversity it offers. Theaters, museums, sports arenas, clubs with live music, and ethnic restaurants are just a few of the common amenities that cities usually offer. You will also enjoy the diversity of people residing in cities. From all walks of life, people of different ages, ethnicities, religions, and lifestyles gather in. If you're looking for variety or to add a little spice to your life, city living may just be the thing for you.

FACT

Many cities have designed parks or wooded areas to bring a little of the country into the city. These are great places to visit if you are looking to take a break from the hectic world of city life.

There are some disadvantages to city living, however. The conveniences are nice, but you'll pay for them. City living is usually more expensive than living outside a city. While commutes are shorter, they are often busier, meaning you'll probably have to fight traffic to and from work. Many people are also concerned about the crime rates in cities. Some, of course, are better than others, so check out the crime rates in your prospective choices. Another aspect of city life that many find to be a disadvantage is the small amount of space you have to work with. Cities are crowded, and it may be difficult to find a lot to build on.

Country Living

Life in the country appeals to many people. Aesthetically, the country offers a picturesque landscape in which to build your dream home. You have the space to create beautiful and elaborate gardens or simply enjoy the sights of nature. If you're an animal lover, the extra space will come in handy if you want to keep livestock or make life better for your family pets.

Away from the hustle and bustle of the city, you can enjoy a peaceful and relaxed lifestyle, complete with fresh air and quiet roads. You will also enjoy the privacy that comes with country living. Your nearest neighbor could be more than a mile away!

Without a doubt, the charms of country living are numerous, but there are also some disadvantages that go along with this lifestyle. For instance, you'll have to make a longer commute to your job, to entertainment venues, and to do everyday chores like buying groceries or visiting the post office. Services that are offered in more populated areas, such as trash pickup and food delivery, may not be available. Also, you may be required to bring in utility services if they aren't already established in the area.

Movin' to the 'Burbs

If the chaos of the city repels you, but you don't want to seclude yourself in the country either, the suburbs may be the perfect solution. These residential communities are situated on the outskirts of a city, but far enough away to capture some of the peace of the country. You are likely to have more lot space to build on, but you will still have neighbors for that added sense of community. Suburbs have tried to capture the best of both worlds, and in so doing have become very popular with many families.

ALERT!

Check building restrictions in your chosen subdivision to make sure they will protect the value of your home. For example, if your house is all brick, make sure restrictions require other houses in the area to have brick exteriors as opposed to vinyl siding.

With the popularity and high residential rates of suburbs, some of these communities are bringing in more and more commercial services to meet the needs of the residents. Because of this, some suburbs are turning into small-scale cities. If you want to get away from the city aspect, check out the development plans of prospective suburbs before purchasing a lot there.

While suburbs are closer to the city's amenities than rural areas, you still have that commute to consider. Sometimes traffic can be quite heavy from the suburbs to the city during rush hour, as many suburbanites work in the city. Suburbs are also often heavily populated because many people have already realized the benefits to living near, but not within, city limits. It may be a little difficult to find a lot to build on, though probably not as hard as finding one in the city.

Location Considerations

Once you've made the general decision about where to live (city, country, or suburbs), you'll need to narrow down the prospective lot locations within that area. Some of these decisions will affect the cost of building your home. Some will affect the future value of your home, and some will affect the quality of life you and your family enjoy. The following sections highlight a few considerations homebuilders usually give to prospective locations, but don't stop there. Come up with your own list of considerations specific to your needs and future happiness in your home.

Utilities

If you have chosen to build in the city, it's likely that utilities, such as water, electricity, and sewer, are already established. However, areas outside the city, especially rural areas, may not have these utilities readily available. Your real estate agent will be able to tell you whether you will need to bring in the utilities or if they have been previously established on the lot. Keep this in mind when considering the price of the lot; while rural areas may be cheaper, you may need to pay more to have utilities set up.

If you are accustomed to having DSL, digital cable, or other such high-tech services, you'll want to find out if these will also be available in the area. While these services are reaching more and more people almost every day, not all areas are yet equipped to offer them.

Future Developments

The future developments of the potential lot area can either work for or against you, depending on how you look at it. Either way, you'll need to find out all you can about any projected developments in the area and how they will affect the quality of life you plan to enjoy in your new home.

For instance, if you plan to live in a rural area because you want peace, quiet, and very few neighbors (if any), but you see that several lots are for sale along the dusty dirt road that leads to your potential building site, then you'll need to be open to the possibility of having more neighbors than you once thought. This possibility probably means more traffic along the dirt road than you reckoned on and also opens you to the risk that cheaper homes will be built on those lots, thus reducing the value of your home. On the other hand, regardless of whether you welcome the thought of neighbors with open arms, you might consider yourself lucky to get such a good deal on the land before it becomes the next hotspot.

It is always a good idea to consider your home's future resale value before building. Take a look at the features of your lot that could affect resale value, such as future developments, neighboring houses, and the overall aesthetic view of your home on the lot.

If you've chosen to live in a suburb or city, you'll need to be on the lookout for commercial properties setting up shop in the area. You may appreciate the development of new businesses, which will grant you more job opportunities and convenience. On the other hand, you may not want to deal with the heavier traffic and general activity that go along with developing commercial areas.

School Systems

If you have children, the local school system is probably one of your biggest concerns. Of course, all parents want their children to get the best education possible. If you have chosen to enroll your children in private school, then visit the private schools closest to the proposed lot location to get an idea of the options available and the quality of education. If your children will be attending public school, then you'll need to find out which school they will be enrolled in. Before you decide to purchase any land, it's always a good idea to find out how schools are rated academically and to make a personal visit. If quality of education is your top priority, you may want to start by locating the best schools, then find out what areas those schools serve and make your lot decision from there.

Finding Available Lots

Take as much time as you possibly can to scout potential lots. Remember, the land you build your home on is just as important as the home itself. The more lots you have to choose from, the more likely you are to find one that suits you perfectly. So how do you go about finding available lots? You have several different avenues open to you. If you take advantage of each, you'll have more options to work with.

People typically start their hunt for a home site at their local real estate agencies. A real estate agent can be a true treasure on a land hunt. As long as you are able to walk into the office with specifics in mind, the real estate agent will be able to tell you what locations will best suit your wants and needs. They know what land is good for building and what land should never have a structure resting on it. They know what you can expect to pay for lots in certain areas and may even have suggestions for less expensive areas you hadn't considered. While the real estate agency may be working for the seller, they will want to protect the buyer—they have a reputation to uphold, after all—so use their knowledge and expertise to your greatest benefit.

FACT

While some people first purchase the land and then design the house they want to build, others scout out lots with house plans in hand. In this way, they are able to find a location that best suits the value, design, and size of their home. They also know how much they are willing to spend on land, as they already have a cost estimate of the house.

If you'd rather not deal with a real estate agent, then you still have some land-hunting options available to you. Since you already have an idea of the area where you'd like to live, take a good long drive around it. Train your eye to search out "For Sale" signs posted by owners. If nothing more, these signs tell you that there is land around for sale, thus answering one of your questions on the spot. Even if you aren't sure that you'd particularly care to live on that particular lot, give the seller a call and find out all you can about the land. He or she may have other lots for sale or know of other sellers. You can also scour the ads in local newspapers to find land for sale.

If you have already designed and planned for your future home, talk with those professionals that you've worked with, such as the designer, general contractor, and supplier. They may know of some prime building spots or land that hasn't yet been advertised as for sale. Again, it's always a good idea to explore all your options.

Evaluating the Lot

Once you've found a few potential home sites to consider, you'll need to inspect the site with a list of questions in hand. Since you're planning to use the land to build your home, you of course need to know that the land can be built upon. Once you purchase the property, it is yours—

meaning all its problems are also yours. Know its strengths and weaknesses beforehand so you can prepare yourself for the work required to create your ideal home.

Not all lots are created equal. It's up to you to determine whether a given lot's strengths outweigh its weaknesses. The following questions will help you determine whether the lot is a prime or poor location:

- Is the lot zoned exclusively residential?
- Will you be able to obtain a building permit for the site?
- Is the building site on a gradual slope up from the road? (If the house is on a down slope, you may have problems with water draining toward the house.)
- Is the lot in a low-traffic area?
- Does the lot allow your dwelling some privacy?
- Is the lot in a flood plain?
- What utility services are established on the lot? Which aren't?
- Is the building site easily accessible from the road?
- Is the lot located in a respectable and safe neighborhood?
- What type of soil base does the lot have? (Sandy or rocky soil may cause problems when building the foundation.)
- Does water collect in spots throughout the lot?
- What is the height of the sewer line, if applicable? (You need to make sure your drain pipe is higher than the sewer line.)
- If a sewer line isn't available, will the lot support a septic system?
- How much landscaping will the lot need?
- Is the lot convenient to your place of employment, shopping areas, schools, etc.?
- Is the lot in a quiet area?
- Are the homes surrounding the lot comparable in value to yours?
- Is public transportation accessible to the lot, if applicable?

Matching Land to Lifestyle

Now that you've determined that you can build on a particular lot, the next step is to figure out if it is suitably equipped to match your lifestyle—or the lifestyle you want to create with your new home. The importance you place on some factors is in direct relation to personal taste. For instance, if aesthetics are important, you may decide that the lot's view, both from the building site and from the road, is a priority in your decision making. Or maybe you enjoy hosting a lot of big parties. In that case, the distance of the building site from the surrounding neighbors and the availability of plenty of parking space may be important to you. Take a look at your current lifestyle. Will the lot be able to support and fulfill your manner of living?

Size

For most people, the size of the lot is a major factor. First and foremost, you'll need to make sure that the lot is large enough for the home you want to build. Even if you don't already have house plans, you should already know the size of the home you want to build and, therefore, be able to determine if it fits within the baselines of the lot. Of course, this is the minimum amount of space you'll need. If you want a large back or front yard, then you'll need to take that into consideration as well.

The owner of the property or the real estate agent should be able to give you the information you need regarding property lines and setbacks. From there you can "place" your home on the lot and see how much additional space you have to work with.

Are you planning to make any future additions to the home, such as an in-ground swimming pool, or build any other structures on the property, such as a barn? If so, make sure the lot has enough room for these added features. Try to look to the future and visualize your home in its ideal, perfect state. While you may not be able to have everything you want right now, adding on later is always a possibility.

Privacy

Another concern many people have is that of privacy. Once the home is built, how much privacy will the lot afford? Is it set back some distance from neighboring homes? Are there trees or other natural features that will give the house some privacy? If not, would you be able to create a screen with landscaping? If you plan to live in the home for several years, you can plant your own trees, as long as you have the room to do so. If you choose to landscape or put up fencing to create privacy, these costs should be added to your total estimate.

Child's Play

If you have children or are planning to start a family, then several additional factors come into play in your decision on whether to purchase a particular lot. You want your children to be safe, so the neighborhood's reputation and its crime rate are major factors. What are the posted speed limits on the roads near the lot? A road with high speed limits and a lot of traffic poses a hazard to the safety of your children, especially if the building site is located close to the road.

Take a look at the type of neighborhood you'll be living in. Are there other children yours can play with? Living in a community of mostly senior citizens might not be as much fun for your children as it would be to live in a community with lots of young families. Does the neighborhood have a playground nearby? If not, will the lot allow for sufficient yard space for a swing set or room to throw a ball? If your children are old enough, you may want to include them in the decision-making process. You may find that their input is invaluable.

Cost Considerations

Unless you get your land as a gift, your home site is going to cost money. The amount you spend will depend primarily on the lot's location. Because lot costs vary so widely, there's no way to accurately define the range you should expect to encounter. One thing is for sure: They're not making any more real estate. Good land is not cheap. You should be prepared to spend quite a big chunk of cash.

Obviously, land prices will play a major role in your purchasing decision, but keep in mind that the asking price can usually be negotiated. Don't let a perfect plot get away just because it's a few thousand outside your anticipated range.

ALERT!

Before purchasing a lot, make sure the land is free of any prior titles or liens. To do this you'll need to pay a fee for a title search of the land. The title officer will then give you all the information you need. Financial institutions will require a free and clear title to the land before they will lend you the money to purchase it.

While you certainly want to purchase a good piece of land, keep in mind that the more you spend on your lot, the less you have available for building the house. It's best to already have a cost estimate in mind for the house itself. That way, as you're shopping for your home site, you can figure approximately how much you're willing to spend on any given lot. Don't go out of your way to scrimp on the purchase; a poorly located lot can have a terrible negative effect on your home's resale value. It's a delicate balance, but one that you should be able to accomplish by doing your homework and making informed decisions.

Costly Alterations

The asking price of the lot is definitely going to claim a lot of your attention, but it isn't the only number that should be swimming around in your head. When considering the overall cost of the land, you also need to take into account any alterations that will be needed before you can build on it. For instance, a piece of land in the country is going to be quite a bit cheaper than the same size plot of land in the city. However, the city lot has utilities already established there, and the rural lot doesn't. You need to know how much it will cost to bring in the utilities. Add that price onto the asking price of the land for a more accurate estimate of rural lot costs. In the same way, you'll need to add costs for blasting rocks, removing trees, and adding soil. Anything that needs to be done to the land before it is deemed ready for building should be added to the overall cost of the land.

Taxes

When deciding whether or not to purchase a lot, you may also want to consider how much of a tax bill you'll be paying on a house in that area. While this isn't directly related to the upfront cost of the land, there's little way to avoid the property and local taxes that will be hitting you in wallet once you build. You might as well try to get the most out of your money. It may be that building the same home on a lot just a few miles down the road will save you a bundle in property tax. Do your homework now, and save money later.

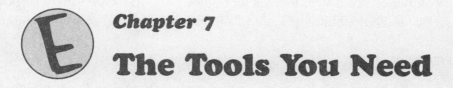

Chapter 7

The Tools You Need

If you are going to participate in the actual building of your home, you'll have to be familiar with the tools that are used during construction. This chapter introduces you to the hand and power tools commonly used in homebuilding and provides you with the information you need to properly and safely equip yourself.

Hand Tools

Hand tools are those that rely on your strength and power to perform at their best. There's no better way to get the most out of a building experience. Yes, they take a little extra sweat and endurance, but that's a worthwhile tradeoff for the satisfaction and pride you'll derive from the experience. Even with today's technology and the wide variety of power tools available, building a home still requires the use of some hand tools.

Hammer

The hammer is the tool most commonly associated with building. Because the hammer is used throughout the building process, it is one of the first hand tools you should get. You probably already have a hammer around the house that you use all the time. However, the process of building a house is quite a bit different from hanging a picture, so before you check off "hammer" on your tools checklist, take a look at your hammer. Make sure it's high quality and comfortable to heft and use.

ALERT!

It is important to find the hammer that best suits you. For instance, if you use a too-heavy hammer for a repetitive job like driving nails, you'll get tired very quickly, thus opening up the possibility that you'll make mistakes and injure yourself. The hammer should have a comfortable grip, balance well in your hand, and be of a weight that fits your physical strength.

Visit any hardware or building-supply company, and you will find a wide variety of hammers to choose from. You'll notice that the hammers have different handle lengths, weights, textured faces, grips, and overall sizes. Some hammers are designed for specific jobs. For instance, a framing hammer, as the name implies, is used for framing and will usually have a waffled face to help it keep from slipping off the nail head. You can get yourself a framing hammer, a drywall hammer, a finishing hammer, and so on, but a high-quality general-purpose hammer with a smooth face will be able to handle most jobs quite well.

Measuring and Marking Tools

Building a home is an exact science with no room for estimates. Therefore, you'll need to have a collection of measuring and marking tools by your side throughout most of the process. A steel tape measure is a necessity. Steel tape measures come in a variety of sizes and lengths. Most builders will have at least two: a 100-foot measure for big jobs and another for smaller jobs, usually 16 to 25 feet. These tape measures read just like a ruler and are designed for convenience and ease of use.

Squares are used to measure and mark—you guessed it—squares. Because you will be working with angles and square cuts often, having a couple of squares on hand will make your job much easier. Again, you will find that squares come in different shapes and sizes. You will probably want to get yourself an aluminum carpenter's square, which is lightweight and easy to handle. You may also want to get a triangular rafter square, smaller than a carpenter's square, which is designed to mark angles quickly and easily.

FACT

A sliding T-bevel is a type of square that many builders find useful. This tool allows you to slide the blade to set any angle you want. Once the angle is set, you can then move the T-bevel to the material you are cutting, making the transfer of the angle easy and convenient.

Measuring won't do you much good unless you have something to mark with. A carpenter's pencil is a good tool to always have on hand. These pencils are more durable than regular writing pencils and are designed not to roll away when you set them down. Another great marking tool is a chalkline. This is simply a piece of string that comes coiled up in a case containing powdered chalk. You pull the string tight between two points and snap it, leaving a straight and accurate line of chalk.

Prying Tools

In addition to tools for putting things together, you'll need tools to tear things apart. A flat bar is handy to have around. It can be used to pry apart pieces that have been previously nailed together, to take out trim, or to pull nails. Another tool that is useful in removing nails is the cat's paw, also called a nail claw. This tool is used to pry out nails that are buried in the wood. The cat's paw is driven under the head of the nail with a hammer and then partially levered out. You then use a hammer to completely withdraw the nail. A crowbar or pry bar can also be used to pry nailed pieces apart or withdraw nails.

Additional Hand Tools

Of course, you'll be using several tools in addition to those mentioned above. The following is a list of the more common hand tools used for homebuilding:

- Levels (a 2-foot level for tight spaces and a 6-foot level for bigger ones)
- Utility knife
- Nail sets
- Screwdrivers (both flat and Philips heads)
- Pliers
- Tin snips
- Adjustable wrench
- Sledgehammer
- Chisels and files
- Shovels (both flat and pointed)

Power Tools

While you certainly *could* build a house using only hand tools, power tools speed up the process and make the work much easier on the builder. Today's technology has placed electric or battery power behind several tools that used to rely on the builder's physical strength. However, because you are dealing with power greater than your own, you need to be especially careful when using power tools. Keep these tools under your control at all times, and be sure you know how to operate them safely and effectively before you even try to use them.

Saws

Power saws are among the handiest tools a builder can have. They reduce the time and energy it takes to cut your materials, making the building process much easier for all involved. The circular saw is probably the most popular power tool on the building site. You can get a direct-drive circular saw, which has the motor on the side, or a worm-drive circular saw, which is a little heavier and has the motor on the front. Get a feel for each to determine which best suits you. Because you will use your circular saw a lot, be sure the brand you get has a reputation for quality and durability.

Many homeowners already have a circular saw in their garage. Most of these saws are intended to be used for various projects around the house. While they handle those jobs very well, it's not a good idea to use your everyday circular saw for building your home. They simply won't hold up as well as a professional grade saw.

A sabre saw is another power tool often found on building sites. This saw is smaller in size and can be used to make cuts in tight places. The sabre saw can also be used to make curved cuts and has blades that can cut through most materials. A power miter saw, sometimes called a chop saw, is used for finishing work. These saws are great to have around as they are great for accuracy cuts, both square and angled. They are also tough tools with the ability to easily cut through materials of varying thicknesses.

Drills

An electric drill (or two or three) is a must-have on a building site. It is most often used to bore holes, but you can also use it to drive screws and mix compounds. Your household drill isn't likely to be suitable for building a home. Most builders prefer a $3/8$-inch reversing electric drill with variable speeds. Electric drills come in both corded and cordless models. For most work, you'll want to use the corded simply because it has more power. However, a cordless drill is portable and handy for the smaller jobs throughout the process.

Pneumatic Tools

Though not essential, some builders find pneumatic tools to be a huge building advantage. Pneumatic tools are air driven, such as nailers and staplers. These tools can increase production time and require less energy and strength from the builder. Because the pneumatic tools are air driven, you will also have to invest in an air compressor in order to power them. The tools are connected to the air compressor with an air hose. This can be an unnecessary and costly investment (though it does cut back on time), so weigh the decision carefully.

Planers and Sanders

Planing and sanding can be done with hand tools, but if you expect to have to do a lot of these jobs, you'll find that power planers and sanders can be very valuable. A power plane makes the job of smoothing surfaces a breeze. Because it has the power of electricity behind it, there aren't too many obstacles that can get in the way (such as knots in the wood). You can smooth surfaces or trim down materials quickly and easily using a power plane.

ALERT!

Consider your purchasing decisions carefully. While power tools do indeed speed up the building process and can make the work much easier for all those involved, they can also be quite costly. If you are working on a tight budget, some power tools (especially those you won't use much) are an unnecessary expense—you can do many of the same jobs with hand tools. You might also want to check your local hardware stores and suppliers; many of them rent power tools at reasonable rates.

Sanders are often used during finishing work. A belt sander is usually used first to prepare the material for finish sanding. It is the heavy-duty sander that takes care of all the greater surface irregularities in the material. These sanders do their job well, so be sure you know how to use them properly before working on quality materials. For instance, if you do not keep the sander moving, it can dig into the material and cause damage.

Finishing sanders are smaller in size and weight than the belt sanders, and, as the name implies, are used to put the finishing touches on certain materials. For instance, you can remove marks left by other tools on the trim of the house using a finishing sander. You can use the finishing sander to remove the scratches and marks left behind by the belt sander. They are designed to smooth out areas, not create flat surfaces, so don't try to use them for big jobs.

Specialized Tools

Depending on how much work you plan to do yourself and what you will contract out, you may need to get your hands on some specialized tools. These are tools that are used for specific jobs, such as plumbing or electrical work. If you are planning to hire out specialized jobs, then you won't need to concern yourself with the tools associated with them—the workers will (or should!) come equipped with their own. However, if you are going to try your hand at doing the work yourself, you'll need to become familiar with some of the specialty tools associated with particular jobs.

It is highly recommended that you leave the more technical and specialized jobs to the experts. Unless you have prior experience with the work, you may end up costing yourself more time and money in the long run.

For instance, if you are going to do the electrical work, you'll probably be using a wire stripper and voltage tester. If you are going to do the plumbing, you'll need to have access to a tubing cutter. The tools specific to specialized trades will be discussed further in later chapters. For right now, you just need to be aware (for budget purposes) that other tools may be needed if you plan to do your own work.

Shopping for Tools

A good rule of thumb is to buy the best tools you can afford. However, this isn't to say that you should go to the building supply store and rack up charges on your credit card immediately. Take your time with this shopping venture. You don't need everything right now, and you may find that you don't need some of these tools at all. While price will likely be on your mind when shopping, always consider these two things when selecting tools: comfort and quality.

Comfort

When shopping for tools, one of the first things to hunt for is comfort. Because you will be using many of these tools regularly, it is important that they feel good in your grasp and match your physical strength. Using tools that are too heavy for you can cause you to tire easily, at best, and at worst can cause injury. Not every tool will fit every person. The best way to figure out if a tool is comfortable to you is to try it out. That's why it's usually better to shop for tools in an actual store rather than ordering through catalogs or the Internet. The hands-on trial will give you a good idea of how well the tool will work for you.

In addition to physical comfort, you'll need to consider your mental comfort with the tool as well. Many power tools can be intimidating to those who are not experienced in using them. Search out those tools that will put your mind at ease. If you are nervous using a tool, you're more likely to make mistakes—not to mention the fact it is simply an unpleasant experience. Try out as many tools as you can before selecting those that will suit your comfort levels.

Quality

You are going to be faced with a wide assortment of tools to choose from. Some of them are going to be so cheap you'll wonder just what they're made of, and others will be so pricey that your mouth will gape wide open. Your purchases will likely fall somewhere in between, but try to stay at the pricier end of things. When it comes to tools, the saying "You get what you pay for" definitely applies.

As a first-time homebuilder, you aren't expected to know which tools are of the best quality. Those who work in the industry will be able to advise you on top-quality brands and styles. Ask around, and note different people's preferences. If all else fails, go with the well-known brands and those that offer lifetime guarantees or warranties.

Because you plan to use most of these tools for a pretty heavy-duty job, they should be reliable and durable. This means that you want professional-grade tools, not those made for occasional household use. The professional-grade tools will cost you more, but in return you will find them easier and safer to use. They will also last longer, and usually they have warranties guaranteeing their performance.

Consider Renting

If you are planning to make this homebuilding endeavor your *only* homebuilding endeavor, then it doesn't make a lot of sense to buy expensive equipment that you'll only use once. A lot of the power tools can be quite pricey and aren't practical for everyday use. In this case, renting those tools that you will use infrequently is a good option to consider. Some tools will only need to be used for a day or two. Compare the cost of renting for two days to that of purchasing the tool, and you may find that you will save yourself hundreds of dollars.

Consider Borrowing

Another option you may want to consider is that of borrowing some of the tools you'll need. As you get further into the homebuilding experience, you will probably meet other people who have built their own homes and have some of the tools you need on hand. Or maybe you have family members or friends who have built their own homes.

Take care when asking to borrow tools. A lot of people are hesitant to lend out expensive or high-quality items—and with good reason. If you have established trust with a person who is lending to you, be sure to maintain that trust by taking good care of his or her tools. Treat the borrowed tools as well as or better than you would your own.

Tool Totes

It won't do to have your tools scattered all around the building site; you'll need somewhere to put them. When visiting the building supply store, take a look at the various tool totes available. You're likely to find toolboxes, tool belts, tool bags, and tool buckets. Toolboxes are the traditional way to carry tools. They are just what their name says: boxes with compartments for various tools. Tool belts are typically made of leather and have straps, hooks, and pockets. They fit around your waist for easy access and also to free your hands. Tool bags have a long strap that goes over your shoulder. These too have various compartments in which to store tools. Finally, tool buckets are simply 5-gallon buckets that are meant to hold larger tools, such as levels and hand saws, and that are usually covered with pouches and compartments meant to hold the smaller tools.

FACT

You'll also need to invest in a few extension cords so you can operate your power tools. Search out the heavy-duty, high-quality cords that are meant for builders. Extension cords come in many gauge numbers. For your purposes, get 10- or 12-gauge cords, as these have the heaviest wire.

The tool totes are used for those tools you use most often, such as a hammer, tape measure, and utility knife. Which you use depends on your personal preference and comfort level. Since you will have the tote with you each time you get to work, make sure it has enough room for all you need and is convenient and easy to carry. If you aren't going to make building homes a full-time job, then there's no reason to purchase the high-priced versions. The less expensive, plainer tool totes will suit your purposes just fine.

Safety Issues

The building site is not a playground; it is a dangerous place that deserves to be treated with a great deal of seriousness and common sense. There are potential hazards lurking everywhere. Even professional builders are injured from time to time. Accidents do happen. However, there are some precautions you can take to lessen the risk of injury:

- Wear appropriate clothing. Good shoes (preferably steel-toed) with traction and comfortable and sturdy soles are a must.
- Tie back long hair so it doesn't get caught in a power tool.
- Always wear goggles or other protective eyewear when using any power tool or when there is a possibility of flying materials.
- Use earplugs or other protectors when operating power tools.
- Wear a hard hat when others are working above you.
- Wear a breathing mask when you are sanding, installing fiberglass insulation, or anytime there is the possibility of breathing in large particles of material.
- Don't allow children to run around unsupervised on the building site.
- Always lift with your legs rather than your back.
- Read the manual before operating any power tool you are unfamiliar with. Pay particular attention to the safety guidelines.
- Unplug electric tools before making adjustments.
- Don't overwork yourself. Take breaks, and drink plenty of water.
- Never drink alcohol or use drugs on the building site. Always work with a clear head.
- Wear gloves when working with materials or tools that could injure your hands.
- Make sure everyone knows where the first-aid kit is stored, and keep it stocked at all times.
- Pay attention to what others around you are doing.
- Keep all electrical tools and cords away from water.
- Protect and secure open holes.
- When using a ladder or scaffolding, make sure it is secure and stabilized.
- Remove any nails that are protruding from boards or other materials.
- Keep your work area clean.

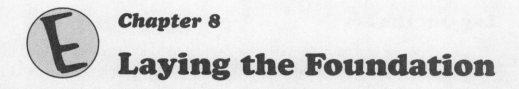

Chapter 8

Laying the Foundation

Take a moment to breathe a sigh of relief. You've made it through all the red tape and to the other side of the sea of paperwork. You have secured the lot, the loan, and the contractors. Now it's time to get down and dirty and start building the house!

Preparing the Site

Yes, there is still some prep work to be done before you can break in those new tools. Your first step is to prepare the site for the foundation. Take your time with this job and make sure you do it right. Mistakes made during this step will be very difficult and costly to fix later.

Lay Out the Lot

Before you can begin digging, you need to know *where* to dig. Pull out your plot plans, and take a look at both the property lines and the location of the house on the site. If it hasn't been done already, you'll first need to stake out the property lines. (You certainly don't want to be building on someone else's property!) Once the property lines are determined and clearly marked, it's time to situate the house on the lot. Again, your plot plans will give you the information you need, but you'll have to transfer that information from paper to land. For right now, just mark the corners of the house.

It is imperative that the property lines and location of the house be clearly marked and accurate. Unless you know how to use surveying equipment, it's a good idea to hire a surveyor to stake these boundaries for you. The surveyor will also be able to do a topographical survey, which will tell you what needs to be done to make the foundation level. This is extremely helpful during clearing and excavation, as spots will be marked where soil needs to be removed or added.

Mark Utilities

In addition to marking property lines and the corners of your building site, you also have to flag the places where utilities come onto the property. For instance, you'll want to place a stake where the sewer and water lines cross into the property. If you will have an underground power line, this will be marked as well. If any utilities will be delivered above ground, mark where they will enter the house. Also mark where a septic system will be installed or a well will be dug, if applicable. To save confusion later, mark each stake with a different color to indicate the utility service it represents.

ALERT!

Don't forget to install a portable toilet on the building site! It will be quite some time yet before the bathrooms of the house are finished, and your neighbors might not take too kindly to construction workers regularly asking to use their facilities.

Your electrical service won't be permanently set up just yet, but you still need electricity at the site to power tools and equipment. So what do you do? Call the electric company, and request a temporary power pole. As this can sometimes take a couple of months, be sure you call well ahead of time. You may also want to consider installing a temporary site telephone. Your local phone company should be able to set you up with a line.

Clearing and Excavating

Before you can begin work on the foundation, you need to clear the land of any unwanted trees, brush, existing structures, tree stumps, and large rocks. This usually requires the use of heavy equipment, so you may want to hire someone to do this for you. Of course, you can do all this by hand, but it will take a lot of time and strength to accomplish what someone with machinery could do in a few hours.

If you do decide to hire someone, make sure you go over the plans with him. He needs to know exactly what areas are to be cleared and what to do with the debris. Mark anything you want kept, such as trees, with a brightly colored ribbon that is clearly visible.

You can save money by cutting down the trees yourself. However, if you choose to do this, make sure you leave at least 4 feet of the tree trunk standing. The bulldozer will need the weight of this to pull the stump and roots from the ground.

Most areas have a toll-free number you can call before starting any excavation to help you locate buried utilities. Failure to comply (by homeowner, excavator, and/or contractor) can cause serious injury and can also leave you liable for the repair of damaged lines.

Outlining the Foundation

Once the land is cleared, you're ready to lay out the foundation. Be sure you check the setback distances from the street, allowable distances for side and backyards from adjacent properties, and easements for utility and drainage.

You've already established the corners of the house. Now you need to connect them to create the outline for the foundation. To do this, install batter boards at each corner. Batter boards are simply three wooden stakes (usually 2×4s) connected with horizontal cross members (usually 1×4s), creating a right angle at the corner. The top of each cross member must be level with the others because the batter boards will determine the height of the foundation.

Position the batter boards 3 to 4 feet away from the stake that represents the corner of the foundation. By stretching string between the opposite batter boards, you create an outline of the foundation. Make sure that each string is stretched over the top of the cross members so that everything is nice and level. Once this is done, run string between the two sets of corners to create two diagonal lines. Measure the length of each diagonal. If the two diagonals measure the same, then your corners are square; if not, then you'll need to make some adjustments.

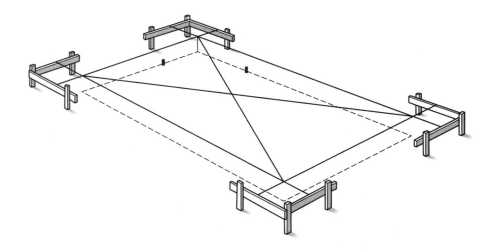

▲ Foundation outlined with batter boards

Excavation

The moment you've been waiting for has finally arrived: It's time to break ground! You are going to be excavating (removing soil) from the building site to prepare for laying the foundation. Use the outline of the foundation that you've just created as a guide for where to dig; however, it is common practice to dig approximately 2 feet out from the foundation outline on all sides, giving yourself room to work and maneuver.

If you plan to install a septic system, you have to dig a hole and trenches during excavation to accommodate it. The septic tank should be installed as late in the construction process as possible to minimize the possibility that material trucks might drive over and damage it.

Refer to your house plans to see how deep you need to dig. Remember, the batter boards mark the height of the foundation top, so use them as a reference point as you take depth measurements. The amount of soil you'll need to remove depends primarily on the type of foundation and whether you are putting in a basement. Don't haul off all the soil you remove during excavation—you'll use it later as backfill.

Foundation Fundamentals

The foundation is the part of the house responsible for supporting and stabilizing the rest of the structure. Laying the foundation is one of the most crucial stages of the building process. Because the house is going to rely on the strength, stability, and levelness of the foundation, a mistake here will result in complications throughout the rest of the building process. While you certainly can do this work yourself, it's a good idea to have an expert who will at least inspect your work, if not to go ahead and hire a foundation subcontractor to do it for you.

Foundation Responsibilities

The foundation carries a lot of responsibility. In addition to simply being the base of the structure, the foundation must create a level building plane. (Refer to your foundation plans for the proper height, elevation, size, and dimensions.) The foundation is also responsible for carrying and properly distributing the weight of the house, as well as protecting the house against water and insect damage. A lot rests (literally!) on the foundation. Take care that this building stage is carried out meticulously.

Factors Affecting Foundations

Some building codes allow only one type of foundation. If your code specifies a certain foundation type, you don't have to worry about choosing one over the others. The types of foundations are discussed in the next section; before discussing specifics, however, there are some general factors you should keep in mind. These are the characteristics that determine the ability of each foundation type to do its job.

FACT

The slope of the site affects not only the type of foundation you choose but also how the house is built. Slopes create a little more complexity and come with their own set of requirements. If you are building on a slope, it's recommended that you consult an expert before commencing building.

First and foremost, find out the requirements for foundations in your local building codes. These codes will tell you what types of foundations are permissible in your area and will specify construction requirements for these foundations. If, after consulting the building codes, you still have a choice left to you, take a look at the soil you'll be building on. Problematic soil—excessively rocky soil, for instance, or heavy clay—can be an important factor in deciding on the type of foundation you need. Of course, you'll also want to consider the weather in the area and whether your location makes your house prone to any natural disasters.

Quite likely the building department has already taken this into consideration and addressed it in their codes. Finally, you'll want to compare the costs of the various foundations and also how each will look supporting your house.

Types of Foundations

There are several types of foundations to choose from. However, your options may be limited by building code restrictions or site complications. It's a good idea to review your options with professionals in the industry to make sure the options you are considering will generate optimum performance for your site and type of house. The three main types of foundations are continuous wall foundations, pier foundations, and slab foundations.

Continuous Wall Foundations

A continuous wall foundation is just what it says—a wall that creates a foundation on all sides of a house. Continuous wall foundations can be built of stone, brick, wood, poured concrete, or concrete block. A concrete continuous wall is the most common form of foundation used today. Using concrete, whether poured or block, is cost effective, easy, and accepted by almost all building codes.

Natural stone looks very nice as a continuous wall foundation and is also inexpensive. However, some building codes won't allow the use of stone, and a stone wall can be difficult and time consuming to build. Brick is also aesthetically appealing. It is allowed by many codes and is durable and performs well. Brick isn't as cost effective as other types and can be quite time-consuming if you are inexperienced with bricklaying. Wood is typically not recommended. While it looks nice, is cost effective, and is easy to build, it doesn't have the lifespan of materials like concrete.

Pier Foundations

A pier foundation is one in which the house is supported by—you guessed it—piers. The piers can be made of stone, brick, wood, or concrete. Again, concrete is the most popular material. Beyond being allowed under many codes, it is inexpensive, permanent, and easy to use. Concrete blocks are more common, but you can also pour concrete into cylinders to create concrete piers.

Though rarely used, you also have the option of constructing steel column pier foundations. However, keep in mind that steel beams are considered unattractive and may affect the resale value of your home. They are also rather expensive and usually require the assistance of a professional engineer.

Stone piers are seen on many older homes, but they aren't common on newer ones. It is inexpensive and looks nice, but stone isn't usually allowed by most codes and doesn't hold up well in earthquakes or tornadoes. Brick piers are also very attractive and inexpensive, but may not be allowed in some areas, especially those prone to earthquakes. Wood piers aren't very common, but they are still a possibility. They are inexpensive and easy to build; however, keep in mind that wood is prone to rot and that the lifespan of this type of foundation would be relatively short.

Slab Foundations

A slab foundation is one that sits directly on the soil. As opposed to the other types of foundations, there is no floor frame or subflooring required with a slab foundation. The concrete slab serves as the rough flooring for the first floor of the house. Because of this, a slab foundation is the least expensive and time-consuming type of foundation you can build.

However, keep in mind that flooring constructed in this way will be very hard underfoot. Also, because the slab sits right on the soil, the house will be close to the ground. This may not be a problem for some houses, but those constructed of wood will be more prone to natural problems, such as moisture, insects, and fungus, if settled close to the ground.

Pouring the Footings

Footings make up the base of the foundation. They are wider than the foundation's walls, providing support and ensuring that the weight of the house is evenly distributed and the house will not settle. Because the quality and design of the footings determines the stability and soundness of the house, your local building codes will have much to say on the matter. For instance, the codes will tell you the depth that footings must be dug to. In all cases, the footings must be below the frost line. If the footings do not extend under the frost line, they will be subjected to a seasonal cycle of freezing and thawing that could weaken or even possibly move them. In colder climates, therefore, the footings have to go much deeper than those in warmer climates.

Your foundation plans, which have been approved by the building department, will give specifications about the footings. Even so, don't be surprised if local building inspectors want to check the location and design of the footings before the foundation walls are built. While this may seem like a hassle, it actually benefits you. Any mistakes you make now constructing your footings can be extremely detrimental to your home later.

ALERT!

Some building codes may require you to embed rebar within the footings to help counteract unstable or problematic soil. Rebar is a steel reinforcing rod that sits vertically in the footing and extends into the foundation wall, adding stability and support.

Footings can be poured into trenches or temporary wooden forms. Most people use the wooden forms, typically made of plywood, which are designed to fit the dimensions of the footings as specified in the house plans. The forms are placed in the footing trenches and held in position with braces and stakes. The concrete is then poured into the forms to create the footings. Once the footings are set and approved, you can then begin building the foundation walls.

Building Foundation Walls

Before you begin building the foundation walls, check your foundation plans and local building codes to refresh your memory of any requirements they must meet. While it is not all that difficult to actually build foundation walls, the job does demand accuracy and time. A foundation subcontractor will already have all the necessary materials, since foundation forms are often reused, and can get the job done quickly and successfully. If you haven't hired a foundation subcontractor, then refer to your plans often to double-check your work.

Foundation Forms

You'll need to use foundation forms to build the walls. Foundation forms are frames—usually made of dimensional lumber backed with panels of plywood—for shaping the poured concrete into a wall. Forms are used for pouring a concrete continuous wall foundation, the most common kind.

If you are building a different type of foundation, such as a pier foundation, you can get forms specific to the type. Some foundations, such as concrete block and brick foundations, do not require the use of forms. Always check your foundation plans for the necessary materials and procedures.

The foundation forms are set up and secured with braces and stakes to keep them from moving out of place. If there are to be any openings in the foundation walls, such as for pipes or windows, be sure the forms account for these spaces. Once the forms are established, the concrete is poured and left to set. After a few days, the forms are removed, and you are left with a foundation wall. Sounds simple enough, doesn't it? Well, there are a couple of things you must also consider.

Other Considerations

Almost all foundations incorporate anchor bolts that are secured within the foundation's walls. These anchor bolts will be used to hold the sill plates in place. (See Chapter 10 for more information about sill plates.) Building codes typically have minimum requirements for the number and location of these anchor bolts. Also take into consideration spaces needed in the wall to act as beam pockets. If your house plans call for a post-and-beam system, you have to leave enough space in the wall for the beam to fit into the foundation.

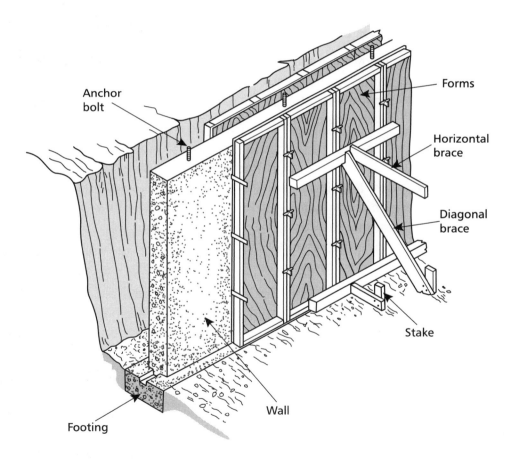

▲ Form for building a concrete foundation wall

Waterproofing and Other Considerations

Now that you've worked so hard to build and perfect the foundation of your house, you want to take steps to protect it against anything that could possibly damage it. Water damage is the number-one concern for most builders. While your foundation plans have accounted for proper drainage, you'll want to take an extra precaution and waterproof the foundation. Waterproof foundation coatings are relatively inexpensive and easy to apply. You can, of course, buy one of the more expensive versions for added protection, and you'll certainly want to do this if your soil is prone to hold moisture for a long time.

It is also recommended that you protect against pests, most notably termites, at this time. A pest-control professional will be familiar with those pests in your area that can do damage to the foundation. A pesticide will be applied around the footings and foundation before backfilling in order to deter pests.

FACT

Many people choose to add a termite shield beneath the sill for added protection against pests. While the shield does not kill the pests, it will help prevent the termites from gaining access to the floor framing. Chapter 11 offers more information about this type of protection.

If you live in a cold climate, you may also want to add foundation insulation at this time. Not only will this make the living environment more comfortable during those long winter months, but it will also help reduce your heating costs. The insulation comes in the form of foam boards that can be glued to the foundation walls. If you have chosen to build a basement, you may want to insulate the inside walls as well.

Backfilling

If your foundation plans and building codes require you to have foundation drains, you'll need to make sure these are installed before backfilling. These drains prevent water from seeping into the basement or crawlspace and from damaging the footings. The plastic drain pipes are situated in a bed of gravel at the footings. They are then covered with more gravel and a filter fabric or tar paper.

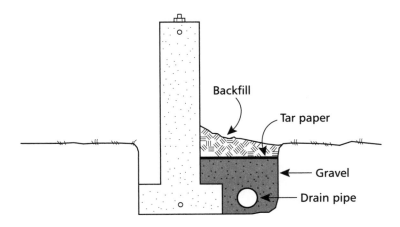

▲ Drain pipe installed at the footing in a bed of gravel

Once the foundation is built and you've taken all the precautions you can against damaging agents, it's time to replace some of that soil you removed earlier. Backfilling is simply placing soil back up against the foundation to grade level. Some foundations may require that you put supports in place to help handle the weight of the dirt. Backfilling can be a very satisfying job as it signifies the end of your first major task: building the foundation.

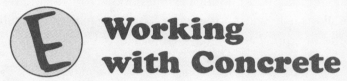

Chapter 9

Working with Concrete

You will probably work with concrete in one way or another when building your home. If you haven't worked with concrete before, it may seem a little intimidating. But you don't have to worry. This chapter gives you the lowdown on concrete and explains the ways in which you can use it to benefit the various structures on your building lot.

Concrete Basics

Concrete is a substance made up of cement, sand, and gravel. Dry concrete mix is combined with water, poured, and allowed to set. It then becomes a strong, durable, and long-lasting material that holds up well to wear and weather. Because it is so versatile and inexpensive (compared with other building materials), many people choose to use concrete when building foundations, sidewalks, driveways, porches, patios, and other structures on the building site.

ALERT!

Concrete is very heavy. When carrying anything heavy, be sure to lift with your legs, not your back. Lifting with your back puts you at risk for serious back injury. Don't hesitate to ask for help if you are having difficulty lifting or carrying anything.

You can buy ready-mix bags of cement and prepare the concrete yourself for pouring. Of course, you'll also need water and a concrete mixer, which you can rent. You can also hire a concrete subcontractor or company to deliver ready-made concrete to the building site. If you have only a small job requiring concrete, it is more economical to do it yourself. However, it is usually better to have the concrete delivered for larger jobs. Concrete is heavy, and all that mixing and pouring for large jobs can be exhausting. Most people are able to justify the expense of hiring a professional simply by considering the time they saved. If you do hire a professional, make sure you schedule for enough concrete to be at the site when needed.

Mixing

Concrete is easy to use, but you need to know what you're doing. If you are going to mix the concrete either using ready-mix or individual ingredients, do so within a half hour of pouring. In other words, don't mix up all the concrete you'll be using for the day in the early morning and expect to be able to pour it in the afternoon or evening. It's also a good idea to mix the concrete as close to the pouring site as possible, thus reducing the time and energy you expend carrying it to the proper location.

The materials you buy will come with directions on how much water you should add for a given amount of concrete to be made. Test a small sample of the concrete before pouring. If you have added too much or too little water, the concrete may not set up properly or may be difficult to work with. The concrete needs to be wet but can't be too soupy. Nor should it be too stiff. To check the consistency, pour a small amount into a miniature form. Use a shovel or other tool to mark the top with shallow gouge marks. If your marks instantly close in, then your concrete has too much water. If the marks hold their shape, then the concrete is the correct consistency.

Pouring

When mixing or pouring concrete, always be sure to wear protective articles. At minimum, you should be outfitted with goggles and gloves. Concrete is a caustic substance, meaning it can burn your skin. Long-sleeved shirts and pants will help protect your skin from splatters.

Before you pour concrete, make sure the soil beneath it drains properly. If the soil has drainage problems, it can't provide all the support that the concrete needs. You can correct for this by spreading a layer of sand or gravel on the soil and then pouring the concrete over that. Concrete should be poured at temperatures between 50–70°F for the best results. When poured in warmer temperatures, the concrete runs the risk of setting up too quickly. If at all possible, schedule concrete pouring for the late afternoon or evening.

FACT

Air pockets form easily within concrete when it is being poured. To remove these air pockets, you can either use a special tool that vibrates the concrete—making it act like a liquid, that is, forcing it to settle so the entrapped air rises to the surface—or you can use a tool like a spade to stir through the concrete to break up air pockets.

Once the concrete is poured and finished—finishing concrete will be discussed later in this chapter—you'll need to give it a few days to a week to set up and cure. If the concrete is out in the open, be sure to set up some sort of perimeter to keep people and animals off its surface. Also, if the concrete is exposed to direct sunlight, it is a good idea to cover its surface with building paper. Mist the surface lightly with water a couple of times a day for the first few days. In two days to a week, you can remove the forms and admire your work.

Basements

Many people choose to add a basement to their house plans. Basements can be a great addition, though you should make sure yours has a practical use or you'll just be throwing away your money. A basement can provide storage space, additional living space, a place to stay during tornado season, and even a garage area. If you're thinking of building a basement foundation, be sure you know what purpose you have in mind for that extra space.

A basement has many advantages, but it also drags along some disadvantages. For instance, a basement is more costly (in terms of both time and materials) than other types of foundations. In areas where the water table is high, you may have to deal with flooding every year. Also, basements can be cold and damp, and they do not get as much natural light as other parts of the house. If you are thinking of using your basement as a storage room, consider flooding possibilities; if you want to use your basement as a living area, consider your comfort levels.

Using Concrete

Most basements are constructed of poured concrete or concrete block. Concrete is the ideal material because it is inexpensive, durable, and easy. It is also safer to use than other materials. For instance, concrete is fireproof. Because many home fires start in the basement, this gives concrete a huge advantage over other materials. Concrete is dense and less porous than other materials, meaning you have fewer leakage problems (when constructed properly). With concrete, you won't have the worries of rotting wood or pest infestation. All in all, concrete is the strongest and most durable material you could use for constructing a basement.

Unfinished basements can be constructed for as little as 20 percent of the cost of upstairs living space, which makes them cost-effective for future use. Remember to think ahead: Don't forget to rough-in any plumbing drains for future use in the basement before pouring the concrete slab.

When deciding whether you should use concrete blocks or poured concrete for your basement, discuss your options with a concrete supplier and your general contractor (if applicable). Keep in mind that one supplier may be biased towards one form or the other. Talk with as many professionals as you can to gather the best information.

Building the Basement

Basements are built using basically the same process as that described in Chapter 8 for building foundations, with a few exceptions. Obviously, the foundation is going to be deeper with a basement. The walls must be a minimum of 8 feet high, though 9 feet is recommended for more head room. Also, you will need to pour a slab of concrete between the walls as flooring. A layer of gravel should be laid between the footings, with the concrete slab placed on top of this. If you are planning for a full walk-out basement, you will need to account for windows and doors as well. Of course, you will also want to waterproof and insulate. As you can see, a lot of work goes into the construction of a basement; however, you may find that the finished product is well worth the expense and time.

Garages

If you are like most people, you've planned to build a garage on your building site. There are several different types of garages you can choose from. When designing the garage, keep the following things in mind. How many vehicles do you want the garage to accommodate? Will you be using the garage for anything other than vehicle storage? Do you need extra storage space or an additional room? Do you want the garage to be attached to the house? Will the garage have utilities running to it? Do you want the garage to have a center drain? Where will windows and doors be located? For such a simple building, you have a lot to think about.

Comparable to Homebuilding

The process for building a garage is very similar to the process for building a house, though on a smaller and less complicated scale. You can purchase ready-made garage plans or garage kits, or you can design the garage yourself. In most places, you have to have a building permit for the garage, and—of course—you must also follow the building codes. The building codes will probably specify the thickness of the concrete slab and footings, whether wire mesh must be used, and the location of foundation anchors in the concrete.

Just like the house, the garage must have a foundation. If the garage will be attached to the house, you'll probably want to use the same type of foundation for both, such as a continuous wall foundation. Even if the garage is unattached, people often choose to use matching foundation types. However, this isn't necessary. Many people opt for the simplicity of a slab foundation.

Building a Slab Foundation

As you recall, a slab foundation is one that sits on the soil. However, when using concrete as your slab foundation material, you'll want to place about 4 inches of sand or gravel on the soil before pouring the concrete. This gives the slab more support and also serves to enhance draining. Once you have the sand or gravel in place, you can lay out a vapor barrier, such as plastic, to keep moisture from seeping up into the concrete slab.

ALERT!

Pay particular attention to building codes. Some will require that an inspection be done before the concrete is poured. Though the garage may not seem as important as the house, you should still go by the book and follow all the rules, thus saving yourself time, money, and energy later.

Because the concrete slab is expected to support the weight of your vehicles, it's a good idea to give it a little extra support. Wire mesh, reinforcement wire, and reinforcement fiber are common options for use in concrete slab foundations. Not only do materials like these give the concrete a little added strength and support, reinforcement also helps to prevent cracking. The wire mesh is usually placed in the center of the slab where it is most beneficial.

Just like a house, a garage must be framed for the walls and a roof. Therefore, anchor bolts are required within the concrete to anchor the sill plate to the foundation. It's important to not forget this little feature—your building codes will likely help you remember, with their own requirements for the anchor bolts—since the sill plate is what anchors the framing to the foundation.

Concrete is the ideal material to use on garage foundations. Because it is strong, durable, inexpensive, and easy to work with, concrete is a favorite with most experienced builders and novices alike. However, be sure you know what you're doing before beginning to pour, as your mistakes with concrete are "set in stone."

Concrete Patios

A patio adds a certain charm to a house. It seems to make it more inviting and improves the overall appearance. There's a lot you can do with a patio. You can put out furniture and create an outdoor living space. You can dress it up with plants and flowers. Of course, you could simply leave it as is. How fancy you get with your patio is entirely up to you.

This also applies to the building materials you choose to use. Many people find that brick or stone work adds a decorative value to their patios. Concrete, though not as aesthetically pleasing, is a common material—it is inexpensive, easy to use, and basically maintenance free. If you are planning to build a patio, seriously consider the advantages of concrete. Its advantages typically outweigh its plain looks, and you can easily dress it up, creating a beautiful and practical addition to your home.

Building a concrete patio isn't very difficult to do, though it can be a little time consuming. By now you are familiar with the process. You must excavate the area that will encompass the patio. Patio floors are usually about 4 inches thick, and you'll need to dig deep enough to accommodate 2 to 4 inches of bedding (typically gravel or sand), depending on how well the soil drains. Most people want the patio to be about 1 inch (or more, as you prefer) above the ground surface.

If your patio is going to extend right up to the house, it's a good idea to design it to slope slightly down and away from your outside walls. This prevents any water that accumulates on the patio surface from draining toward the house. Typically the slope is ¼ inch per foot.

Since you don't want the concrete to flow out of control all over your yard, you'll need to build a form to contain it. As you know, forms are typically made of wood. They use braces and stakes to give them enough support to hold the weight of the concrete. Be sure to position the form exactly where you want the concrete to go. For instance, if you want the concrete to stick up 2 inches above ground level, make sure the top of the form is set at 2 inches above ground level.

Once the forms are placed, a layer of gravel or sand is spread along the bottom to create the bedding. If you are planning to use wire mesh as reinforcement, you can lay that out on top of the bedding. Place a few rocks under the mesh to raise it up from the bedding a little. The mesh needs to be inside the concrete, not simply lying underneath it.

Now you're ready to pour. After pouring, level off the concrete and smooth the surface. Use an edger to create the edges of the slab. You can finish the concrete any way you like (as we discuss later in this chapter).

Cover the concrete, and allow it to set and cure. In about a week, you can remove the forms and the covering and admire your handiwork.

Sidewalks

Sidewalks aren't just for public areas. Many homes have sidewalks that surround them, lead to and from outbuildings, and make paths through gardens. Whatever your use for a sidewalk, you'll want to consider using concrete to build it. Most people find this to be the most inexpensive and practical material to use.

Sidewalks are not difficult to install and are a good project for the novice builder. Typically, sidewalks are 4-inch concrete slabs with 2 to 4 inches of gravel bedding underneath. Before excavating, decide whether you want the surface of the sidewalk to be flush with the ground or elevated slightly, and include this consideration in your measurements. You'll want to make sure that the sidewalk is level with the driveway or other sidewalks, unless of course you want to build a step from one to the other.

ALERT!

Before installing a sidewalk, check with your local building department. Some areas require a building permit for residential sidewalks. Most do not, but it's always a good idea to make sure before pouring.

Use forms to contain the concrete. The forms should be nailed to stakes that are no more than 4 feet apart. While most forms are made of lumber, if you have curves in the sidewalk, you'll need to use a more flexible material. Discuss your options with a professional at your local building supply company or with the concrete supplier. When laying the forms, take into account the need for a slight slope for proper water drainage. Also be sure to install pipe under sidewalks to accommodate features like downspout drains, sprinkler lines, or low-voltage wiring.

Once the forms are set, lay a bed of sand or gravel. It's a good idea to use wire mesh for added support and to help prevent against cracking. This should be suspended slightly above the bed so that the concrete can flow underneath it. (The mesh needs to be in the middle of the concrete slab.)

Pour, level, smooth, and edge the concrete. Allow it to cure, keeping it moist and covered for a few days. You have several different finishes available to you depending on how fancy you want the sidewalk to be. (Finishes are discussed later in this chapter.)

Driveways

When properly installed, concrete is the most durable of all materials you can use for a driveway. However, keep in mind it is also the most expensive. Even so, many people find that the advantages of a concrete driveway more than make up for the expense. Since the driveway is going to be the first thing people notice when visiting your home, you want to make sure it makes a good impression. Because concrete is so durable and can be finished in many different designs, it is usually a good choice for both practicality and aesthetics.

The first thing you'll need to do is determine how wide you want the driveway to be. For instance, if you have a two-car garage, the driveway needs to be at least wide enough to accommodate two cars in front of the garage, but it doesn't have to be that wide at the entrance from the road since only one car will be entering at a time. You can design the driveway to be approximately 9 feet wide at the entry and then widen it to approximately 17 feet closer to the garage.

FACT

It is recommended that the concrete mix you use for your driveway has a load capacity of 4,000 psi (pounds per square inch). Also, the driveway should have a slight slope off the sides so that water can drain off properly—a slope of 1 inch per every 10 feet is sufficient.

When excavating for the driveway, keep in mind that most driveways are 4 to 6 inches thick. You will want the surface of the driveway to line up with any sidewalks leading to and from it, as well as with the garage entrance. A layer of bedding is typically not necessary; however, you may need to use gravel if the soil is expansive. Dirt or sand fill is the least desirable material for bedding because it needs to be compacted; rock or gravel needs no compaction. Whether you decide to use dirt or gravel, make sure it is compacted before pouring.

You will of course need to use forms. It is a good idea to space the supporting stakes no more than 4 feet apart. This is necessary if the forms are to support the weight of the concrete. Before pouring, moisten the subgrade (soil or gravel), but do not allow water to stand. After pouring the concrete, cut or trowel joints no more than every 10 feet. These joints can help conceal cracks in concrete that might appear in the future. Level off the concrete, and smooth the surface. It is imperative that you allow the concrete to cure before permitting vehicles to use it. Curing can take anywhere from three days to a week. Keep the surface moist and covered during this time.

Types of Finishes

Many people are under the impression that to use concrete they are stuck with a boring, gray, plain slab. Today, however, there are several concrete finishes available to you that change the color, texture, and overall look of the concrete. You can make the concrete as fancy or as simple as you want. Talk with your concrete supplier or a professional at your local building supply company. They will be able to give you information on the various finishes available. To give you an idea of what your options are, let's take a look at some of the more common types of finishes. Each of these can be used to enhance the look of your driveway, sidewalks, and patios.

Stamped concrete. Made to resemble other materials, such as stone, brick, wood, slate, and tile, it is available in a wide variety of patterns and colors.

Stained concrete. Just as the name implies, this is concrete stained in different colors. Stained concrete is often used in conjunction with different textures to create a specific look. You can get quite creative with stained concrete as there several color options available.

Stenciled concrete. You can now use stencils to create patterns, logos, borders, and so forth in the concrete. You can choose from premade stencils or make your own to create a unique design.

Exposed aggregate. This option gives the concrete a decorative texture. You decide how much or how little aggregate is brought to the surface. The natural colors of the aggregate also add to the design and look of the finished product.

Textured finishes. There are several ways to create a textured finish. You can use rock salt to create small holes in the concrete. A broom can be used to create grooves in the concrete in a swirling or straight pattern. You can also create various patterns and textures using tools such as floats and trowels, available at your building supply company.

Chapter 10

Framing

Once the foundation is built, you are ready to give your house its shape. In this chapter, you will learn how to attach the sills and frame the floor, walls, roof, windows, and doors. The framing is the skeleton of the house. It provides you with a bare-bones vision of what your house will look like.

The Sills

The sill (also called sill plate or mud sill) is the lowest member of your house's frame. It sits on the foundation and gives support to the floor joists. The sill is pressure-treated wood (typically a 2×4 or 2×6) that is anchored to the foundation with anchor bolts.

This is going to be the first and lowest wooden part of your house. As such, it runs the risk of being damaged by pests (namely termites). To help combat this, many people install a termite shield between the foundation and sill. This metal shield prevents the pests from gaining access to the sill and framing. You may also want to add a sill seal, or sill insulation, to the top of the foundation (beneath the sill) to help protect against drafts of air.

Sill Position

Before installing the sills, you'll need to see if the foundation is straight, square, and level. It's unlikely that your foundation is going to be perfect, regardless of the amount of preparation and hard work put into building it. Luckily, the house's frame is going to sit on the sills, not the foundation, so all you need to do is adjust the sills to make up for any imperfections in the foundation. For example, if you find that the foundation is not square, adjust the sills so that they are square, even though this means they will not be perfectly aligned with the foundation.

FACT

Typically sills are positioned flush to the outside edge of the foundation. However, there are some instances in which you may want to set the sills inside a bit. For instance, if you are going to be sheathing the frame with ½-inch plywood, you can set the sills a ½ inch inside the outside edge of the foundation.

You'll need to mark the foundation to show where to install the sills. The best way to do this is to use your chalkline. Determine where the inside corners of the sills will be located, and then simply stretch and snap a chalkline between these points. This line will indicate the inside edges of the sills. Be sure to make allowances for any foundation imperfections that need to be rectified.

Attaching the Sills

Once you've checked that the chalklines are square, you're ready to install the sills. The sills will be attached to the foundation with the anchor bolts, so you'll need to mark where holes need to be drilled in the sills. You can do this in a couple of different ways.

Place the sill up against the inside of the bolts, and make a mark across the width of the sill for each side of the bolt. You'll then mark a line in the center of these two lines, which marks the center of the bolt. Measure from the center of the bolt to the chalkline, and then transfer that measurement to the sill along the center line, marking where you will need to drill the hole for the bolt. You can also do this using a bolt marker. This tool allows you to transfer the location of the bolt holes onto the sills easily and accurately.

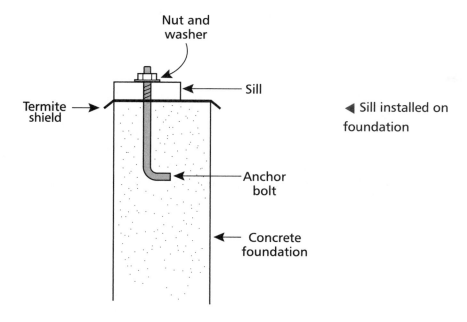

Nut and washer

Sill

Termite shield

◄ Sill installed on foundation

Anchor bolt

Concrete foundation

Drill holes for the anchor bolts in the marked locations. Clean the foundation and situate the sills, aligning the holes with the bolts. Also, as you are doing this, make sure the inside and corners of the sills are aligned with the chalkline you made earlier. Put on the washers and nuts, and before tightening completely, check to see if the sills are level. Once level, tighten the nuts, and you've installed the sills. (Remember, if you have opted to install a termite shield or sill seal, these should be placed on top of the foundation and beneath the sill.)

Floor Framing

Your first framing job is going to be the floor of the house. This is a relatively easy process that is usually done pretty quickly. During this stage of construction, you will be building a frame consisting of girders, joists, and bridging. Girders are large beams of wood or steel that provide midspan support for the joists. Joists are parallel beams, typically boards 2 inches thick, that provide the support for the floor. Bridging is the material (wood or metal) placed between the joists either perpendicularly or diagonally to add rigidity to the frame and brace the joists.

Girders

A girder will be installed along the length of the house, down its center, from one foundation wall to the other. You may need more than one girder, depending on the size of the house and how much support is needed. Without the girder, the finished floor would sag in the middle. Refer to your house plans for the number and location specifications for the girders.

FACT

While girders are most often used, they can be replaced with a continuous wall foundation, which spreads the weight of the floor system more evenly on the ground than a girder-and-pier system.

Always check with your local building codes for any requirements that must be met. Often building codes will have specifications regarding size and spacing of girders and joists. Your house plans should reflect these specifications, though it's always good to double-check.

Girders are typically supported by wooden posts, which are set upon concrete piers. The ends of the girders are either set into notches in the foundation walls or attached to the walls with fasteners. The posts are typically set about 6 feet apart. The height of the posts depends on how the joists will be attached to the girders. If the joists are designed to hang from the girder, then the posts need to be set at a height that makes the bottom of the girder level with the top of the sill. If the joists will be placed on top of the girder, then the top of the girder needs to be level with the top of the sill.

The posts must be as wide as the girder, and they must sit directly beneath it. If two girders are to be joined, this must be done over a post, and the post needs to be a bit wider. Once the posts are cut to the appropriate height and set in place, simply toenail the girders to the posts. Toenailing is a process of nailing at a 60-degree angle to penetrate two pieces that cannot otherwise be nailed directly.

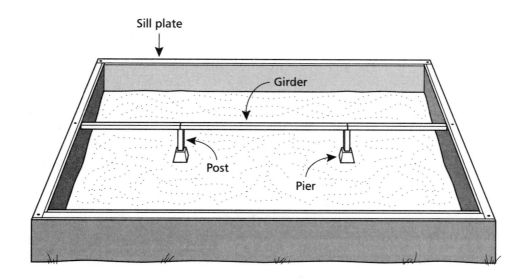

▲ Girder supported by posts, attached to foundation walls

Joists

You will begin the process of installing joists with the header joists and then the first and last joists. This creates "the band," a name for the joists that form the perimeter of the joist system. The header joists are those that run perpendicular to the joists of the frame. The first and last joists are those that run parallel to the joists of the frame. The band needs to sit flat on the sill, so try to get joists that are straight. When nailing down the band, make sure the outside edges of each joist are flush with the outside edges of the sill. Toenail the header, first, and last joists to the sill with a nail every 16 inches.

If your house plans call for any opening in the joists, such as for stairs, you will cut the joists to allow for the amount of space needed for the opening and then attach header joists to the parallel joists. Take into account the thickness of the header joist when cutting the joists to make sure the opening is appropriately sized after the headers are attached.

Once you have secured the band, you are ready to lay out the joists. Check your plans to see how far apart the joists should be spaced. Typically, plans call for 16-inch spacing. In that case, you measure off 16 inches along the header joists and girders, marking the measurement with a line. Because the lines mark the edges of the joists, not their center, you'll need to place an **X** on one side of the line to determine where the joist will be positioned. Joists often overlap on a girder. In order for this to occur, one header will mark an **X** to the right of the line, and the other will mark an **X** to the left to allow for the overlap.

It isn't likely that all your joists will be perfectly straight, so you'll need to check each individual one to find the crown, or top, of the bow. The crown should always be placed up when installing the joists. Position the joists so that they are aligned with their corresponding lines, and nail them to the header joists using two nails, one near the top and the other near the bottom. You may also want to toenail the joists to the sill. The joists must be toenailed to the girder as well. Once all the joists are installed, check them for symmetry and to make sure they are parallel.

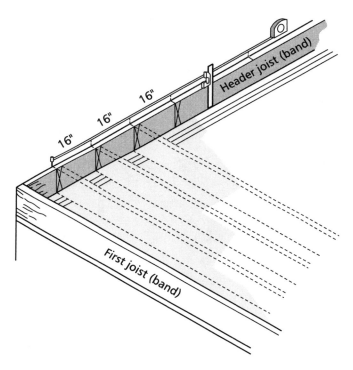

▲ Joists laid out along the header

Bridging

Several building codes call for bridging between the joists. Typically bridging is done with wood, but metal is sometimes used as well. There are two common types of bridging: solid bridging, and cross, or diagonal, bridging. In solid bridging, the bridges are usually of the same thickness and width as the joists. These pieces of wood are secured perpendicularly between the joists. In cross bridging, metal or smaller pieces of wood (typically 1×4s) are positioned diagonally between the joists. When installing cross bridging, you secure the top of the diagonal first and the bottom later on during construction, which gives the crowns time to settle. Bridging is usually spaced approximately 8 feet apart, but of course you'll want to refer to your house plans for this information.

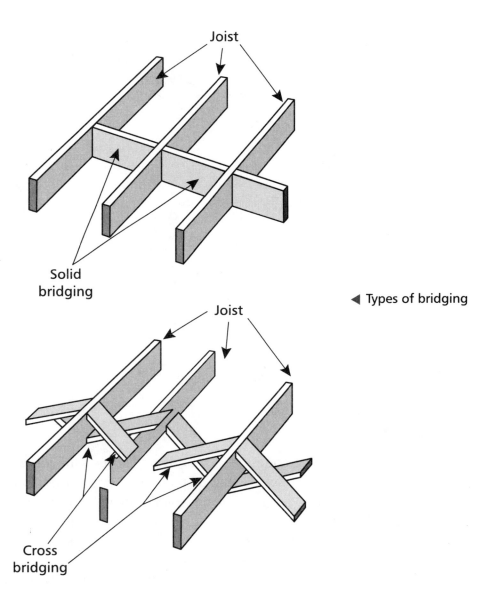

◀ Types of bridging

Installing Subflooring

The subflooring is installed over the joists. It acts as a platform for subsequent work to be done on the house. A finished floor will be installed on top of the subfloor later on during construction. Plywood (either tongue-and-groove or butt edge) is the most common material used for subflooring, and because of this, it's the material we will discuss here. However, plywood is not your only option; you can also use tongue-and-groove boards or oriented strand board (abbreviated as OSB).

A Simple Process

Installing subflooring is relatively simple process. The boards are placed perpendicular to the joists, so that the grain direction creates a right angle with the joists. The boards should be staggered so that the boards end on different joists. In other words, you should use a full sheet for your first panel and a half sheet for the adjacent panel, and so forth, so that you end up with a staggered pattern. Each sheet should also end on a joist so that you are able to secure the ends. The smooth edge of the plywood should be facing up. If you are using tongue-and-groove panels, point the tongue edge toward the outside edge of the frame, making it easier for you to pound one panel into the other.

FACT

If you are using tongue-and-groove boards or plywood, you must pound one sheet into the other. Use a block of wood as a buffer so that you do not damage the grooves. Always make sure the two panels are fit together tightly before moving on to the next pair.

You will begin at a corner of the frame and lay the subflooring in rows, working from the first joist to the last joist. While not necessary, many people choose to use a subflooring adhesive in addition to nailing. This adds to the strength of the floor and also helps eliminate squeaks. If you choose to use an adhesive, spread glue over the area to be covered one panel at a time. Once the panel is placed, use a chalkline on the panel to mark where the centers of covered joists are. Nail the panel into place even if you have used an adhesive. The typical nail pattern is every 6 inches around the perimeter of the house and where panels meet, and every 12 inches throughout the middle. Continue in this manner until you've reached the last joist, then start back at the first joist and begin a new row with a half sheet.

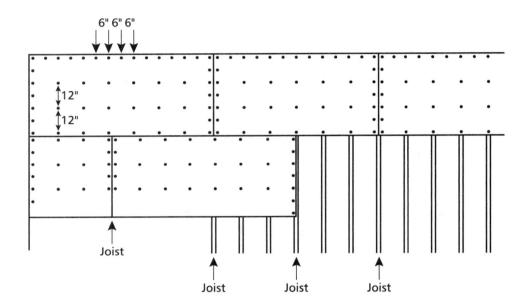

▲ Installing the subflooring

Underfloor Utilities

You may need to allow spacing for underfloor utilities in your subflooring. If pipes have been installed before the subflooring, you'll have to cut holes in the panels to allow the pipes to go through. This adds a bit of a complication to the process of laying the subflooring, but it isn't too difficult to manage. Many people simply measure the distance from adjacent panels that have already been laid to the pipe and transfer that measurement to the panel that needs to be cut. For instance, let's say a panel that will be adjacent to two already laid needs a hole cut for a pipe. Measure the distance from the end of the side panel in to the center of the pipe, then measure the distance from the end of the end panel in to the center of the pipe. Take those measurements and use them to find the center of the pipe on the panel to be cut. Cut a hole for the diameter of the pipe. The panel should fit nicely over the pipe and up against the edges of the adjacent panels.

Wall Framing

Framing the walls is an exciting part of the building process. Once the frames are up, the house actually looks like a house. You'll be able to see individual rooms and walk through the house to get a feel for the layout. Though exciting, the process is also more time consuming and labor intensive than framing the floor. So strap on your tool belt, and get ready to work up a sweat.

Marking the Layout

Before you begin building and erecting the walls, you need to mark the floor to show where the walls will go. Pull out your house plans, and study them carefully. You are going to transfer the dimensions from the plans to the subfloor you just installed. Begin with the exterior walls. Mark the corners by measuring in from the edge according to the type of material you'll be using for the frame. If using 2×4s, measure in 3½ inches from the edge; if using 2×6s, measure in 5½ inches. When the corners are marked, stretch a chalkline between them and snap. This line marks the inside edge of your exterior walls.

Be sure you understand how to read dimensions from your house plans. Some plans measure from the center of one wall to the center of another, while others measure from the outside edge of one wall to the outside edge of another. Understanding how the dimensions are laid out is critical if you're going to successfully transfer them to the subflooring.

Next you'll mark the interior walls. Mark the longest walls, such as hallways, first and then move on to the shorter walls. Using the house plans as your guide, measure in from the outside walls the distance indicated. Use a chalkline to mark straight lines between points. Mark the side of the line where the wall will be located with an **X**. Once you've chalked all lines marking the dimensions of the walls, recheck them against the plans to make sure everything is worked out correctly.

Plating the Walls

Plates are the horizontal framing members that will become the tops and bottoms of the walls. The studs are vertically attached to the plates to finish off the wall frame. The best way to begin plating the walls is to carry the plates to the subflooring and use those layout lines you marked to cut the plates to length. Again, starting with the exterior walls, tack (that is, temporarily nail) the bottom plate to the subflooring, and then tack the top plate to the bottom for each wall. Work your way from the longest to the shortest walls.

Once the two plates are tacked together, you can easily mark the location of studs on both at once. The plates can then be separated and nailed to the studs. Keep in mind that the ends of the plates must always land in the middle of a stud. This keeps the wall frame sturdy and more secure. (Check your plans for the locations of studs.) Studs should be placed in the wall with crowns turned up to help achieve a straighter wall. Once the studs are nailed to the plates, you attach a double top plate. This additional plate ties the whole wall frame together. Where another wall will be intersecting, leave a gap of approximately $3^3/_4$ inches in the double top plate on each through wall to allow for the extended double top plate of the butt wall.

Of course, it isn't quite as easy as this. You'll have to mark the plates for corners and intersecting walls. You'll also have to take openings into consideration, such as those windows and doors, but we'll get to that in a moment. As long as you follow your house plans closely and make the marks accurately, plating the walls isn't difficult— just time consuming.

Erecting the Walls

Building codes often require walls to be braced. They will have specific requirements regarding bracing, but you can usually use metal angle braces. These braces should be positioned so that there is a 45-degree angle from the bottom plate to the double top plate. A brace needs to be placed at every corner and every 25 feet from the corners of the exterior walls. You'll need to cut slots in the studs along the angle so that the brace fits into the stud. Nail the brace to the bottom plate, but don't secure the brace to the double top plate just yet. That will be done after the wall has been raised.

QUESTION?

What are through walls and butt walls?
Through walls and butt walls intersect one another. The through wall spans the entire length of the appropriate measurement—it is the wall that continues on *through*. The butt wall is cut short so it can *butt* up against the through wall.

Raise the exterior through walls first. When raising, remind everyone to lift with their legs, not with their backs. Raising walls takes a lot of manpower but can be accomplished easily if everyone cooperates. Once the wall is raised, hold it steady while the temporary braces are secured. You can use a stud nailed at a diagonal from the corner stud to the band as a brace on either end. This will hold the wall in place while you erect the others. (Corner bracing can also be done with 4×8 sheets of plywood or OSB.) Make sure the wall is lined up accurately, and drive a nail through the bottom plate into the subflooring between each stud (except of course in doorways, as the bottom plate will be cut away). Also drive nails through the bottom plate into the band or joists.

Once both through walls are raised and in the appropriate position, then you can erect the butt walls in the same manner. Nail the end stud of the butt walls to the through walls, making sure the corners are flush. Next comes the interior walls. Again, work your way through the house, first securing the longest walls and then moving on to the shortest. When all walls are erected, you will then pull it all together by securing the overlapping double top plate of the butt walls to the through walls.

At this point, you'll need to check to see that the walls are plumb (vertically level) and straight. This is important, as crooked walls will cause you all kinds of problems later on. Use temporary braces to straighten the walls. These braces will need to stay in place until the sheathing has been completed to ensure that the walls stay in place.

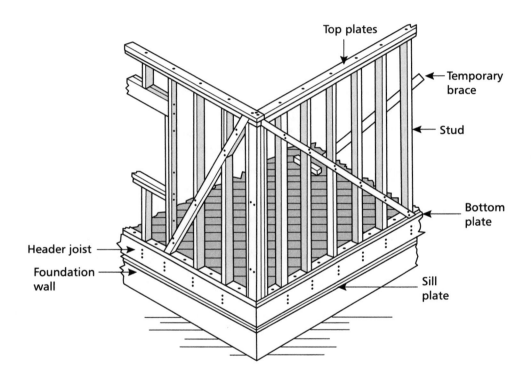

▲ Framing the walls

Door and Window Framing

As we mentioned earlier, you are going to have to accommodate openings such as windows and doors within the wall framing. This is to be done before the walls are built and raised. Refer to your house plans for the dimensions of the windows and doors. Keep in mind that these are the dimensions of the windows and doors themselves; the opening you leave in the wall framing must also account for other features, such as the trimmer studs.

Let's first take a look at the anatomy of windows and doors. Because these spaces in the framing don't have studs to support the weight of the roof, headers must be placed at the top of the opening. Headers are typically made of wood, and your local building codes will determine their size based on the size of the opening. A king stud is secured between the top and bottom plates on either side of the headers. The headers are supported by trimmer studs, which are placed inside the king studs on either side of the opening. Windows also require a rough sill, which extends the length of the bottom of the opening. Cripple studs are used for support between the plates above the headers and below the rough sills. Cripples are simply shortened studs.

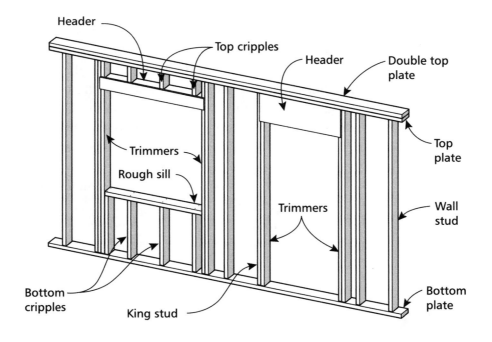

▲ Window and door framing

Before marking the locations of the studs on the top and bottom plates, mark the locations of the specific parts of the windows and doors. People differ in their marking systems. Some use the first letter of the feature to mark its location. For instance, you could mark the plates with a K where the king studs will be located and with a C where the cripples are to be placed. Whatever system you choose to use, make sure you are consistent and that all who are working on the frame are aware of it.

It's unlikely that all your studs are going to be straight. Many will be plagued with bows and warps. Find the straightest studs, which will be used as trimmer studs and king studs. This will make things a lot easier later on, when you are installing the finishing trim.

To assemble the frames for these openings, begin with the top cripples. Toenail the top cripples to the header at each marked location. Then, nail the bottom cripples to the rough sill, making sure there are cripples on each of the ends of both the header and sill. Next, nail in the window trimmer studs—the door trimmer studs will be installed later. Finally, nail the king studs to the trimmer studs and the headers. Line up the window and door frames on the subflooring where they will be nailed to the plates. This makes for easier work when you are ready to put the wall framing together.

After you have attached the window and door frames and raised the walls, nail the trimmer studs to the door frames. It's a good idea at this time to make sure the trimmer studs for both windows and doors are plumb. Keep in mind you will also need to cut out the bottom plate from the door openings.

Roof Framing

Once the walls are erected, it's time to put up the roof. There are several different styles of roofs and a few different ways to frame and install them. (Chapter 12 discusses the different types of roofs in greater detail.) As most roofs today are built using trusses, that is what will be discussed here. If you'd rather cut and build your own roof framing on site, you can of course do that; it just takes more time and energy than simply ordering the trusses. Your house plans will give you most of the information you need to build your own roof frame; however, there are several decisions that are typically left to be made at the building site. If you choose to take the do-it-yourself route, it's a good idea to hire an experienced hand to help you with the frame.

What Is a Truss?

A truss is a structure that consists of a pair of rafters attached to a bottom joist chord by webbing (short pieces of wood). Gussets are steel plates that are attached at the joints to hold it all together. A number of trusses will be installed atop the wall framing to create the roof frame. Trusses transfer the weight of the roof to the outside walls, thus minimizing the need for interior support walls and allowing for more "open" floor plans.

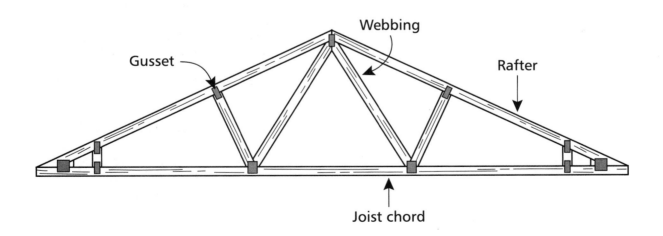

▲ Anatomy of a truss

Trusses are factory made, and they will be delivered to the building site. You must order the trusses approximately three weeks before they are needed. Be sure to give the supply company the exact specifications for your roof design from the house plans, including the pitch, the span between exterior walls, the rise, and information on the house's eaves. Of course, you will also need to know how many to order. Generally, trusses are spaced approximately 2 feet apart.

FACT

There are several different types of trusses available to you. For instance, if you want more space in the attic, you can use a scissor-type truss, which allows for a higher ceiling. Consider your design preferences, and have a lumber supplier show you the different options.

Installing Trusses

Before installing the trusses, mark the wall plates to indicate the position and location of each truss. You certainly don't want to be stuck high up in the air managing a truss while trying to figure out where it goes. Installing the trusses is pretty easy to do; you just need to be comfortable with working at such a height. Simply hoist the truss up to the top of the wall plates (if they weren't already unloaded there), position them according to your marks, and nail them to the top plates of the wall.

When you have a few trusses installed in position, you'll want to begin bracing the roof. Install a diagonal brace (typically a 2×4) from the top plate of an exterior wall to a rafter at a 45-degree angle. Usually this type of brace on both ends of the house is sufficient; however, if the roof is rather long, you may want to add a brace in the middle as well. Next you need to nail a long brace along the top of the joist chords, as near the center as you can get it. Nail the brace to each joist chord with two nails to make sure it is secure enough to offer optimum stability.

Framing for Special Features

This chapter has provided information on framing for the basics of any house. However, you are building your home to be unique and individually suited to your needs and preferences. Therefore, it's likely you will have other features to frame as well. For instance, if your house is more than a single story, you'll need to frame the upper floors just as you did the first and also frame for the stairway. Your house plans will give the dimensions and materials needed for this job. Also take into consideration features such as skylights, sunrooms, and fireplaces. Study your house plans carefully. They will give you construction instructions needed to frame any special features unique to your house design. (E)

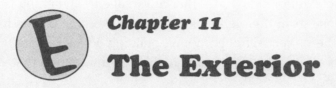

Chapter 11

The Exterior

Having framed the house, you now have a big wooden skeleton. It's time to cover that skeleton with some skin to truly give your house its definition. This chapter walks you through the process of sheathing the walls and discusses some of the different types of exterior finishes available to you.

Wall Sheathing

After the walls have been framed, they are covered with boards or panels. This is called sheathing. Sheathing is especially important in areas prone to earthquakes, as it helps hold the house together. Sheathing also acts as a wind barrier, adds strength to the house, and provides a surface for nailing on the exterior siding. Another advantage to sheathing is that it protects your house from the elements as you are working on the interior and completing the project. Though not all building codes require sheathing, due to all its advantages, it is highly recommended that you sheathe the exterior walls.

Types of Sheathing

You have a variety of materials to choose from when sheathing. The most commonly used are plywood, fiberboard, and foam board. As you will see, not all of these offer the same advantages of rigidity and strength. However, you can combine materials to get the optimum performance of sheathing.

Plywood is the most popular sheathing material. It is one of the more expensive, too, but it is by far the strongest. If you live in an area that is prone to earthquakes, tornadoes, or hurricanes, it is advised that you use plywood to sheathe your home as it can hold the house together better than any other material. Plywood comes in large sheets and is easy to install and cut. Most people use exterior-glued plywood for sheathing because it can get wet during construction and not be damaged.

FACT

Many people choose to combine materials for sheathing. For instance, you can sheathe the corners of the house with plywood and finish sheathing the walls with foam board. This gives the house the extra strength and rigidity of the plywood and the ease and economy of the foam board.

Fiberboard is composed of wood fibers and a chemical for water-proofing. It does not have the rigidity or the strength of plywood, but is a little cheaper. This is a common sheathing material in areas not prone to destructive natural forces like earthquakes or hurricanes. While it has little structural strength value, fiberboard does reduce moisture and air penetration. It will also serve as a nailing surface for exterior siding provided you choose a fiberboard with nailing-base density.

Like fiberboard, foam board is less expensive than plywood and lacks the advantages of rigidity and strength. It is very lightweight and easy to break. Many people choose to use foam board because it is easy to handle and install and offers a barrier for air and moisture penetration. Before deciding to use foam board (or fiberboard) be sure to check your local building codes. There may be requirements regarding the type of sheathing that can be used.

Installing Sheathing

Installing sheathing is an easy task, though a little monotonous. The good thing about this simple project is that because it will be covered with an exterior siding, you needn't worry about being perfect in your cuts and measurements. No one will ever see it, so it doesn't have to look good. This doesn't mean you should be sloppy; the sheathing does have a purpose after all. But you don't have to stress out over accuracy, either.

The sheathing can be installed before or after the roof is framed. Starting at a corner of the house, apply the sheet of sheathing vertically. (The sheet can be installed horizontally, but you lose strength.) When nailing, work your way from the outside of the sheet to the inside. Nailing patterns typically call for nails to be spaced 4 inches apart on the perimeter of the walls, 6 inches apart where the sheets meet one another, and 12 inches apart in the middle. The end of each sheet should fall in the middle of a stud. If it doesn't, either cut the sheet to fit or add another stud.

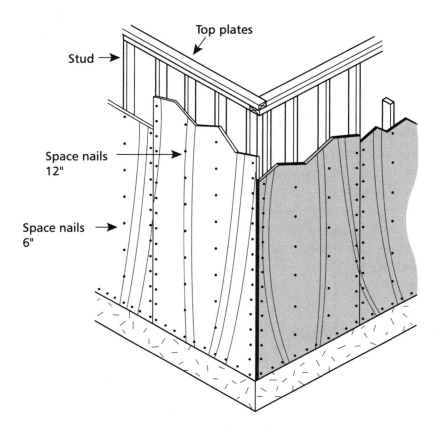

▲ Installing wall sheathing

Some people start with the corner sheet and work their way around the house. Others secure sheets at each corner and then work to fill in the walls. Any way you prefer will work just fine. Just make sure you check to see that the sheet is level and plumb before moving on to the others. If you live in a humid area, you can leave a ⅛-inch gap between sheets to allow for expansion.

You can use the scraps from cutting out openings in the sheathing to cover smaller areas, such as under windows. This saves you the hassle of cutting a large sheet down to size for a small area.

Your walls will have openings, and these must be transferred to the sheathing. You can do this in one of two ways. You can cover the entire wall with the sheathing, then go back and cut out the opening from the inside of the house using a reciprocating saw. Or you can cut the opening in the sheathing before installing it. The best way to do this is to temporarily tack up the sheathing, outline the opening on the sheet from the inside, take it down, and cut out the opening. This ensures that the opening is of the appropriate size.

Horizontal Vinyl Siding

Horizontal vinyl siding is probably the most popular form of siding used on newly built homes today. Compared to other types of siding, such as masonry veneer, vinyl siding is inexpensive and can be used anywhere. It is also easy to install, easy to clean, and virtually maintenance free. While many people tend to think of vinyl siding as a second-rate and boring form of siding, this is far from true. There are now several styles, colors, and textures to choose from, and it is used on all types of homes from the simplest structure to the most elaborate and expensive styles. Vinyl siding offers several advantages you may want to take into consideration when choosing a siding.

Before you can begin installing the siding panels, you must install the trim. Your order of vinyl siding will come with starter strips, J-channels, undersill trim, and inside and outside corners. The starter strip is the first to go up. This long strip should be nailed along the bottom of the sill. To allow for expansion, leave at least 1/4-inch gap between strips, at least 1 inch from the end of the strip to the outside corner, and at least 1½ inches from the end of the strip to the inside corner. The J-channel is the trim that goes around the tops and sides of doors and windows to hide the ends of the siding panels. The undersill trim fits beneath the windowsills and serves to both cover and lock the siding panel in place. The inside and outside corners are just that—corner trim that fits along the corners of the house. These pieces also serve to hide the ends of the siding panels to make everything look nice and neat. Install these as instructed by the manufacturer.

To install the siding panels, start at a bottom corner of the house. Fasten the first panel into the starter strip, and slide it under the corner trim. To secure it in place, drive a nail through a precut slot in the panel and into a stud. Keep the nail a little loose to allow for expansion. You should put a nail into each stud the panel covers. Once you've secured the panel, test it to make sure it has a little give and will slide back and forth. Slide it out so there is between ¼ and ½ inch between the inside of the corner trim and the end of the panel.

When you've reached the end of one panel and need to begin another, you'll first have to cut back the nailing flanges. This is the strip with the precut holes you use to nail the siding to the studs. The nailing flanges shouldn't touch, so trim each back enough to leave 1 inch of space between the two when the panels overlap. There should be about 1 inch of overlap. Finish a row, and then work your way up one row at a time. The higher row always overlaps the lower. Joints in siding should be staggered or offset by at least 16 to 32 inches. You should also avoid lining up splices in a vertical line to make the siding more aesthetically pleasing.

You'll have to make cuts in the siding to allow for openings, such as doors, windows, and vents. Cutting vinyl siding isn't difficult. You can use a variety of tools, including a table saw, hacksaw, or even a utility knife, depending on the type of cut you need to make. Just be sure you measure for the siding to slide beneath the trim.

Depending on whether the eaves are to be open or closed, you'll use either a strip of undersill trim or a J-channel for the final row of siding. If the eaves are to be left open, use the undersill trim to secure the final panels. If the eaves will be closed, use the J-channel trim to secure and cover the final panels.

Brick and Stucco

Some people choose to go all out for aesthetic appeal. After all, the first thing people are going to notice about your new house is the outside. For this reason, some people find that the extra expense of masonry siding pays out in the end. The most common masonry siding materials are brick and stucco. You will often find brick homes in the eastern states where there's little chance of an earthquake occurring. (Brick doesn't hold up well in earthquakes.) Stucco homes are more often found in the western or southern states where they won't be susceptible to freezing weather. (Water that freezes in stucco will cause it to crack.)

Brick

While brick is expensive to purchase and install, it makes for a very beautiful siding and is maintenance free. Although brick is initially much higher in price than other exteriors, the cost will easily be recovered during resale of house. Brick is heavy and will require some sort of footing to support it. For instance, you can build a lip off of the foundation that will serve to hold the weight of the brick. Because the brick does not bear any of the load of the house, it is considered to be a veneer, or covering.

Because brick is expensive compared to other sidings, many people choose to cover only part of the house in brick, such as the side facing the street. You might even use brick to accent certain features of the house, such as a bay window.

Brick is very difficult to install and takes a great amount of skill. You can do it yourself if you have the patience and time to learn to do it correctly. However, most people wisely choose to leave bricklaying to the professionals. Skilled bricklayers are able to do the job effectively and efficiently. Though more costly, hiring a brick mason saves you the time and frustration of doing it yourself. If using brick, you will need to create a brick-ledge, which is an offset in the foundation that the brick rests on. This space is allotted for when you pour your walls or lay your block foundation.

Stucco

Stucco is essentially just an outer layer of mortar. Even so, it makes for a very attractive siding. You have a lot of style options with stucco. It can be as rough or smooth as you like. It can be patterned and dressed up with decorative work, and it can also be mixed with pigment or painted. Another advantage to stucco is that it is very durable and strong, if applied correctly.

Two to three coats of stucco are spread with a trowel over wire mesh that is stretched over the house. It is applied wet and must be given time to dry. Be sure to check the weather forecast on stucco day. Stucco shouldn't be applied when it's raining or if there's a lot of moisture in the air.

It is often difficult for the novice builder to do a good job applying stucco. This is a job that takes a lot of skill and experience to do correctly. Because stucco is known to crack when not applied properly, it's a good idea to hire a professional if you haven't done this type of work before. If you do decide to do it yourself, it's recommended that you do a few trial runs on another building first and get a feel for the process.

Plywood Siding

Another type of siding that is gaining popularity is exterior plywood siding, otherwise known as T1-11. While T1-11 can be used as sheathing, it doesn't look like the plywood you would normally use for sheathing. It comes in a variety of textures, designs, and thicknesses. You can choose from grooved, smooth, rough, painted, stained, or untreated boards. Aesthetically, T1-11 usually gives your home a rustic appearance.

This type of siding is relatively inexpensive compared to other types, though the cost varies depending on the style you choose. For instance, those panels that are composed of redwood plies are going to run much higher than those composed of southern pine. Your costs will also be higher if you choose to have your panels treated with a water repellent. Your best bet is to just shop around. You have a lot to choose from and should be able to find an exterior plywood that is both economical and pleasing to the eye.

FACT

T1-11 is not as durable as other forms of siding and will usually require sealing every few years. Should you decide after a time that the maintenance is just too much to keep up with, you can always install other forms of siding, such as vinyl siding or shingles, right on top of the T1-11.

One of the greatest advantages to T1-11 is that it is quick and easy to install. It usually comes in 4×8 panels and is installed vertically. The installation process for T1-11 is just the same as for plywood sheathing. Using rust-resistant nails, nail the panels to the studs and plates of the house. You can also install the panels horizontally, but that is usually not highly recommended as you run the risk of allowing water to get between the plies.

T1-11 does require regular maintenance to protect it and keep it from delaminating, and it usually doesn't hold up as well as some other types of siding. You'll need to apply a sealing approximately every three years. While the upfront cost may be cheaper for exterior plywood, you'll have more maintenance costs in the years ahead for this type of siding. Keep this in mind as you think about the long-term consequences of your decision.

Other Sidings

There are, of course, other sidings you can choose from. It's likely that one of the reasons you decided to build your own home is because you wanted it to be unique and individually suited to your taste and style. The exterior of the house is going to be your signature for everyone to see. Plus, the type of siding you choose can have a profound effect on your budget. That's why it is important to make this decision carefully. Luckily, a wide variety of options are available to you. You should be able to find a siding that meets both the needs of your budget and aesthetic preferences.

Shingle Siding

Shingle siding is thought to be quite attractive and can give your home a very distinct look. Shingles are typically made from redwood or cedar, but can also be made of other woods. Because they are made of wood, you'll need to consider possible problems with termites. Shingles are easy to install, but because each shingle covers such a small area, it is very time-consuming work. If you are going to hire out the labor, it can get to be quite expensive. The shingles themselves can also be expensive, depending on the grade you choose and whether you opt for any decorative features. The good thing is that shingle siding appeals to a lot of people and could increase the resale value of your home.

When shopping for shingles, be sure you know the difference between shingles and shakes. Shingles are cut by a machine to lie smooth, flat, and uniform. Shakes are split and are rougher, more irregular, and thicker. Shakes and shingles will give your home two completely different looks, so know what you're buying!

Metal Sidings

Metal sidings are a good option if your main concern is the impact on your budget. Aluminum and steel sidings are relatively inexpensive and quick and easy to install. These types of siding usually come in horizontal panels, though you can find some vertical styles. The main advantages to metal sidings are the cost, easy installation, and low maintenance. They aren't going to rust or blister, nor will they catch fire. However, you will want to paint these sidings and make sure you repaint according to the manufacturer's instructions to prevent rusting.

Wood Board Siding

Siding with wood boards gives your home a nice natural look that is often admired for its beauty and high quality. These boards are available in several different types of wood, including redwood, cedar, pine, cypress, and fir. The price for this type of siding ranges from moderate to expensive. Your final cost will really depend on the type and quality of wood you choose to use. For instance, redwood boards that are clear of any knotholes are likely to be pretty pricey. The boards are easy to install, though they take a bit longer than other types. A nice feature of this type of siding is that you can either install the boards horizontally, vertically, or even diagonally for greater style and design options.

Painting the Exterior

Depending on the type of siding you've chosen for your home, you may need to paint it. Painting isn't all that difficult. It makes for a good do-it-yourself project—not to mention a good money-saver—but you have to know what you're doing. Choosing the wrong type of paint or a poor grade will affect the overall look and quality of the paint job.

Types of Paint

You can use either latex paint or oil-based paint on the exterior of your home. Latex paints are easy to use, produce few fumes, and dry quickly. Recent improvements in latex paints have made them more durable, and they are becoming popular choices for exterior projects. Oil-based paints are the traditional first choice for use on home exteriors, as they are the most durable of all paints. The oil base adheres well to almost all surfaces and repels water. No matter which type of paint you choose to use, make sure it is exterior grade.

ALERT!

If you choose to hire out the painting project, make sure that the workers have liability insurance and worker's compensation. Painting the exterior of a home can be a dangerous task, and you don't want to be liable for accidents.

Paint comes in three quality grades: premium, budget, and professional. To get the best quality and durability, purchase premium grade paints. Don't be fooled by the "professional" label. Professional-grade paint is actually the cheapest and lowest in quality. These paints are meant to be sold in large qualities and to keep costs down for contractors.

Painting Equipment

If you are going to do the painting yourself, the type of equipment you use depends on what you are comfortable with. Most professional painters use sprayers to apply the paint as they can get the job done quickly and effectively—often, a house can be done in one day when using sprayers. However, using this type of equipment requires skill, so if you haven't used sprayers before, it's not a good idea to try it out on your home.

Many amateur painters enjoy the use of power rollers for exterior jobs. This tool is easy to use and is good for large jobs. The power roller pumps paint up a hose and to the roller, eliminating the need to continuously go back to the paint can. (Rollers are notorious for holding very little paint.)

Of course, you can always stick to tradition and use brushes to paint your home. Purchase good quality brushes and follow their instructions for proper care. A good brush will do a good job; a poor brush will do a poor job. You can buy specialty brushes for the type of paint you are using. However, nylon brushes will work for both latex and oil-based paints. For large flat surfaces, get brushes with the bristles cut straight across. For smaller jobs such as trim and touch-ups, get brushes with the bristles cut at an angle. You'll likely want to purchase a variety of sizes. E

Chapter 12

Roofing

The exterior of the house is nearly complete. But unless you want to leave the inside unprotected from the elements, you'll need to finish the roof. This chapter takes you through the different types of roofing. We will discuss sheathing and the process of installing roofing material, as well as how to finish the small but important details.

Styles of Roofs

The style of roof you choose will have a tremendous impact on the overall look of your house. The roof can be as simple or as complex as you like. Of course, the complexity of the roof will affect your budget so you need to take that into consideration as you are going over your options. As you are designing your home, try out several different styles to see which you prefer. The same house will look entirely different with each roof design you put on. You'll soon see that while it is undeniably an important functional part of the house, the roof is also an important aesthetic element.

Gable Roof

When most people think of roofs, they usually form a picture of a gable roof in their minds. A gable roof has two sloping roof planes that intersect at a ridge to form an angle. It is a very basic roof style and is easy and quick to build. A gable roof's greatest virtue is its ease of venting, by use of a continuous ridge-vent, which ventilates heat and moisture out through the peak of the roof. It eliminates the need for powered attic ventilators or static roof vents, which can cause unsightly clutter on the roof system. While you will often see the gable roof centered over the house, it doesn't have to be. You can build a gable roof that is off center with a longer roof plane on one side. You can even create multilevel gables on the same house, creating a more complex design.

Flat Roof

Flat roofs are the easiest to build, as the roof is all one plane. A flat roof isn't technically "flat." Instead, it is still built with a slight slope so that water can run off it instead of pooling on top. Even so, the flat roof needs special considerations for sealing. Typically, hot tar is applied to flat roofs to create one continuous sealant, thus reducing the chances that water will find its way into the house. (It's highly recommended that you hire a professional to apply the hot tar.) Flat roofs should be avoided in parts of the country where there is a great variation in temperature. Expansion during summer months and contraction in winter can cause the tar structure of a flat roof to crack open and separate.

Less Common Styles

You shouldn't worry if you find you don't care for either of the options above; there's lots of room to get even more creative with your roof design. Some other styles you can choose from include the gambrel roof, hip roof, and mansard roof. These styles are each more complex than the typical gable or flat roof, so as you consider these for design purposes, also consider the fact that they will cost more to build.

If you are planning to install a complex roof design, it's a good idea to hire a roofing subcontractor to do the work. While this may be more expensive than doing it yourself, complex designs lend themselves to more opportunities for mistakes, which may cost you considerably more in the long run.

The gambrel roof is one that consists of more than one ridge. A gambrel roof may have its main ridge at the top and another ridge, farther down, that interrupts the slope of the roofline. This type of roof isn't terribly complex, but it does add character to the appearance. The hip roof is a little more difficult to build. In this style, the ridge doesn't extend all the way along the house. It is cut short, and hip rafters are installed diagonally from the shortened end of the ridge down to the corners of the walls. The mansard roof is a fancier style of roofing with a charm all its own. It has a double slope on each of the four sides of the house. Typically, the upper slopes are designed to be nearly flat and the lower slopes are nearly vertical.

The Overhang

The overhang of the roof is another functional yet aesthetic element. The overhang is that section between the edge of the roof and the exterior of the house. It typically "hangs over" the edge of the house, hence the name "overhang" (though it is also sometimes called the eave or cornice). The overhang is made up of the soffit and fascia board. The soffit is the underside of the overhang; the fascia board is a board that is nailed to the edge of the overhang.

Depending on your preference, you can either have an open or closed overhang. An open overhang leaves the underside of the roof exposed. This is sometimes a nice design element for homes that have impressive structural members, such as log homes. A closed overhang covers up the underside of the roof. If you choose to have a closed overhang, you'll likely want to install vents to allow for air circulation beneath the roofline.

FACT

Some roofing designs call for a drip edge. A drip edge is a piece of metal that is attached to the edge of the roof. It directs water to the outer edge instead of allowing it to find its way into the roofing material and from there into the house.

The soffit and fascia board can also be used as design elements. While they probably won't get as much attention as the siding and roofing material, you can still make them look nice and complement the rest of the home. Although soffits are usually made of plywood, you can also easily find them in aluminum. Some houses have fascia boards, and others don't. The fascia board is used both as support for the gutters and as trim for the overhang. While the fascia board finishes the edge of the overhang, if you have a wide gutter, you don't need it.

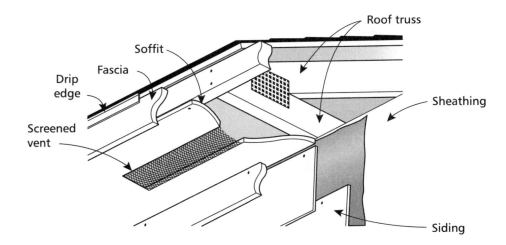

▲ Anatomy of an overhang

Roof Sheathing

The roof frame needs a protective covering. Roof sheathing adds rigidity and strength to the roof and provides a surface for nailing the roofing material. Like wall sheathing, roof sheathing is easy but monotonous work. Because the sheathing will be covered with roofing materials, you needn't be concerned too much with accuracy or how it looks. This work is a little different in that you won't have as many openings to cut out. Because you will be working up high, the work should go a little more slowly and carefully.

Materials

You can choose from a variety of materials to sheathe the roof. Visit your local building supplier and discuss your options with an expert. You will find that some sheathing materials work better than others for the type of roof and roofing materials you plan to use. For instance, if you are installing a shingle roof, you may find that horizontal wooden strips are best. In any case, it's a good idea to be informed of the options available. This will help you decide which sheathing material is the best fit for your house.

ALERT!

Safety when building a home cannot be stressed enough, and this is especially true of roof work. Always make sure you stay well hydrated, take frequent breaks, and are alert at all times. Even a short fall can result in serious injury.

Plywood is the most common material used for sheathing a roof. Plywood is inexpensive and easy to install. It comes in large panels that cover big areas, thus making the work move along quickly. Plywood comes in a variety of thicknesses for you to choose from. Check your building plans to see if there are any specifications for thickness. If not, keep in mind that the minimum thickness for roof sheathing is $5/16$ inch. However, it is usually a good idea to go a little thicker and use plywood that is between $3/8$ and $3/4$ inch thick.

Installation

The plywood panels should be installed perpendicular to the rafters. Starting at the eaves, apply the panels and work your way up to the peak. Make sure that the row is exactly perpendicular to the rafters; to do this, it's a good idea to temporarily tack down the first row, and then—once it is laid—go back and check to make sure it is perpendicular. Once any needed adjustments are made, you can permanently nail the first row down. The nail pattern for roof sheathing is typically to drive the nails 6 inches apart around the edges and 12 inches apart in the middle.

Before beginning to lay the second row, you'll need to attach H-clips to the first row panels. These clips should be placed in the center between each rafter. The clips are used to hold the rows together and add strength to the roof.

Just as you did when installing the subflooring, you'll need to stagger the panels. So, since you started with a full panel as your first in the row, for the second row, you'll start with a half panel. Work your way along the row using the same nailing pattern as before, and attach this row to the first using the H-clips. Continue this pattern of staggered rows all the way to the peak.

Sealing the Roof

Once you've applied the sheathing, you're ready to seal the roof. Sealing protects the sheathing from the elements and ensures that the finished roof is weather tight. You will be using a breathable roofing felt, sometimes referred to as tar paper or builder's felt. You can use either 15 pound or 30 pound roofing felt, though it is advisable to use the heavier weight for the added protection it offers.

FACT

If your roofing design calls for drip edges—which are typically used with asphalt shingles—apply the roofing felt over the drip edge at the eaves and under the drip edge at the edge of the slope.

Roofing felt is easy to install. It comes in large rolls with horizontal lines marked on it as a guideline. As you did with the sheathing, you work your way with the roofing felt from the bottom up. Starting flush with one edge, simply unroll the felt, smoothing it as you go to get rid of any bumps, and secure it using roofing tacks. Allow a 4-inch overlap as you unroll the next row over the first.

If you have vents or intersections in the roofing, you'll need to allow for extra protection around these areas. For vent pipes, cut out a square of roofing felt with a hole in the middle. Fit the felt around the vent, and seal it around the pipe with roofing tar. For intersections in the roof, tack down an extra layer of roofing felt in the valley area. Adding the extra felt will provide optimum protection from water and help prevent against leaks.

Flashing

Flashing is a material—usually metal—used in valleys, around chimneys, skylights, and vents, and at any intersection in the roof, such as where a roof butts into a wall. The purpose of flashing is to divert water. As these areas tend to gather more water than other areas of the roof, it is essential that you use some type of flashing to waterproof the intersections. The flashing is installed on top of the roofing felt and covered by the roofing material, such as shingles. Always install the flashing per the manufacturer's instructions for optimum performance.

There are different kinds of flashing made to be used for the various areas that need to be flashed. Valley flashing is typically made from long strips of metal with a center crimp. You may need more than one piece of flashing to cover a long valley. If so, install the bottom piece first, and then overlap the next piece by at least 8 inches. When covering the valley flashing with roofing material, angle it out so that the exposed flashing gradually gets wider as it goes down to the bottom.

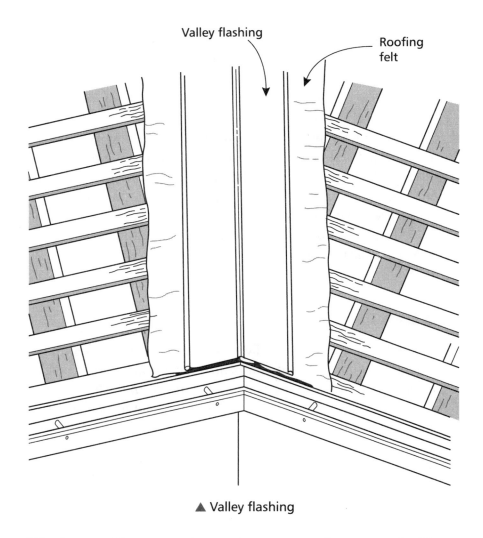

Valley flashing

Roofing felt

▲ Valley flashing

Wood-stove chimneys and vent pipes are usually protected with flashing that is premade to fit different sizes of pipe. This type of flashing is relatively easy to install as it is simply slipped over the pipe and fitted into place. To fit it into place at the bottom, try to slip a portion of it under the roofing felt. If you aren't able to do this, cut out some more felt and cover the bottom edges of the flashing. Once this is done, you can apply the roofing material up to the pipe, leaving a gap of 1½ inches between the roofing material and the neck of the flashing.

ALERT!

Metal flashing usually has several sharp edges. It's a good idea to protect those hard-working hands by wearing gloves when handling this type of material.

Skylights, chimneys, and areas where the roof intersects a wall require step flashing. Step flashing is composed of several long, L-shaped pieces of metal that are overlapped to create a trough. One edge of the L is laid flat along the roof, and the other edge works its way up the intersecting wall (or curb, in the case of chimneys and skylights). To install step flashing, work your way up from the bottom, overlapping the second piece over the first by 2 inches. (When using shingles as the roofing material, the step flashing will be placed on top of the lower course and then covered by the next course. Shingle courses are discussed later in this chapter.)

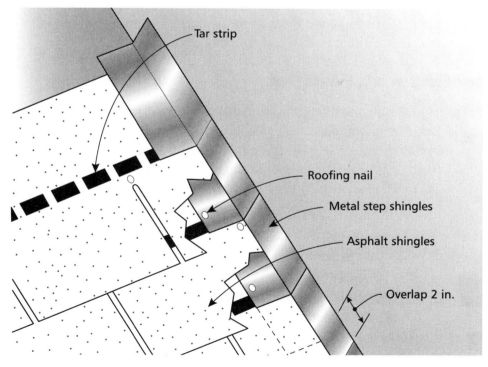

▲ Step flashing

Installing Roofing Material

You must take several things into consideration when choosing a roofing material. As roofing materials don't come cheap, the amount of money you want or are able to spend will likely be a big factor. You will need to think about how easy the material is to install. If you choose to hire labor to do the installation, the price will go up if the material is complicated to install or requires a lot of time. And, of course, the roofing material will greatly affect the overall appearance of your home, so you'll want to seek out a material that will complement both the style of roof and siding you've chosen.

Material Choices

Some of the materials you can choose from include metal (aluminum, copper, galvanized, or terne), rolled roofing (mineral-surfaced asphalt), hot tar, tile, shingles (asphalt, fiberglass, wood, or slate), and wood shakes. Because shingles are the most popular, that is the material we will discuss here. To install other kinds of roofs, consult or hire a professional roofer so that your roofing is installed correctly and efficiently.

Roofing with Shingles

As with sheathing and sealing, you'll want to start at the eaves. The first row of shingles you'll install is called the starter course. This course is installed differently than the others. Cut about 3 inches off the tab side of the shingles, and trim about 6 inches from the end of the first shingle. This will allow you to create a staggered pattern with the next course. Turn the shingles upside down so that the tabs are facing away from the eaves, and keep the mineral surface facing up. Nail this starter course down approximately 3 inches above the eaves.

If you haven't shingled a roof before, it's a good idea to snap chalklines to act as guidelines as you are working. Most people apply a chalkline vertically every 36 inches and horizontally every 10 inches. These lines will help you to install the shingles straight.

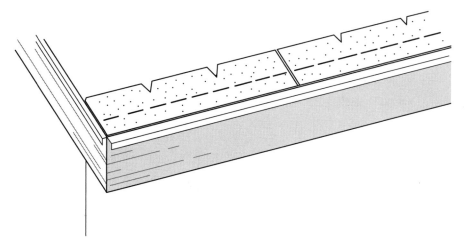

▲ Starter course

The first course is installed on top of the starter course. Don't trim down any of these shingles. The shingles of the first course are full-sized, thus offsetting the joints of the starter course. These shingles, and all the rest, will be installed with the tabs facing the eaves. Nail them down working from left to right, driving nails 1 inch from each edge and using a nail about every slot.

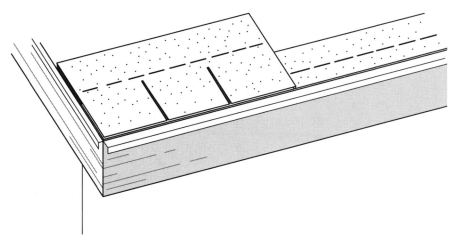

▲ Installing the first course

The remaining courses will need to be staggered, so trim 6 inches off the first shingle of the second course, 12 inches off the first shingle of the third course, 18 inches from the first shingle of the fourth course, 24 inches off the first shingle of the fifth course, and 30 inches off the first shingle of the sixth course. For the seventh course, start over with a full shingle, and repeat the same staggered pattern as you work your way up.

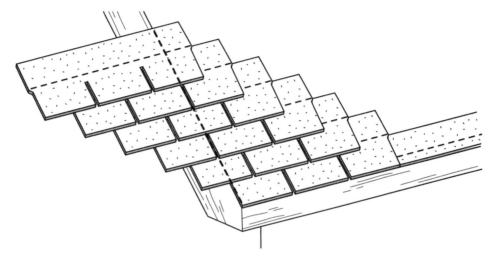

▲ First six courses of shingling

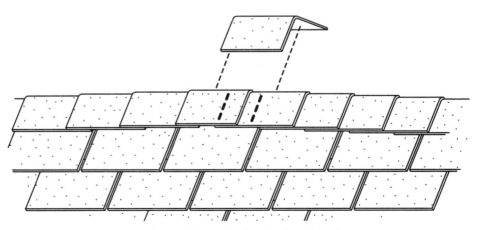

▲ Installing the final ridge shingle

Once you reach the top, you'll need to install ridge shingles for the final application. A ridge shingle is one tab (12 inches) of a full shingle. You can either buy these shingles or cut them out of full shingles yourself. Install these shingles working from both ends of the ridge towards the middle. Where they meet in the middle, you'll need to install one final ridge shingle, called the saddle, covering the joint. Nail it down with four nails and cover each of the exposed nails with roofing tar.

Don't Forget the Gutters

Check with your local building codes, as they may require the installation of gutters along the roof's edge. Gutters collect rain runoff from the roof and carry it along to downspouts that direct water away from the house. Without gutters and downspouts, some houses would be at risk from water that could pool and erode the foundation.

You can hire a contractor to install the gutters for you, but as it is a relatively easy job, this is a good do-it-yourself project. Gutters, downspouts, and all the elements needed for installation are available at most building supply stores. Be sure to read the manufacturer's instructions for proper installation. Keep in mind that in order for the runoff to channel properly, you need to install the gutters with a slight slope running from the top edge to the downspout. You'll also need to find out where to channel the runoff from the downspouts—it may need to go to a ground sewer.

If you have a little extra money lying around, you may want to consider investing in gutter guards. These handy devices keep leaves and other debris out of the gutters, while still allowing the water in. This will significantly cut down on the number of times you need to get up on the ladder to clean out the gutters. You can find an image of the anatomy of the gutter system on page 160.

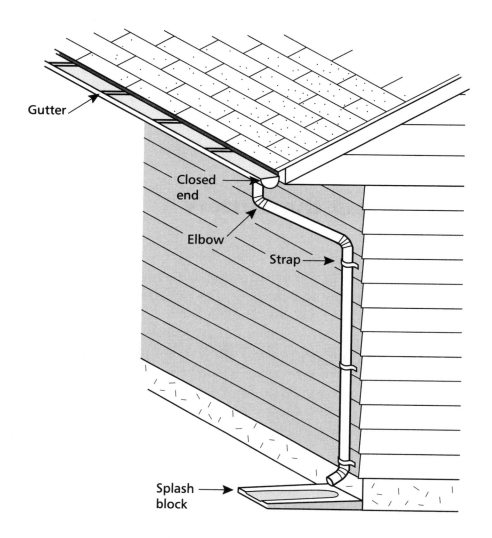

Gutter

Closed
end

Elbow

Strap

Splash
block

▲ Anatomy of the gutter system

Chapter 13

Electrical and Plumbing

Your house will be uninhabitable until you install the electrical and plumbing. These two building systems require a great deal of knowledge to be installed correctly. This chapter gives you the information you need for a basic understanding; however, it is highly recommended that you hire professionals to do the actual installation unless you are experienced with this type of work.

Electrical Materials

Your first lesson in understanding electrical work is to become familiar with the materials. Once you know the materials and what they are used for, you will be better able to understand how they fit together to create the electrical system. While electrical systems are unique to the design of individual houses, all of them use certain standard materials.

Wires

The primary material used in electrical systems is wire. Wires come in different sizes to do different jobs. You will see the wire's size indicated by its gauge. Larger wires have smaller gauge numbers; the smaller the gauge number, the more electrical current the wire can carry without overheating. For instance, 10-gauge wire is larger and able to carry more electrical current than 14-gauge wire. The wire sizes used in homes typically range from 10 to 14, depending upon the appliance or fixture that a particular wire serves.

Check your electrical plans or electrical codes to find out what gauge to use for particular applications. You must never use a higher gauge than what is approved by codes; however, you can use a smaller gauge. The smaller gauge can handle more current and is thus safer.

Wires are insulated and are either made of copper or aluminum. (Copper is more common as it is more conductive than aluminum.) The wires are also color coded to indicate their function. Red, black, and blue colors signify the hot wire. White is used to indicate the neutral wire. Green or bare wire is the ground wire. These colors are standard and shouldn't be changed. All electricians are familiar with the color code, which makes it easier for them to do their job.

Cables

The wires are grouped together within a nonmetallic (NM) cable, which is often referred to by the brand name Romex. Cables are labeled according to two main properties: the size of the wire, and the number of conductors it holds plus ground. Therefore, a cable labeled 12-3 w/G is holding three 12-gauge conductors plus ground. A 14-2 w/G cable is holding two 14-gauge conductors plus ground.

Electrical Boxes

Electrical boxes are installed in the walls to hold the wires going to and from receptacles and switches. These boxes are typically metal but can also be made of fiberglass or plastic. (Many codes enforce the use of only metal boxes.) The box protects any wiring joints and splices and allows room for the heat from a splice to dissipate. Wiring splices can only be made inside the boxes; the wires outside the boxes must be continuous.

Boxes come in different sizes, depending on the number of wires they can hold. The electrical code will specify how many wires are allowed in each box. If you need more room for the number of switches or outlets you are trying to accommodate, some metal boxes can be joined together to make a larger box.

Other Electrical Fixtures

Other fixtures you will encounter as you install the electrical system are receptacles, circuit breakers, fuses, and switches. You are already familiar with receptacles—these are the outlets you plug your television, lamps, and computers into. When you plug in your computer, the receptacle taps into the circuit to provide the electricity that lets you power up.

FACT

Receptacles are designed to take two- or three-pronged plugs. You'll notice on the receptacles that one slot is smaller than the other. The smaller slot is for the hot wire; the bigger is for the neutral wire. On those that take three-prong plugs, the third slot (or hole) is for the ground wire.

Switches are devices that control the flow of electricity by turning it on or off. When you come home at night, how do you turn the lights on in the house? You flip a switch. The switch controls whether or not that particular light fixture, for instance, gets a flow of electricity. One particular fixture can be controlled from different locations, depending on the type of switch you use. For instance, you may have two locations in the kitchen that can each control the kitchen light. In this case, a three-way switch is used.

Fuses and circuit breakers are safety mechanisms designed to interrupt the flow of electricity if a circuit carries too much electricity for too long. Fuses are small pieces of metal that are found in encasements where a current passes into a circuit. Cartridge fuses are used on large appliances that have short bursts of electricity (such as an air conditioner). They can accommodate these short bursts, but only for a certain amount of time. Circuit breakers are located in the breaker box. The current passes through a metal spring, and if this spring gets too hot, the breaker trips, causing the circuit to be interrupted. The breaker then switches to reset. The problem must be fixed and the breaker turned back on before the circuit can resume carrying its flow of electricity.

Understanding the Electrical System

Now that you know the materials used, it's time to learn how they all come together to create the electrical system for your home. Your house plans will include a set of electrical plans. This is the guide that tells you where the breaker box (or main service panel), meter, circuits, receptacles, and switches are to be installed.

These plans won't mean much to you, though, unless you understand how the electrical system works. You are able to tap into electricity from the service line of your local electric company. The electricity from this service line runs into the house through the meter and then into the main service panel. Within this panel are the breakers that control specific circuits. The hot wires are attached to these breakers, and the neutral wires are all tied together. The ground wires also meet up in the service panel. Cables exit the service panel and run to the electrical boxes, where they give power to the switches.

ALERT!

If you plan to do your own wiring, it is essential—for your own safety but also to reduce the risk of a fire hazard—that you understand how electricity works in conjunction with the materials you'll be using. If you don't understand the process in its entirety, consider taking a class or hiring a professional.

Now that you know the basic layout for the path of electricity, let's take a look at how the electricity works. The hot wire is what delivers the electrical current. The neutral wire brings the current back to earth. The ground wire is basically a safety backup. Electricity has to run in a loop—in order for your electrical devices to work, the power that comes into them must have a way back out. For instance, your fixtures are attached to the neutral wire, and the switch is connected to the hot wire. When you flip the switch, it allows electricity to flow to the fixture, giving it power. Then the neutral wire brings that power back to earth, creating the loop. Each circuit is its own loop, running through the main service panel, out to its switches and receptacles, and then back to the service panel.

Wiring the House

Installing the electrical system is one of the most difficult tasks you'll take on when building your own home. It requires a great deal of knowledge, not only about the electrical system itself, but also about the codes the system must meet. The National Fire Protection Association has published the National Electric Code (NEC), which gives information about basic safety and installation procedures. Your local building codes will likely use the NEC and supplement it with their own additions. Local codes differ somewhat, so it is essential that you visit the building department to find out what codes your system must meet, what permits you must get, and when inspections are required.

Some codes will not allow you to do the installation work yourself. And, unless you know what you're doing, it's a good idea not to. If you really want the responsibility of this job, consider taking some classes, reading a few texts, and hiring a professional to inspect your work. Make sure you are comfortable with the work before taking on the job yourself.

You can always opt to hire a professional. A licensed electrician will be familiar with the local codes and will be well equipped to install a system that is unique to the design of your home. You can always work with the professional and do some of the smaller and less complicated jobs to save money and learn along the way.

The installation of an electrical system is done in two phases: rough-in, and finish. Rough-in is completed before the interior walls are installed and the electricity is turned on. During this phase you install the electrical boxes and wires, the parts that will be hidden when the house is completed. Finishing is connecting all the wires to the receptacles, switches, and the main service panel, and bringing in the electrical service.

Install the Boxes

Your first task is to install the main service panel, or breaker box. As you know, the main service panel serves as the central command area. It provides power to the circuits running through the house and contains the breakers for these circuits. You need a service panel that is large enough to hold all the circuits you'll need. These panels can either be installed between two studs, leaving enough room for the box's face to extend past the drywall, or they can be mounted on the surface, leaving the entire box exposed. Your electrical plans or local code will specify where the main service panel should be located.

Once you have the main panel installed, it's time to install the subpanels, or electrical boxes. These boxes will house the wiring for switches and outlets. Be sure you install boxes that will be big enough to accommodate the appropriate wiring and connectors. The boxes typically come with their own nails, which are used to secure the box to a stud. When installing, make sure the boxes will be flush with the final wall covering. The best way to do this is to measure against a piece of the wall covering you hold up while installing the box. Refer to your electrical plans for the locations of boxes.

Install the Wiring

The cables will be running through the studs, so you'll need to drill holes or cut notches large enough to accommodate the individual cables. When drilling holes, use a right-angle drill and make a hole in the center of the stud. When cutting out notches, use a circular saw to cut a ½ inch-deep notch. Cover the notches (after the cable has been placed) with nail guards.

FACT

This book does not aim to give you the detailed information you need to properly install the electrical and plumbing systems. Such work requires extensive knowledge and familiarity with local codes. Instead, the goal here is to give you an overview of each system and information for a basic understanding of installation.

Lay out the cables according to the specifications on your electrical plans. You must pull the cables through the holes or notches in the studs, being careful to keep it free of kinks. As you are doing this, make sure you do not pull too tight. Enough slack needs to be left in the cable lines to allow for expansion and contraction of the house. At each box, the wires will be exposed. The best way to do this is with a cable stripper. This tool will cut the cable but ensure that the wire coatings are not cut. Secure the cables to the studs using staples or horseshoe nails in accordance with the specifications of your local code. At the main service panel, there must be enough exposed wire for each to reach its appropriate locations. At the individual boxes, you'll need to pull the cable through the knockout hole in the box and then cut and expose at least 6 inches of wire.

Once you have installed the electrical boxes and laid the wire, it's time to call for a rough-in inspection. The rough-in must be approved before you can complete the connections and bring in the electric service.

Connecting Wires

Some wiring connections are easier than others. Some switches and receptacles use push terminals. With these terminals, you simply need to strip the insulation off the wire and push the wire into the correct terminal, which then clamps down and holds it in place. Other switches and receptacles use screw-type terminals. Again, you will need to strip the insulation off the wire and, using pliers, make a loop on the end of the wire and attach it to the appropriate screw. Tightening the screw tightens the loop and secures the wire. Remember that the hot wires should be connected at the terminals labeled with a plus sign (+), and the neutral wires will connect at the terminals labeled with a minus sign (-).

Wiring gets a little more complicated when you are working with several wires or cables. In this case, you will need to learn to *pigtail* the wires, creating one wire to connect to the outlet or switch. Pigtailing involves binding all wires of the same color together with a 6-inch pigtail wire. The pigtail wire is the one that connects to the receptacle or switch. Twist the ends of like-colored wires together tightly with the pigtail wire in a clockwise direction. Once you have done this, slip the bare ends into a wire nut and twist the nut clockwise to secure the wires. Then all you need to do is connect the pigtail wire to the appropriate terminal in the receptacle or switch. The pigtailed wires should fit nicely into the electrical box.

ALERT!

Always make sure you install individual outlets and switches according to the manufacturer's instructions. Though it may seem straightforward and easy enough, you don't want to take any chances where electricity is concerned.

When you have installed all receptacles and switches and have connected the wires to the main service panel, you are ready for the final inspection. The inspector will scrutinize your work, so prepare yourself. If the electrical system meets with approval, you can then call the electric company and set up service.

Safety Issues

Safety is always of the utmost importance, and this is especially true when you're working with electricity. If you have chosen to install the electrical system yourself, or if you're helping the professional electrician, here are some pointers and precautions you need to keep in mind:

- Never wire the house when the electricity is turned on. This includes working with circuits, fixtures, switches, and receptacles.
- Never use a higher gauge wire than what is approved for a particular application.
- When working with electricity, it's a good safety precaution to wear rubber-soled boots.
- Do not splice wires outside of an electrical box.
- Label the circuits at the main service panel.
- Always make sure the working area is dry.
- Double-check that wires are assigned to their appropriate jobs. For instance, don't install a neutral wire to supply power.
- Know the electrical plans inside and out before beginning to install the electrical system.

Understanding the Plumbing System

The basic concept behind a plumbing system is to bring fresh water into your home and carry used water out of your home. Sounds easy enough, doesn't it? Well, it's a bit more complicated than that. There are several components that make up the plumbing system, and it's important that you understand the purpose and workings of each. There are two main subsystems you'll be working with: the supply system and the drain/waste/vent (DWV) system.

The Supply System

The supply system is what carries fresh water into your home. A pipeline carries water in from a water main or well. Where this pipe enters your house, there is a water meter for the water company to measure how much water you've used and a shutoff valve that allows you to stop the flow of water into the house. The main supply line enters the house and goes to the cold water inlet. From here, several lines branch off to carry cold water to the various fixtures in the house. The main line continues on from the cold-water inlet to the water heater. Again, lines will branch off from here to carry hot water to the fixtures in the house.

Some houses have a water softener installed. If your house plans call for this, then it will become part of the supply system. Typically it is the hot water that is softened; however, some people choose to soften some cold water supplies, such as the one for the kitchen sink.

Pipes run both vertically and horizontally. Those that run vertically from one floor to another are called risers. The supply lines must be pressurized in order to get the water to flow up the risers and throughout the system. The supply system typically runs through the floors, up through the walls, and out to the fixtures.

The DWV System

The DWV system is more complex than the supply system. Its job is simple enough: to remove the used water and waste from the house. The waste/drain pipes lead to the main drain, which leads to the sewer. Pretty simple. However, there are several details that need to be nailed down for it to work properly.

Because the DWV system is not operated by pressure, it has to rely on gravity to move waste materials through the pipes. Therefore, the pipes must be installed with a slight slope, typically a minimum of $1/4$ inch per foot. Installing the pipe with insufficient or too much slope will cause the pipes to become clogged. Plumbing professionals realize this and have the sloping system down to a fine art.

The DWV system also requires the installation of vents and traps. Vents allow atmospheric pressure into the DWV system so that waste materials can move through the pipes and out of the house. Vents also ensure that gases within the system are released safely outside through vent pipes that exit through the roof. Traps are necessary to ensure that gasses do not escape into the house through the pipes. Each fixture has its own trap, which is essentially a dip in the pipe where water blocks the escape of any gasses. In the case of toilets, the water that pools at the bottom of the bowl performs the trap function.

Installing Plumbing

Even more difficult than installing the electrical system is installing the plumbing system. Again, it is highly recommended that you hire a professional to do the installation to ensure that all codes are met and the system is functioning at its optimum level. As with the electrical system, you will do a rough-in first and then the finish work. The rough-in includes the installation of the water supply and drainage pipes, vents and traps, and fixture supports. Finishing is installing the fixtures themselves and connecting them to the supply and drainage systems.

The DWV pipelines are usually installed first. This system typically uses plastic pipe, such as PVC (polyvinyl chloride) or ABS (acrylonitrile-butadine-styrene). You'll need to purchase a special solvent to glue the plastic pipes together. Refer to your plumbing plans for the proper layout and location of the DWV system. The piping will have to run through studs, plates, and joists. To drill big enough holes through these elements, you'll need a pretty heavy-duty drill. (There are bits and saws available that are specially designed for plumbing projects.) Keep in mind that you will need to install this piping at a slope as mentioned earlier. This system also includes traps and vents—don't forget these as you install the DWV system!

QUESTION?

What size of pipe should be used?
The plumbing plans will specify the sizes of pipes to be used for both the DWV and supply systems. Typically, a ³⁄₄-inch pipe is used for the main water supply line, ³⁄₄- or 1-inch pipe for the cold and hot water mains, and ¹⁄₂-inch pipe as it gets close to the fixture.

The water supply system is usually installed after the DWV system since the piping is smaller and able to maneuver out of the way of the DWV piping. Most use copper pipe for the supply system. Again, you'll need to refer to your plumbing plans for the layout of the supply lines. It's generally best to begin the installation where the water supply enters your home and work your way through the network of piping. Copper pipes need to be cut with a tubing cutter and soldered together.

After you have installed the water supply system (including all cold and hot water lines) and have tested it for leaks, you can install the various plumbing fixtures. Always follow the manufacturer's instructions for installing sinks, bathtubs, showers, toilets, and washing machines. Each fixture has its own set of requirements and installation procedures.

Chapter 14

Heating, Ventilation, and Air Conditioning

Your home's heating, ventilation, and air conditioning (HVAC) system is responsible for creating a comfortable atmosphere inside your house. It will be one of your bigger expenses, and you should consider your selection very carefully. To make your home energy efficient, it's essential that you install an HVAC system best suited for the house, the climate, and your family's needs.

Understanding the HVAC System

The HVAC system controls the temperature and quality of the air in your home by providing heat, air conditioning, and ventilation as needed. There are several different systems on the market, and it's important that you find one that is suited to the needs of your home. A contractor will design a system made up of several components that will reflect your individual requirements. The components of an HVAC system are a heating system, an air conditioning system, a ventilation system, and often a humidifying or dehumidifying system. These systems work through a series of ductwork that circulates the air in your home, along with a thermostat to give you control over the system. To better understand the HVAC system, let's take a look at its individual components.

Heating System

The heating system is responsible for keeping your house warm when it's cold outside. Sounds simple enough, right? It would be, except that there are several different heating systems to choose from. Most houses have a furnace that is installed in the basement or in a utility closet. This furnace heats the heat exchanger and then blows the resulting warm air through the ductwork into your living areas. This is called a direct heat system. The furnace can be fueled by propane, oil, natural gas, wood, or electricity. You'll need to compare the costs of each to find out which would be the most economical for your home. These costs often depend on how close you are to the source of energy.

FACT

The filtration system on most forced air systems can be upgraded in two ways: by the use of a larger and more efficient air filter, or by the use of electronic air filters, which can take almost all dust, pollen, and allergens out of the ducted air supply.

Though it is the most common, the direct heat system isn't your only option. You could also opt to use a heat pump. A heat pump is actually both a heating and cooling system combined into one unit. This unit is essentially a regular air conditioner; however, it has a valve that can be switched to reverse the flow of the refrigerant. When this happens, the heat pump takes heat from the outside air and circulates it through the ductwork in your home. It uses electricity and the refrigeration cycle to accomplish this.

Of course, you have other options available, such as baseboard heating systems, solar heating systems, radiant heating panels, or wall and ceiling heaters. These types of systems are less common in newly built homes as they aren't always as reliable and may cost more to operate. Even so, you may want to take a look at them just so that you are aware of all your options.

Air Conditioning System

The air conditioning system is responsible for keeping your house cool when it is hot outside. Most people choose to install a central air conditioning unit in their home as these are more energy efficient than room air conditioners. The central air conditioning unit is that big box that sits outside the home, sometimes making kind of a lot of noise (though newer models have cut down on the noise level a bit). The air conditioner uses two coils and a pump to cool your home. The evaporator is the cold indoor coil that pulls heat out of the house, using the refrigerant. The condenser is the hot outdoor coil that releases the captured heat into the outside air. The compressor is the pump that moves the refrigerant between the evaporator and condenser, thus aiding the transfer of the heated air outdoors. The central air conditioning unit will utilize the blowers on the heating systems to circulate the cool air through the ductwork and into your living areas.

Ventilation System

The ventilation system is responsible for providing fresh air and limiting air pollution inside the home. While indoor air quality is important for all homes, people with allergies, asthma, or special needs should definitely think about installing high-quality ventilation. Your HVAC system will come equipped with filtration, which will cut down on the amount of contaminants that get into the air; however, you'll want to include a mechanical ventilation system in addition to this to ensure the air inside the house is kept fresh.

ALERT!

Don't rely on your local building codes for adequate minimum ventilation requirements. Residential ventilation system requirements have fallen behind in standard quality. It's best to consult an HVAC professional to find out what type of ventilation system will provide the best indoor air quality for your home.

Mechanical ventilation systems are comprised of several small fans placed in prime locations throughout the house to pull out stale and contaminated air and vent it to the outside. Often these fans are placed in areas where moisture and odor in the air is a concern, such as in the kitchen and bathrooms. Your HVAC contractor will be able to advise you of the best locations for ventilation.

Humidifying/Dehumidifying System

Humidifying or dehumidifying systems control the amount of moisture in the indoor air. The normal humidity range is between 35 and 45 percent relative humidity within a home. In dry areas or during the winter when the heating system can dry out the air, a humidifying system replenishes moisture to the air. In humid areas or during the summer when moisture tends to collect in the air, a dehumidifying system will pull out excess moisture from the air. Depending on where you live, you may need one, both, or neither of these systems. Your HVAC contractor should be able to advise you on the best strategy for your home.

Selecting a System

While you can certainly go out and shop for your own HVAC system, your best bet is to hire a reputable contractor to do the work for you. An HVAC contractor will be familiar with the residential systems available and will perform a thorough study of your home and its needs in order to find the best fit. The key here is to find a *reputable* contractor. A reputable contractor is experienced in working with residential HVAC systems, courteous and willing to answer any and all questions you have, licensed (if so required in your state), and up to date on all new technologies associated with HVAC systems.

When seeking out a contractor, ask friends, family, and other building specialists for recommendations. Word of mouth is one of the most useful tools in finding a reputable contractor. Be sure to ask for references from the contractor, and check up on each and every one of them. If a license is required, get the license number and check up on this as well. Most importantly, you should be comfortable in discussing your needs with the contractor and not feel pressured by a "sales pitch" attitude.

Find out if the contractor is a member of any HVAC associations, such as Air Conditioning Contractors of America. Typically, if the contractor is involved in associations, this shows that he or she keeps up with new developments.

Once you find a contractor (or if you have decided to go it alone), you'll need to make sure you take an active role in the decision-making process. Several factors are involved in your selection of an HVAC system. You should consider each one of these factors when selecting a system on your own or when discussing what best meets your needs with an HVAC contractor. Keep in mind that if the contractor tries to dance around any of these topics, it's time to find a different contractor.

Energy Efficiency

One of the first things most people look for in an HVAC system is energy efficiency—at least, that's what they *should* look for. The systems available today are much better than they were just a few years ago. Some systems will be much more energy efficient than others, but these will also cost you a lot more up front. You'll need to decide for yourself how much you are willing to spend and then try to find the most energy-efficient system for that price. Keep in mind as you are shopping that the more energy-efficient the system, the lower your energy costs in the long run. As with any high-efficiency energy purchase, make sure that the added expense can be recouped in energy-cost savings in a reasonable amount of time (usually seven to ten years).

Size

The size of your unit makes a big difference in how well it works to control the temperature and air quality in your home. While many people often think that bigger is naturally better, this isn't so when it comes to HVAC systems. A system that is too big for your home will not only cost you more to purchase and install, but it will also cost you more in repair and energy costs. It will switch on and off more frequently, which can suck up energy and cause it to break down more quickly than a smaller unit that is designed and sized to fit your home. The system should be sized to properly handle the calculated heating and cooling loads for each room. (Your HVAC contractor can perform these calculations.)

Cost

Of course, cost will be a main factor in choosing a system. Costs of HVAC systems will vary widely considering how the system is tailored to your home's individual needs. The factors most responsible for driving price up are the size of the system and its energy efficiency.

Local utility companies will often give you information about local energy efficiency ratings. They may even be willing to give you HVAC suggestions for your home if you bring in the house plans. It's a smart move to contact these companies to see if they can do an energy audit of your home.

Do a little comparison shopping on your own, and have a price in mind when you discuss your options with the contractor. If you are dealing with a reputable contractor, he will be able to find you the best system for the price you are willing to pay. Keep in mind that you must think both about the initial cost as well as the operating cost. Spending a little more now may save you a lot in the long run.

Ductwork

Ductwork is the transportation system for your HVAC system. It is comprised of ducts (pipes or vessels) that circulate the conditioned air in the house. There are two different elements of ductwork: air supplies and air returns. Air supplies are those ducts that transport the conditioned air to the living areas. Air returns are those ducts that carry old air back to the heating and air conditioning system to be cleaned and conditioned.

Ducts are usually made of either fiberglass or sheet metal. Most new homes use insulated fiberglass ducts. The insulation adds to the energy efficiency of the entire system. Also, fiberglass is quieter than sheet metal. If you've ever been in an older home that was equipped with sheet metal ductwork, you know the strange noises the ducts can make as air moves through. At the same time, sheet metal with fiberglass insulation is probably the most durable ductwork option. The fiberglass insulation eliminates the noise problem.

FACT

There is an air filter between the return air duct and the heating and air conditioning unit. This filter catches and traps dust and dirt, preventing it from entering the HVAC system and being blown back into the living areas.

Make sure that you or your contractor designs the ductwork to match the capacity of your heating and air conditioning system. Ductwork that is too small or too big won't be able to operate at its optimum level. This could easily affect the energy efficiency of the entire system. Also, if the ductwork isn't the proper size, your local building inspector may not give it his stamp of approval. Again, it's a good idea to consult an HVAC specialist, as this is a specialized trade and not easily taken on by the novice builder.

As stated before, the ductwork impacts the energy efficiency of your HVAC system. To make the most of this, it's a good idea to install your HVAC system as close to the center of the house as you can get it. This minimizes the length of the ductwork required to reach all rooms. Also, you'll want to have as few turns and bends in the ductwork as possible. Bends and turns slow down the airflow, thus decreasing the energy efficiency of the system.

Registers

The ducts lead up to registers. A register is a device through which the conditioned air enters a room. The airflow can be controlled at the register by opening or shutting it. (There are fixed registers that are less expensive, but these give you no control over the airflow.)

Even the registers have an impact on the energy efficiency of your home! The placement of registers is not done at random. The designer will have carefully thought out where each register should be placed in each room. Typically, registers are installed under windows and near doors. Since windows and doors are where a home incurs heat loss, placing the conditioned air near these problem areas promotes even air distribution.

Each register must be sized to fit the needs of the room, just as the duct is. The size and number of registers per room is designed to be in direct relation to the calculated heating and cooling loads of that room. In other words, bigger rooms will require more air to be brought in; therefore, larger and more registers are needed in the bigger rooms compared to the small rooms. This way each room is equipped to maintain a comfortable atmosphere.

As the ductwork and registers are being installed, make sure there is a tight and secure fit between the duct and the register boot. If any air is allowed to escape the ductwork system, it will significantly decrease the energy efficiency of the house and force the HVAC system to work harder.

The registers are typically placed along the exterior walls of the house. If you have two different ductwork systems for the heating and air conditioning systems, then you'll want to consider the placement of the registers for each. For instance, because heat rises, it's a good idea to place the heat supply registers near the floor, under windows and close to doors. Air conditioning supply registers should be placed as high as you can in each room since cooler air falls. Of course, most heating and air conditioning systems use the same ductwork. In which case, many designers decide to stick with the lower exterior wall placement of registers. Discuss size, placement, and number of registers with your HVAC contractor.

Up until now, we've been discussing the air supply ducts. Of course, you'll also need to consider the placement of the air return ducts, which will pull the old air out of the room and take it back to be conditioned in the HVAC system. These ducts are typically covered by grills and are larger but fewer in number than the air supply ducts. Again, if you have separate ductwork for the heating and air conditioning units, the placement of the air returns should be different. Warm air returns should be placed lower in the room to take out the cooler air; cool air returns should be placed higher in the room to take out the warmer air.

Installing Additional Ventilation

In addition to the ventilation fans you'll have installed in the kitchen and bathrooms, other areas of the house will also require ventilation. For instance, if you plan to have a clothes dryer, you'll certainly want to install a vent from the dryer to the outside. Otherwise, hot air and lint will be blown back into the basement or utility room. Insulated attics will also require ventilation to ensure that condensation doesn't have a chance to collect and cause damage. Also, since heat rises, attics can get extremely hot during summer weather. Ventilation will allow that hot air to escape.

Installing a Vent for a Dryer

Most driers require a ventilation hole of 4 inches. This hole needs to be cut above the bottom plate through the wall sheathing. (Of course, before you cut this hole, you'll first need to know where you are going to put the dryer.) Once the hole is cut, you can attach the vent pipe—preferably galvanized steel or rigid aluminum—to the dryer and insert it into the vent hole. Be sure to seal the hole so that air and water can't get inside. It's best to seal it on both the inside and outside for added protection.

Installing Attic Vents

To ensure that moisture doesn't get trapped and hot air can escape, the attic needs to be ventilated. There are several different ways in which you can ventilate the attic; ridge vents, gable vents, soffit vents, roof louvers, and wind turbines are among the most popular.

FACT

Many people choose to use a combination of vents on their roofs, such as a ridge vent with soffit vents as well. This allows air to escape through both the top and sides of the roof, creating an optimal ventilation system.

Ridge vents are those that span the length of the roof. They are installed along the peak. You will often see these on new homes as they are often recommended for their efficient ventilation capabilities, appearance, and ability to keep rain out. Gable vents are louvered vents that are installed in the gable end of the roof. While they do allow hot air to escape, they aren't as effective as other types since they provide only limited airflow. Soffit vents are louvered vents installed in the soffits of the roof. These are always installed in conjunction with another type of vent. That's because soffit vents are designed to allow fresh air to get inside the roof, but they don't allow for proper elimination of hot air and moisture. Roof louvers are small covered openings that come in a variety of styles. While they do allow air to escape, there must be several placed across the roof to adequately ventilate the roof. Wind turbines are sphere-shaped projections that are installed near the peak of the roof. They are designed with specially shaped vanes that catch the wind, causing the turbine to spin and pull air out of the attic. Without wind the turbine loses power, but still allows air to escape the attic. (E)

▲ Anatomy of a ridge vent

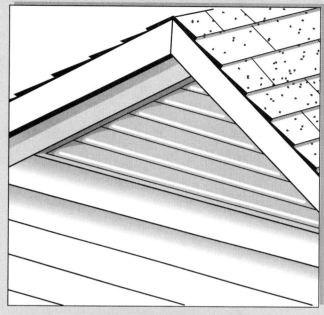

▲ Gable vent

▲ Soffit vent

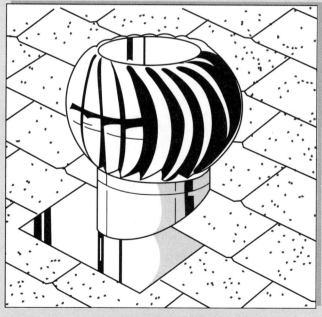

▲ Wind turbine

Chapter 15

Insulation and Sealing

You've taken your time in choosing a heating, ventilation, and air conditioning system to control the temperature inside your home. However, you must use insulation and sealing if you want to maintain that temperature and make your home energy efficient. Otherwise, the fluctuations of the temperature inside your home will be at the mercy of the climate outside.

Housewraps

One of the first steps you should take toward protecting your house from air infiltration is sealing the exterior. You do this by covering the framed or sheathed house with housewrap. Housewrap is basically a big 12-foot roll of a slick, lightweight material; the common brands are Tyvek, Typar, and Barricade. This fabric-like material keeps water and air from coming into the house, but it allows water vapor to escape from inside. Visit your local building supply company to compare types of housewraps. Some will be better than others for your particular climate area.

Installing the Housewrap

Housewrap is fairly easy to install, but it does take more than one person to accomplish the job. It's a bulky material that would be too awkward for someone to handle without help. Housewrap can be attached to the wall studs, if you haven't chosen to sheathe the exterior, or it can be attached on top of the wall sheathing.

If you have opted not to sheathe the exterior, it's a good idea to give the corners a little added protection. You can do this by doubling up the housewrap and stapling it to the outside corners, bringing it in to staple it in on the inside of the corners as well.

Before attaching the housewrap, cut it down to the height of the house. This will not only make covering the house easier, but will also save you the trouble of trimming the wrap after it has been attached. Unroll the edge and use a staple gun to attach it to a corner of the house. Unroll the housewrap to cover as much of the house as you can. At least one person should be stapling the wrap to the studs or sheathing as you unroll. Don't worry about openings right now; just cover them up as you go.

Cover as much as of the house as you can with the first roll, taking it around any corners. If you need to use another roll to finish the exterior, overlap the ends by at least 16 inches. You'll need to seal this joint with a tape made specifically for housewrap. Continue until the entire house has been covered.

Finishing Touches

Inspect your work, keeping an eye out for tears in the wrap. If you have any tears, these will need to be repaired. Simply cut off a length of the wrap and apply it over the tear, starting at the top of the wall. Doing the repair this way ensures that water flows off the wrap properly and doesn't seep into the joints. Use the housewrapping tape to seal the tear securely.

Finally, cut the housewrap from the openings. The best way to do this is to cut diagonal lines from one corner of the opening to the other, creating an **X**. Pull the flaps back from the opening from inside the house, and staple them to the inside header, trim, or sill. Once this is done, your house is successfully housewrapped. That wasn't so hard, was it?

Types of Insulation

Once you've installed an HVAC system, you'll naturally want it to do its job. It will heat and cool your house accordingly; however, your house's capacity to maintain the desired temperature is dependent upon the amount and quality of the insulation installed. Insulation is what cuts down on heat transfer through the walls, doors, and windows of the house. Heat always flows toward cooler areas. During the winter, heat wants to escape the house, and during the summer, heat wants to get in. Insulation is used to force the air to stay put. This will not only make your home much more comfortable, but it also cuts down significantly on energy costs.

ALERT!

Some types of insulation are flammable. Your local building code may have restrictions regarding the use of these types of insulation. It's always good to be on the safe side and opt for insulation that is nonflammable or that has been treated with a fire retardant.

Visit your local building supply company and take a look at the various types of insulation. You will find that you have a choice of materials for insulation as well as a choice of the type of insulation to be used for particular applications. Before you make a purchase, check with your local building department to find out what insulation requirements must be met.

Insulation Requirements

Insulation requirements differ according to area. Climate dictates how much insulation is necessary to effectively insulate your home. For instance, a home in Fargo, North Dakota, requires an insulation with a greater resistance to heat transfer than a home in Nashville, Tennessee.

Building codes aren't likely to stipulate the exact type of insulation you should use. They will, however, require a particular R-value. The R-value measures the amount of resistance to heat flow. This measurement is a standard across the board for all types of insulation. The higher the R-value's number, the more resistance to heat transfer it will offer. For instance, an insulation with an R-19 rating will have greater insulating properties than an insulation rated R-11. You have to insulate with at least the minimum R-value as stipulated by your local building code. However, it is a good idea to purchase the highest R-value insulation you can afford. While it may be more costly up front, you will save more in energy costs in the long run.

Batt Insulation

Fiberglass batt insulation is one of the most popular forms of insulation. It's quite likely you've seen this type of insulation before. You can get sheets of batt insulation in varying thicknesses, lengths, and R-values. The width of this material is typically either 15 or 23 inches, made to fit 16- and 24-inch stud and joist spacing. Some batts come with a paper backing that acts as a vapor barrier. The paper is stapled to the studs or joists to hold the insulation in place. Other batts (called friction batts) do not have this paper backing and are held snugly in place by friction.

Blanket insulation is very similar to the batt type. The only difference is that blanket insulation comes in large rolls that need to be cut to size. Batt insulation comes in precut sheets, often sized to fit common wall and floor dimensions.

Blown-In Insulation

Blown-in insulation is most often made of cellulose, but you can also find it as glass fiber, rock wool, perlite, or vermiculite. This type of insulation comes in bags and must be poured or blown in using a special blower. You can usually rent blowers at building supply stores. Blown-in insulation is often used in attics as well as odd-shaped and hard-to-reach cavities. You don't need to be as stringent in the application of blown-in insulation as you do the other types because gravity helps out and causes it to settle down into cavities and crevices.

Foam Insulation

Foam insulation, sometimes called rigid insulation, is a foam board that comes in different sizes and thicknesses. This type of insulation is used as an exterior sheathing. Of course, it isn't as stable as other types of sheathing, so if you live in an area prone to destructive elements such as earthquakes, you may not be able to use this insulation as sheathing. As foam insulation usually has a lower R-value than the other kinds, you may want to use it in conjunction with batt or blanket insulation. Foam insulation is nailed to the studs and installed much like sheathing. However, you will need to seal the joints with tape to ensure that unwanted air does not get through.

Insulating Walls and Ceilings

Fiberglass batts are most often used for insulating walls and ceilings, so that is the technique we will discuss here. Installing insulation is an easy task and great for the do-it-yourselfer trying to save some money. However, you need to take some precautions when working with fiberglass insulation. The fibers can damage your lungs and eyes and cause skin irritation. So, before you begin installing, let's take a look at some safety precautions.

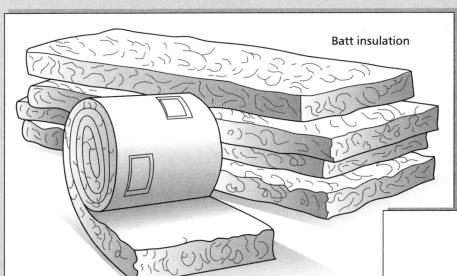

Batt insulation

Blanket insulation

▲ Batt and blanket insulation

▲ Blown-in insulation

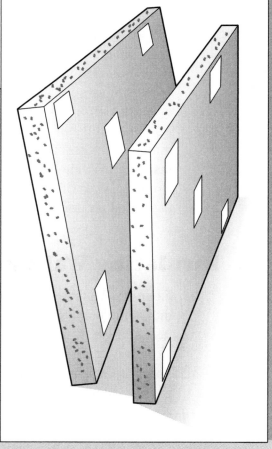

▲ Foam insulation

Working Safely

You should be properly outfitted to work safely with fiberglass insulation. Though you may get hot, you have to wear a long-sleeved shirt (preferably with sleeves that gather or button at the wrists), long pants, and gloves. This keeps the majority of your skin protected from the tiny fibers that can and will escape the insulation. Because you don't want to stifle yourself, wear loose-fitting clothing.

If you do get fibers on your skin, you will likely begin to itch. Don't give in to the temptation and scratch; this will only serve to embed the fibers into your skin. Instead, take a break from the work and wash the area well. Using vinegar as a rinse will help reduce the itching.

Because the fibers can damage your eyes, always wear a pair of high-quality goggles. Make sure they fit snugly but are not too tight. If they are too tight, no air will be able to circulate, and they will keep fogging over. This will make you stop your work so you can leave the area to clean them or momentarily expose your eyes to the fibers as you wipe them down.

It is also essential that you wear a dust mask because it is very easy to inhale those dangerous particles, which ultimately will be damaging to your lungs. Visit your local building supply store for a good mask. If you'd rather, you can use a respirator, which is more comfortable and allows you to breathe easily while at the same time protecting your lungs. When insulating the ceiling, wear a hat to keep the fibers from getting into your hair.

Installing Insulation

Install the fiberglass batts snugly between the studs of the walls and between the joists in the ceiling. While they need to fit snugly without any gaps, don't cram them in there too tightly. Batts usually come in dimensions cut to fit standard walls, making the job much easier. If the insulation is faced with craft paper, staple the paper tabs to the face rather than the inside of the studs. Stapling the foldout tabs to the inside of the studs can leave gaps that will diminish the insulating value.

In warm climates, you're advised to purchase batts that do not have the paper facing. These are called "unfaced batts." The paper facing acts as a vapor barrier, which is not recommended in warm areas with high levels of humidity. You install these batts in the same manner as the paper-faced kind, except you won't have anything to staple. These batts are held in place by friction until the drywall is installed to hold them permanently.

Cut to Fit

The insulation will not be sized to fit perfectly. You'll have to cut the fiberglass insulation for cavities such as those above and below windows. To do this, measure the area to be insulated, and add ½ to 1 inch on all sides. This will ensure that the insulation fits the area snugly and doesn't leave any gaps.

ALERT!

When you're cutting insulation, always be sure to use a sharp knife. A dull knife can create tiny tears or holes in the insulation or tear the paper facing. Even the smallest of holes can reduce the effectiveness of the insulation.

Cutting the insulation is easy. Lay out the fiberglass insulation with the paper side down, if applicable, on a flat surface. Line up a board with a straight edge along the measurement line and press down. Then use a sharp utility knife to cut along the edge of the board. Be sure to make a clean cut. If you happen to tear the paper facing, you'll need to cut another piece.

Insulating Floors

Insulation is installed between the floor joists and beneath the subflooring to keep cold air from coming up through the floor. This helps make the floor more comfortable to walk on, and it also keeps more heat in. The process of installing floor insulation is very similar to that for wall and ceiling insulation, as fiberglass batts are often used. However, there are a couple of differences.

Installing Batts

The way you install your insulation depends on where you live. The paper facing of insulation must face the heat. If you live in a colder climate and heating is a concern, you'll want to install the insulation with the paper facing the floor, or towards the inside of the house. If you live in a warmer climate where you are more concerned with keeping the house cool, you'll want to install the insulation with the paper facing the ground.

As you are installing the batts, keep in mind that the insulation needs to fit snugly and be in contact with the subflooring and headers to keep air from finding its way into unwanted spaces. Because the insulation needs to be held against the subflooring, you will need to provide supports for it as gravity would otherwise cause it to fall, leaving gaps. Your best bet is to use thick batts. This will make the installation of supports much easier and will provide you with even greater insulation.

FACT

When insulating the floor, you will have several obstacles, such as pipes, to work around. Take your time to ensure that you leave absolutely no gaps. Spray-foam insulation is handy to have around when insulating the floor as it easily fills small spaces and gaps around obstacles.

Once you have filled the space between the floor joists, making sure it butts snugly up against the header joists, you can then install the supports to hold the insulation in place. There are a few different materials you can use for this. Wood laths can be nailed in strips every 12 to 16 inches across and perpendicular to the joists for a very sturdy support system. Polypropylene twine can be stapled in a zigzag fashion every 12 to 18 inches between the joists and beneath the insulation to hold it in place. This material is mildew and rot resistant. You can also use a plastic or wire mesh, stapled to the bottom of the joists, as a support for the insulation. Whatever method you choose to use, make sure the insulation is fitted up against the subflooring, but is not compressed.

Using Blown-In Insulation

Many people choose to use cellulose blown-in insulation for the floors of the attic. Blown-in insulation is easy to use as you can simply pour it in between the floor's joists. However, you have to rent a blower or hire a subcontractor to blow the insulation in those hard-to-reach areas of the attic floor. It's recommended that you get enough blown-in insulation to fill the cavities all the way to the top or over the joists. Then run a long, straight board over the top of the joists to make an even surface and to push the insulation down into unfilled areas. Cellulose insulation may cost you a little more, but has a higher R-value per inch than fiberglass insulation. Its ease of use and great insulation value make it a popular choice for attic floors.

Insulating Small Spaces and Around Obstacles

Installing insulation would be a quick and easy job if not for all the small spaces you must fill. Plus, you'll come across obstacles such as pipes and electrical boxes that you must insulate around. This can be rather frustrating, but it doesn't have to be. Follow these tips to help make this tedious job a bit easier:

- To insulate around electrical boxes, split the insulation in half and tuck the back part underneath the box. Place the front half over the box and use a utility knife to cut the insulation to fit snug around the box.
- Use a screwdriver to pack scrap insulation into those narrow spaces around window and door frames. Or, even better, spray foam insulation into these spaces.

- You can insulate a pipe or wire by cutting a slice halfway through the batt long enough to fit the pipe or wire and simply enclose it in the insulation.
- Use expanding spray-foam insulation in any narrow gaps you come across and around pipes and wires that enter the house from the outside.

Vapor Barriers

Vapor barriers are often used on houses in cold climates and in high humidity areas. (Consult your local building department if you are unsure of whether you need a vapor barrier.) Vapor barriers are installed to prevent moisture buildup in the attic and exterior walls where trapped moisture can cause wood to rot.

There are different types of material that can be used as a vapor barrier, but polyethylene sheeting is the most commonly used. Polyethylene is a thin clear plastic that comes in rolls. This material is usually readily available at local building supply stores. (It is also often used in landscaping and on greenhouses.) Make sure you purchase the polyethylene sheeting that is used for construction projects, which is typically specified as "6 mil."

The paper facing on insulation is used as a vapor barrier. However, in order for it to do this job, the paper must overlap at the studs to create a continuous barrier that will not allow moisture to penetrate.

Installing a vapor barrier isn't difficult, but you need to make sure the material you use forms a continuous barrier without any tears or holes. Like housewrap, it requires more than one person to do the job. The polyethylene sheeting is big and bulky, and you'll need at least one person to hold the sheeting up and another person to attach it. This is another good job for the do-it-yourselfer. Just make sure to carefully inspect your work once you've finished.

Covering the Ceiling

The vapor barrier is installed after the insulation. You'll want to cover the ceiling first. Because it would be difficult and awkward to unroll the polyethylene along the ceiling, measure out the area you need to cover, and cut pieces of the sheeting to fit. Be sure to allow enough material for an overlap at least a joist-width wide. You should also take the ceiling sheeting down the walls at least 3 inches to allow for an overlap of the wall sheeting.

Attach the sheeting to the joists with staples spaced approximately 12 inches apart. Start in the middle of the ceiling and work your way out toward the walls. Completely seal the areas where the sheeting overlaps with housewrap tape. If you happen to cut or tear holes in the sheeting, tape these openings as well. It is imperative that the polyethylene sheeting forms a continuous barrier.

Covering the Walls

Once you have finished the ceiling, you can then move on to the walls. Just as you did with the ceiling, work your way out from the middle of the wall to the edges. At the top, overlap the wall sheeting to cover the ceiling sheeting. Staple it to the top plate, and seal the overlap with housewrap tape. Take the wall sheeting down past the bottom of the wall and allow it to lap over the subflooring by approximately 3 inches. If you need to use more than one sheet of polyethylene, overlap by at least a stud's width. Again, you seal the lap with housewrap tape.

Go ahead and cover all openings such as windows and doors. Once you have covered the wall, you can go back and cut out the openings. Seal the edges of the openings by wrapping the polyethylene over the headers, sills, and trim. Staple it securely. For electrical boxes, cover the box and then go back and cut out an opening for the size of the box. Spread a bead of caulk around the box's edge to seal the polyethylene. Ⓔ

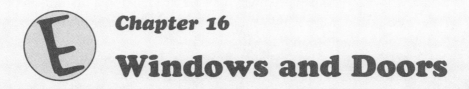

Chapter 16

Windows and Doors

Windows and doors have a huge impact on the design and overall appearance of your home. Of course, they are also functional and meant to serve a purpose. You'll need to carefully consider all the consequences your decisions on windows and doors will have on the finished product. This chapter helps you explore your options and implement your plan.

Types of Windows

Windows are an important part of your home. Not only do they drastically affect the overall exterior look and the feel of a room from within, but they also determine the amount of natural light and airflow that penetrates the house. You'll need to carefully consider the effect each window you are considering will have before making a final decision. Take into account the window's size, style, quality, use, maintenance, insulating value, and even the manufacturer.

It's a good idea to get windows that are prehung. This means that the window is all one unit, with trim, sill, weather stripping, and molding already put together at the factory. Prehung windows are easier to install and take less time than older windows that you must assemble yourself.

A plethora of window styles are available on the market, and deciding among them can be overwhelming. However, knowing what type of window you want to use will narrow down the options. The following sections discuss some of the more common types of windows. Try to visualize each type for use in your home.

Casement

▲ Casement window

Casement windows are hinged on the sides. While you'll most often find that these windows open outwards, some models are available that will open inwards. They are equipped with either a push bar or cranking mechanism that allows you to open them. They provide excellent ventilation because you can open them all the way up. You can also open them just a little to catch refreshing breezes.

Casement windows are considered to be very energy efficient. When closed, the sash is pressed against the frame, which reduces the amount of air leakage/penetration. They are also easier to clean than other types since you can reach both sides of the window from inside the house.

Double-Hung

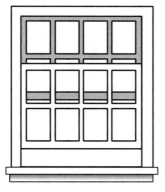

▲ Double-hung window

Double-hung windows are probably the most common type. These allow both sashes to slide open vertically—the bottom half slides up, and the top half slides down. They use spring-tension devices to hold the open sash in place. Though they provide less ventilation than casement windows—since only half the window can be opened at one time—you can create an airflow strategy by opening the top half of the windows on one side of the house and the bottom half on the other side. Cool air will be pulled through the bottom halves, and warmer air will be drawn out through the top halves. (Single-hung windows are similar to double-hung except they allow only the bottom half of the window to open.)

Horizontal Sliding

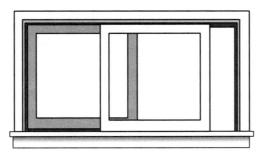

▲ Horizontal sliding window

Horizontal sliding windows are typically made up of two sashes (though some styles have more) that slide open horizontally on a track. Often, only one sash can open while the other is fixed. Like the double-hung window, only half of the window area can be opened at one time, so ventilation is more limited than in the casement style. These aren't as common as double-hung or casement, but you should be able to find them from most window manufacturers. As horizontal sliding windows are usually less expensive than other types, they offer an economical option while still providing adequate ventilation and energy efficiency.

Awning

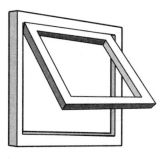

▲ Awning window

Awning windows are similar to casement windows except they are hinged at the top instead of on the sides. Like casements, awnings use a push bar or cranking mechanism to open them. They typically open outwards, though you can sometimes find models that open inwards. Because the sash is pressed against the frame when the window is closed, they reduce the amount of air leakage/penetration, thus making them energy efficient. They are also easy to clean as you can reach both sides of the window from the inside. (A variation of the awning window is the hopper window, which is hinged on the bottom.)

Fixed

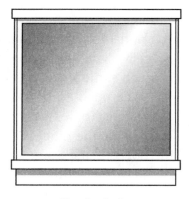

▲ Fixed window

Fixed windows do not open. They are often used in conjunction with other types of windows, adding to the view, entrance of natural light, and overall appearance, without adding the expense of windows that do open. Because fixed windows are permanently fixed in their frames, their tightly sealed edges make great barriers against air leakage/penetration. The flip side of that is that they do not offer any ventilation. You can get fixed windows in almost any size and can even construct them onsite to fit your particular design.

Less Common Types

While the above-mentioned windows are the most commonly used, there are other types available that may better suit your design. Rotating windows pivot open from a central point in the window. They provide excellent ventilation, as the majority of the window area can be opened at once. They are also easy to clean since you can reach both sides from indoors.

Jalousie windows are made up of several horizontal slats of glass that are fitted together like the slats on Venetian blinds. The slats tilt open to allow for ventilation. The disadvantage of jalousie windows is that they are not energy efficient. The slats simply lie on one another when closed—there is no seal that blocks air leakage/penetration.

FACT

The number of panes in a window is a significant factor in its energy efficiency. A window with a single pane of glass is a very poor insulator. As you add more panes (as with double- and triple-paned windows), the insulating property increases considerably.

Bay windows are a great addition for their aesthetic appeal. A bay window is a series of three or more windows that together create a projection outward from the house. The center window or windows are parallel to the house's wall and the flanking windows are set at an angle (typically 30, 45, or 90 degrees) out from the wall. You get to decide whether the windows can be opened and how—or if—they are fixed.

Installing the Windows

You've already completed the hard part of window installation back in the framing stage. But you'll need to take a moment now to reinspect your work. Check the window opening to make sure it is square and has the proper dimensions for the window that is to be installed. Next you'll want to check the window itself. Carefully remove the window from its packaging. Check the measurements of the window to make sure it will fit into the appropriate opening. It's also a good idea to go ahead and make sure that the window itself is square.

Add Flashing

Before actually installing the window, you should install flashing around the opening to ensure that water won't seep into the wall through the window sill. Many builders choose to use roofing felt as the flashing for windows since it does the job well and is easy to install. Cut four strips of the felt paper at least 6 inches wide. The length of the strips will be equal to the length of the window, plus a couple of inches on each end so that the strips can overlap for added protection.

You'll attach the first strip along the bottom of the rough sill. You can use staples or nails, your choice. The side flashing is next. Make sure that the bottom end of each strip overlaps the flashing beneath the sill. The top strip is left until the window is installed. This strip will then cover the side flashings and the window's top flange.

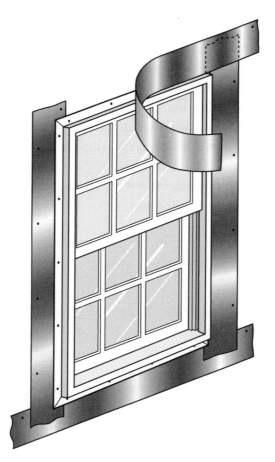

◀ Flashing a window

Inserting the Window

Most windows come prehung these days, which makes installation a snap. Once you've made sure that the window is in fact what you ordered and that it will fit into the opening, you're ready to begin installation. Because you want to make sure that water and air aren't going to penetrate your house through the windows, apply a bead of caulk along the backside of the window's flanges. Working from the outside, lift and set the window into its opening. Push the flanges against the wall's surface.

QUESTION?

What are window flanges?
A window's flanges are the rims that project out from the perimeter of the window. The flanges are nailed to the walls to secure the window in its proper position.

Set a few ¼-inch shims on the rough sill beneath the window. (This can also be done right before the window is inserted). Shims are small, thin wedges of wood that are used to align parts of a structure. The shims will help you center and level the window. Attach the top flashing over the top flange and side flashings. Before permanently securing the window in place, take the time to make sure it is level and plumb.

Once the window is properly positioned, you can nail it in place using galvanized finishing nails. Put a nail into each corner of the window flange and then every 8 inches along the flanges. For added insulation, apply spray foam insulation in the narrow spaces between the window and the trimmer studs. You can also seal the edges of the flanges with waterproof tape.

Types of Doors

There are two types of doors: exterior and interior. Exterior doors allow entrance to your home from the outside, like your front door or the doors from your patio. Interior doors are found within the home, such as the bedroom and bathroom doors. Each type serves a different purpose and is constructed a little differently. For instance, exterior doors will need to provide more security and weather tightness than interior doors.

Like windows, the doors you choose for your home make a design statement and can dramatically affect its overall appearance. In addition to being stylish, they serve a purpose, so it is essential that you make an informed, careful decision. As you shop for doors, consider the impression you want them to make, how you want them to open, and, of course, how much you are willing to spend. Shop to compare styles, designs, materials, and price. The following sections will help you get started by giving you an idea of what is available.

Exterior Doors

As you drive along on your shopping trip for doors, take a look at the houses you pass. You will see a wide variety of entrance doors, some more elaborate than others. This is just a glimpse of what you will have to choose from. Think about what kind of statement you want to make with your exterior doors. Also consider the style of your home. You'll want to purchase exterior doors that complement the house.

Building codes often have different requirements for interior and exterior doors. For example, exterior doors are usually required to be at least 32 inches wide, and interior doors are usually required to be at least 24 inches wide. Check your local codes for any requirements you must meet.

Exterior doors come in two basic forms: swinging and sliding. Swinging doors are hinged on one side and swing out or in. Sliding doors are set on tracks and wheels and slide open. Swinging doors are typically used on main entranceways, whereas sliding doors are typically used to open out to patios or backyards. Within each category, there are several styles and designs to choose from.

Exterior doors are usually solid wood; however, they can also be made of steel, fiberglass, aluminum, or a combination of these materials.

They can be paneled, flush, with or without glass, single or double. While most doors are made to look like wood, you can paint or have them painted to add a colored accent to your home.

Interior Doors

Interior doors come in three basic forms: swinging, sliding, and folding. As you know, swinging doors are hinged on one side, and sliding doors are set on tracks with wheels that let them slide open. Folding doors are pushed or folded to the side to allow entrance to a closet or room. These are often used in small areas where there isn't room for a door to swing open.

The restrictions for interior doors are more relaxed since they don't have to protect against weather or provide security. You can find interior doors in solid wood, solid core, or hollow core. Solid wood doors are the most expensive, but they offer a beautiful appearance and are the best for soundproofing. Solid core doors are composed of a light frame that is filled with laminated wood strips or particleboard. These are more lightweight than solid wood, but they still offer some soundproofing quality. Hollow-core doors are also composed of a light frame. The inside is typically filled with compressed cardboard. These doors are the least expensive, least durable, and offer the least soundproofing quality.

You have a wide variety of styles and designs to choose from. For instance, you can install French doors opening to the study or salon-style swinging doors opening to the kitchen for a decorative touch. Or perhaps you want to be more practical and install doors for their soundproofing qualities. Consider all your options to find the best fit for the interior of your home.

Ordering Doors

Most doors now come prehung, meaning that the door comes in one unit that includes the jambs, threshold, and sometimes the trim. This makes installation much easier. When ordering, make sure you are purchasing prehung doors. The prehung doors will state the dimensions of the unit itself and of the jambs. Although doors come in standard sizes, as your house plans will probably reflect, you should double-check that the door you order fits the dimensions of the opening you've framed.

Your house plans will tell you how the doors swing, so it's a good idea to take your plans with you when ordering doors so that there isn't any confusion or miscommunication.

You also have to stipulate how you want the door to open when ordering. That means deciding on which side of the door the hinges should be placed and whether you want the door to swing in or out. Most exterior doors swing in, to the house, and most interior doors swing in, to the rooms. Closet doors rarely swing into the closets, but swing out to the room instead. Also specify whether the door will swing open to the left or right.

Installing Exterior Doors

Hopefully, you have purchased prehung doors as recommended. Because these doors come as one unit, they are easy to install and do not take a lot of time. However, installing doors does take precision and accuracy, so don't rush the job. Before you begin work, double-check that the door you have is what you ordered. Its dimensions should fit the opening you have framed, and it should be designed to swing in the direction the house plans show.

Flashing

As you did for the windows, you install flashing around an exterior door's perimeter before actually installing the door. The flashing serves to redirect water so that it doesn't find its way beneath the threshold and cause the wood to rot. You can use the same 6-inch-wide strips of roofing felt that you used for the windows for the door's sides and top. However, it's a good idea to use 12-inch-wide metal (preferably aluminum) flashing for the threshold.

Cut the roofing felt into strips that measure the length of the sides and top of the door plus a couple of extra inches on either end to allow for overlap. Staple the strips along the sides of the door first. Then staple the last strip along the top, overlapping each side strip. The threshold gets special treatment, as this is where you want to protect against water the most. Cut the metal flashing that measures the length of the threshold plus approximately 3 inches on each end. Use galvanized nails to secure the flashing in place, allowing the flashing to extend up the trimmer studs.

Setting the Door

After removing all the packaging material, do a quick test-fit of the door. Set it in place, and make sure it opens and closes easily. If you are satisfied with the results, remove the door and grab your caulking gun. Run a bead of caulk along the back of the casing and along the length of the threshold flashing. Set the unit into its opening, pressing the casing against the wall sheathing. Drive a nail into each corner of the casing to hold it in place.

◀ Setting a prehung door

Before you finish securing the unit, test the door to make sure it opens and closes properly. Also take a moment to check that it is level and plumb. If you need to, you can add shims between the jambs and trimmer studs to make a tight fit. To finish securing the unit, drive nails around the perimeter of the door through the casing, spaced 2 feet apart.

FACT

Some codes require insulation to be placed between the jamb and frame for exterior doors. If this is required by your local building code, you can use spray-foam to insulate that narrow space quickly and easily.

When the unit is secured, drive nails along the hinge side of the jamb through to the trimmer stud. Move to the lock side and again drive nails through the jamb to the trimmer stud. To finish installation, screw the hinges to the jamb and through to the trimmer stud. If you put long screws through the jamb of the frame to fasten the unit, you'll make later adjustments easier.

Installing Interior Doors

You follow the same general procedures to install interior doors, but there are a few minor differences. Again, before beginning work, make sure you have received the correct door and that it swings according to the house plans. After carefully removing the packaging, take out the nails, plugs, or blocks that are temporarily attaching the door to the jambs.

Set the prehung assembly into the opening, and drive a nail approximately 3 inches down from the top into the hinge-side jamb through to the trimmer stud. Check to make sure the jambs are level, plumb, and square. Also take a moment now to make sure that there is ⅛-inch gap between the door and the underside of the top jamb. Use shims to correct any inaccuracies. Then drive another nail in the center and one near the bottom of the hinge-side jamb. Line up the door's hinge plates with the jamb's hinge plates and secure them with the hinge screws that came with the unit.

If your hinge-side jamb is plumb, then the lock-side jamb will be plumb. Install this jamb just as you did the hinge-side jamb, using shims to perfect the gap widths. There should be a consistent ⅛-inch gap all around the door. If the door came with built-in casing trim, drive nails through the casing into the trimmer studs all around the door. Keep in mind that you should be constantly checking to make sure the door is opening and closing correctly as you are working, not just when you are finished.

ALERT!

Don't forget to install the locksets! You should purchase quality locksets, especially for your exterior doors. Most prehung doors come predrilled for the locksets, which makes installation easy. Simply follow the manufacturer's directions.

Trimming Windows and Doors

After you have installed the drywall or other interior wall covering, you'll need to install the trim around the windows and doors. The trim hides the area where the wall covering meets up with the door and window jambs. Properly installed trim makes the windows and doors look nice and neat and can add a decorative touch suited to your tastes. Visit your local building supply store and check out the various styles and designs of trim.

When trimming windows, the first piece you install is the sill. The sill must be long enough to cover the window's rough sill and wide enough to project out from the wall at least 1½ inches. Of course, if you plan to set items on the sill, you will likely want the projection to be even greater, and in that case you will extend the sill width as needed. The sill must be long enough to extend 1 inch past the trim on either side of the window. Secure the sill to the rough sill using finish nails and construction adhesive.

Next you'll measure for the side and head trim. Most trim is mitered, which means that its end is cut at an angle so that two pieces can be fitted together. You can purchase premitered trim, or you can cut it yourself. Just make sure that the angles allow the two pieces of trim to fit together tightly without any space between. The flat bottom edges of the side trim will butt to the sill. The head trim will be installed between the two pieces of side trim. Secure all trim with finish nails, making sure to nail the mitered joints in from both directions (top and side).

Most carpenters leave a reveal—meaning the trim is set back approximately ¼ inch from the inside edge of the jamb, leaving part of the jamb exposed. Make sure you measure carefully and, using a combination square, mark guidelines where the trim should be installed.

Once you have secured the side and header trim, finish off the window by installing the apron. The apron is simply a piece of trim that is installed beneath the windowsill to cover the area where the wall covering and windowsill meet. The apron isn't as long as the sill itself. Instead, the ends of the apron should line up with the outside edges of the side trim. Nail it into place using finish nails with its wider edge up against the sill.

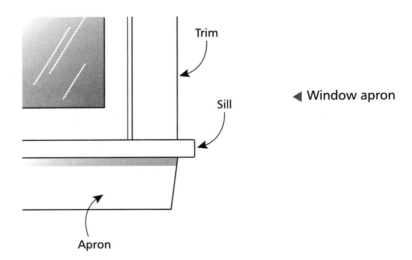

Trim

Sill

◀ Window apron

Apron

Doors are trimmed in the same manner as windows, with a couple of exceptions. The doorway, of course, doesn't have a sill, and doesn't require the installation of an apron. Many prehung doors are already equipped with trim, which of course makes your job much easier.

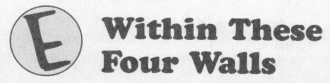

Chapter 17

Within These Four Walls

The exterior of the house is complete. Take a moment to admire your hard work. Don't take too long, though—there's still a lot to do inside! This chapter walks you through some of the finish work required to make your house functional and stylish. Strap on that tool belt, and let's get to work!

Drywall

Drywall is the superstar of the interior wall and ceiling coverings. It is made of gypsum core sandwiched between two pieces of heavy-gauge paper. It has many virtues, including low cost; ease of use (simple to cut, install, and repair); decorative flexibility (can be painted, wallpapered, or paneled over); and flame resistance. With all these advantages, it's no wonder most homes today use drywall to cover their walls and ceilings.

Drywall panels are large and heavy. You should always pair up with at least one other person to carry a panel to avoid injury. Standard panels are 4 feet wide and come in varying lengths, the most common being 8, 10, and 12 feet long. For walls, the standard thickness is ½ inch. Ceilings typically require a ⅝-inch thickness to avoid sagging. High-moisture areas, such as bathrooms, require a special water-resistant drywall, typically called greenboard because of its green-colored paper facing.

Prep the Area

Before you can begin installing drywall, you need to complete a few tasks to prep the area for the work to be done. First of all, you need to make sure that all the studs and joists are dry. Because wood will shrink somewhat as moisture evaporates, the nails and screws you use to install the drywall can come loose and cause noticeable marks in the drywall surface. Unless you are sure the wood is dry, run a dehumidifier or turn on the heat inside the house for a few days or weeks, depending on how much moisture content the wood holds.

ALERT!

It's a good idea (as well as a requirement, under many codes) that you use nailguards to protect all wires and pipes from potential drywall nailing. These are simply metal plates that are placed over wires and pipes and attached to the studs.

Because you'll be nailing the drywall to studs and joists, you have to be able to tell where these are located as you're installing the drywall. To do this, make a mark on the floor indicating the location of studs and a mark on the top plate to indicate the location of the joists. At this time, you'll also need to check the studs and joists for bows. A bowed stud or joist will cause the drywall to protrude, creating an uneven surface. Correct any problems with shims, planing, or by replacing the stud or joist.

Ceiling Drywall

You should install the drywall for the ceiling before doing the walls. This way the drywall on the walls can add extra support to the edges of the ceiling drywall. Working overhead with drywall isn't an easy task because of the material's size and weight. As a safety precaution, always have extra support as you are working. You can use other people to hold up the panel as you install it, or you can set up two or more 2×4 T-supports along the panel to brace it in place as you work to screw it down. It's best if you can use both the T-supports and other people.

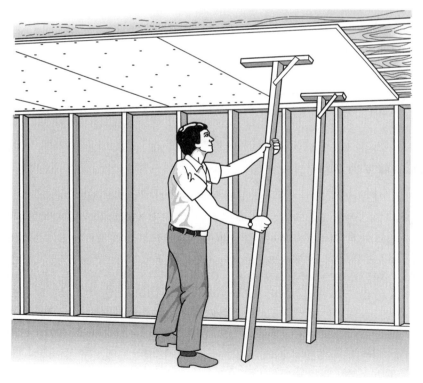

▲ T-supports to install ceiling drywall

The drywall panels should be installed perpendicular to the ceiling joists. The smooth white paper facing is the "good" side and will be exposed to the room; the rough, darker paper facing is the "bad" side. Keep in mind that you should use ⅝-inch panels for the ceilings. While longer and a little more difficult to work with, 12-foot-long panels usually cover the expanse of ceilings in smaller rooms. You may prefer to use 8-foot panels, though you will likely have to create more joints with those.

> The joints where two panels meet should always be aligned over a joist. Also, leave an approximately ¼-inch gap between the two panels. (This will later be filled in during finishing work.)

You can use either drywall nails or screws to install the drywall panels, though most prefer screws for ceilings because they are easier to work with. Whichever you choose, make sure you drive the nail or screw slightly below the surface of the panel, creating a dimple in the drywall. Be careful not to break the facing paper as you do this. This dimple will later be filled with compound to create a smooth surface. Check your local building codes for the fastening pattern. Typically, you should drive a nail or screw every 6 inches along the edges of the panel and every 12 inches in the middle.

Wall Drywall

Once you have installed the ceiling drywall, you can start on the walls. You can hang the panels either horizontally or vertically. The choice is yours, but you will have fewer joints in the wall if you hang them horizontally. Hanging drywall horizontally makes it easier to finish the tape joints. Also, the horizontal positioning of the 4×8 or 4×12 sheets can actually add strength to the walls. To hang the drywall horizontally, install the top row of panels first and work your way down. This top row must butt up snugly against the ceiling drywall. Start nailing or screwing in the center and work your way out to the edges of each panel. Again, refer to your local building codes for the fastening pattern. If you are going to hang the drywall vertically, start at one end of a wall and work your way to the other end, always installing the topmost panel snugly against the ceiling drywall first. Don't worry if the drywall doesn't extend all the way to the floor. Any small gaps will be covered by baseboard later.

Cut the Drywall

The drywall panels aren't going to measure to the exact dimensions you need to cover a wall or ceiling perfectly. Therefore, you'll have to cut panels to fit. Cutting drywall is easy, but must be done correctly to ensure an even and square edge. Measure and mark the good side of the drywall, or you can position a T-square to ensure a straight edge. Using a utility knife, score the drywall by making a cut along the mark or square by slicing through the paper facing and slightly into the core. You don't need to drive the knife very far into the drywall. Once you've scored along the mark, snap the drywall open along the cut and fold it back onto itself. This will create a crease in the back paper. Use the utility knife to cut along the crease, separating the panel into two pieces. If needed, plane the edge to make it even and smooth using a drywall shaping tool.

FACT

Tools are available that are specially designed for use on drywall. A drywall hammer has a curved face that allows you to create a dimple in the drywall when you drive the nail. A drywall saw has a pointed tip that easily penetrates the drywall, allowing you to make cuts easily and accurately.

Of course, you will also have to cut the drywall panels to allow for openings like windows, doors, electrical boxes, or pipes. You can accomplish this in a few different ways. When cutting openings for doors and windows, you can cover a portion of the opening with drywall and then simply cut along the edge of the opening. Make sure the joint falls in line with the center of the window or door. A drywall saw is best for this type of work. When you have one side cut appropriately, do the same thing for the other side, ensuring an opening of the proper dimensions.

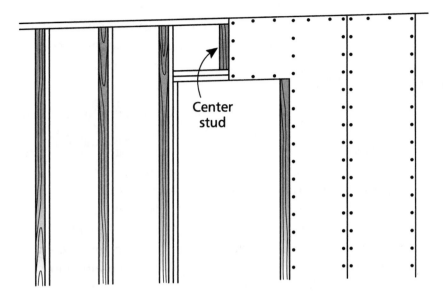

▲ Installing drywall around a doorway

Smaller openings, such as electrical boxes or pipes, can be measured from drywall panels that you've already installed or from the ceiling or floor. Transfer the measurements to the panel that will be installed, and cut the proper opening using a drywall saw. You can also cover the box or pipe with chalk and fit the panel into place, applying pressure to the box or pipe. This will leave a mark on the panel so you can easily see where the opening needs to be cut once you've removed the panel.

Finish Work

Once you've hung the drywall, you will go back and complete the finish work. First, you'll protect the corners from impact by installing corner beads, which are basically pieces of metal trim. You can find these at your local building supply store. Nail, screw, or staple the corner beads along all outside corners and around windows and doors. Install them by working your way from the top down, driving in a nail, screw, or staple every 8 inches and making sure they lie flat and are straight. The corner beads will later be covered with compound.

Once the corner beads are installed, it's time for the lengthy process of taping and floating. The floating process involves the spreading of joint compound, available in either premixed or powder form. For the novice, it's best to go ahead and get the premixed version. The "tape" is a paper tape that will be embedded in the compound. You can also get a self-adhesive fiberglass tape that doesn't require an undercoat of compound. Because this finish work will affect the visual smoothness and evenness of the drywall, you may want to hire a professional to tape and float. If you'd rather do it yourself, take your time, and make sure your work creates a smooth finish.

ALERT!

As you are applying the joint compound, always make sure you use your knife to smooth the coat and to remove any excess. The compound should be flush with the panel and free of any bumps. Use your knife to feather the compound out from the center of the joint, thus concealing it.

First fill in all dimples with the compound, making sure you use your drywall trowel to smooth the compound flush with the panel. Next, you'll move on to the joints. If you are using paper tape, you'll start by pressing a layer of compound into the joint with a drywall trowel. Soak the tape in water for a moment and then apply it to the joint, using a drywall trowel to smooth and embed it into the compound as you work along the joint. Apply another coat of compound over the tape, and use your trowel to press down and release any air that may be trapped beneath the tape. If you are using self-adhesive tape, you can apply this directly to the joint without putting any compound underneath. Once the joint is covered, apply a layer of compound over the tape.

Corners are covered in much the same way as the joints, except the tape must be folded to fit into the corner. Embed the tape just as you did with the joints, working with one side of the corner at a time. Floating over the tape takes a little more patience because you must be careful to not allow the drywall trowel to damage the finished side of the corner.

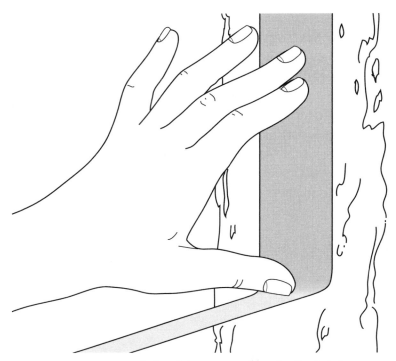

▲ Applying paper tape to the joints

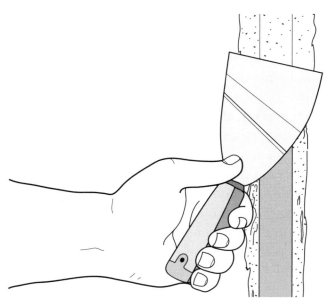

▲ Apply the joint compound over the paper tape

Joint compound is applied in three coats. Allow each coat to dry overnight. Before applying the next coat, sand the dry coat to a smooth surface, using 100- or 120-grit sandpaper. Be careful to sand only the joint compound and not the actual drywall. Each coat should be a little thinner than the previous one. Add a little water to the compound to make it a bit thinner. After you allow the final coat to dry, once again sand it down to create a smooth and even surface.

Cabinets

The cabinets in your home are important for both functional and aesthetic purposes. There are many styles and materials available for you to choose from. It's a good idea to visit home centers or cabinet-supply stores and examine your options before making any decisions. You'll want to find cabinets that both accent the design and style of your home and also make the most of the space you have available. Because of the number of appliances found in homes today, we don't have as much cabinet space as we once did. To counteract this, many cabinetmakers have created designs that allow cabinets to fit around these appliances and that also make better use of the space allotted.

The walls should be painted before installing cabinets and appliances. If you are installing a tile or hardwood floor, these should be installed beforehand as well. Vinyl flooring can be installed either before or after the cabinets are installed. You should always follow the manufacturer's instructions when installing cabinetry.

Cabinets can be expensive, depending on the type of materials used and whether those you order are custom built or prefabricated. If you are planning to resell your house in the future, you may want to go the extra mile in purchasing cabinetry, as quality cabinets and good kitchen and bathroom designs can increase the resale value of a home. There are two main types of cabinets you'll want to take a look at: base cabinets and wall cabinets.

Installing Base Cabinets

Base cabinets are those that are measured up from the floor. Typically, base cabinets are manufactured to have a countertop height of 36 inches. (You can always special-order cabinets of a different height.) To fit a base cabinet in your particular kitchen space, measure up from the highest spot on the floor to the height specified in the manufacturer's instructions. While the countertop height is usually 36 inches, the actual cabinet height can vary. Mark a level line along the wall indicating the cabinet's height.

Before installing cabinets, do a quick check to make sure they fit within the specified area. You'll need to know where the appliances will be placed in order to do this. Make sure there is a little bit of space between the cabinets and appliances. You don't want them to butt up against one another.

Beginning with a corner cabinet, predrill the holes that will secure the cabinet to the studs. Screw the cabinet to the wall studs and check that the top of the cabinet is level all the way across. You can use shims if necessary to level the cabinet. When the first is installed, move on to the next. Join any two cabinets that will be placed next to one another. Using clamps, hold the stiles (the vertical frame members) together, and drive screws through the two stiles. Again, you'll need to make sure the cabinets are level all the way across. Continue in this manner until all base cabinets are installed according to the manufacturer's instructions and your kitchen design layout. Make sure you cut or drill holes in the backs of those cabinets that will have pipes or lines going through them, such as the kitchen sink base cabinet.

Installing Wall Cabinets

Wall cabinets are just what they sound like—cabinets that are hung on the walls. These cabinets usually measure 54 inches from their bottom edges to the floor. Measure up from the floor, and mark level lines indicating both the top and bottom edges of the cabinets. It is also important that you know the exact location of the studs. It's essential that you secure the wall cabinets to studs. Otherwise, the weight of dishes and other kitchenware may cause the cabinet to sag or, even worse, to fall.

FACT

It doesn't matter which you choose to install first, the base or wall cabinets. However, it may be easier to install the wall cabinets first so you don't have to work over the base cabinets to reach them.

Wall cabinets can be heavy, so it's a good idea to remove the shelves and doors before lifting them into place. You'll need to make sure the cabinet is stable and level as you are installing it. The best way to do this is to use a T-support to hold it in place as you screw it in. This will leave your hands free to do the work and reduce the risk of injury or damaging the cabinets with a fall. Start with a corner cabinet, and work your way around the room. Double-check that the cabinets are level and plumb after installation.

Countertops

The most common and least expensive type of countertop is laminate. However, if you want to spend more or make your kitchen look fancier, you can choose from other materials, such as tile, granite, or marble. There are many styles and colors of laminate countertops to choose from. Keep in mind that laminate can be scratched, and on darker colors scratches will be more noticeable.

The standard depth of a countertop is 24 inches, and most come with a built-in backsplash of 3 to 4 inches to go against the wall. Measure your base cabinets to get the right measurement for your countertops. Make sure you add 1 inch for counter overhang on the exposed ends and at the front. You can also give the supplier the size and location of the sink; often, the supplier will go ahead and cut out this opening for you.

Installing countertops is pretty easy for straight surfaces. First do a test fit to make sure the countertop fits properly and is level. Once everything is fitted properly, drive screws up through the top frame of the base cabinet into the countertop. Be careful to not allow the screw to penetrate the countertop surface. Follow the manufacturer's instructions for screw locations.

If the backsplash isn't secure up against the wall, you can either attach the accompanying scribing strip to fit the backsplash to the wall or use caulk to fill in the gap after the countertop has been installed.

If you plan to install an L-shaped countertop, have the supplier make the mitered cuts. These types of cuts are difficult to make yourself and are a little harder to install. Not only do they need to be secured to the base cabinets, but they also need to be fastened together. They typically come with slots for draw bolts cut into the bottom edges. You'll use the draw bolts to fasten them together, but before tightening the bolts, make sure you coat the two meeting edges with waterproof silicone caulk to help seal the joint.

Appliances

Your house just wouldn't be a home without the standard—and sometimes cutting-edge—appliances that none of us could live without. So be sure you make room for these devices, such as the refrigerator, dishwasher, range and oven, washer and dryer, microwave, garbage compactor, and so on. If you have planned carefully, your house plans will reflect the location of these appliances.

Choosing to purchase brand new appliances or making do with your older ones is entirely up to you. However, you need to keep in mind future wants and needs. For instance, if you own a small refrigerator that works just fine now, you may be thinking you'll make it last a few more years to save costs. But you are planning on expanding your family. This of course means that those growing children may need more food than your little refrigerator can accommodate. Unfortunately, you designed your kitchen around that small refrigerator, not leaving any room for a larger model without having to pull out cabinetry and either cutting it down to size or replacing it entirely. The moral of the story is this: Design for your future, not present, needs.

You must also keep in mind that not all appliances can be set down just anywhere. For instance, your dishwasher will require access to the hot water supply line and a waste line. A gas range will require access to the gas supply line. Some ovens will need to be installed on top of a low base cabinet for support. The washer will need a water supply line, and the dryer will need a vent to the outside.

You have a lot to consider when it comes to appliances. Cost, model, size, and location in the home all need to be carefully planned for. Once the decisions are made, changing your mind can turn out to be difficult, time consuming, and expensive.

Baseboard Trim

Baseboard trim is trim that covers the gap between the bottom edge of the drywall and the floor. You install the finish flooring (though not the carpet) before installing the baseboard trim. Baseboard trim is most often made of wood, and a wide variety of styles are available, as well as varying thicknesses.

The first piece of baseboard trim you'll install within rooms will be cut square on both ends and will fit in between the door's casing and the wall. Drive nails approximately 16 inches apart into either a stud or the bottom plate. If this is a short piece of trim and fits snugly, you don't need to nail it in. Simply glue it into place; the next piece of trim will secure it.

FACT

If you are planning to install carpeting, you'll need to leave room for the carpet to slide beneath the baseboard trim. Use temporary supports to hold the trim up approximately ½ inch as you install to allow for this room.

The second piece of trim butts up against the first and is fitted along the adjacent wall. If the trim has a flat rectangular profile, you can simply butt this second piece of trim into the first. However, if the trim has a curved or otherwise shaped profile, you'll need to cut it to create a coped joint. A coped joint is made by using a coping saw after the trim has had an angle cut into it. Coped joints are difficult to cut, so it's recommended that you seek out the help of an experienced worker to do this. The coped trim will butt up snugly against the first piece of trim in the inside corner.

Continue in this fashion all the way around the room. The last piece of trim will have only one coped end, as the other end will be a straight cut that butts up against the door casing.

Outside corners will require the baseboard trim to be mitered, not coped. Typically, outside corners create a 90-degree angle. Therefore, the butting ends of the baseboard trims will each need to be mitered at a 45-degree angle in order for the two to come together at a perfect joint. Of course, you aren't always going to have perfect 90-degree angled corners, so you must adjust the mitered cut appropriately.

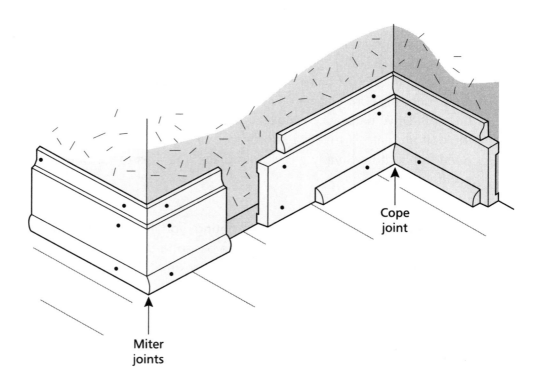

Cope joint

Miter joints

▲ Installing baseboard trim around corners

Closet Shelving

Most people like to be organized, or at least they like to give the semblance of organization. As closets are renowned for their untidiness, many people now are choosing to install closet organizers or maybe a few shelves to help make better use of the space available. You can visit a home center and purchase a prefabricated closet organizer and simply install it according to the instructions. You can also build your own shelving to accommodate your specific needs.

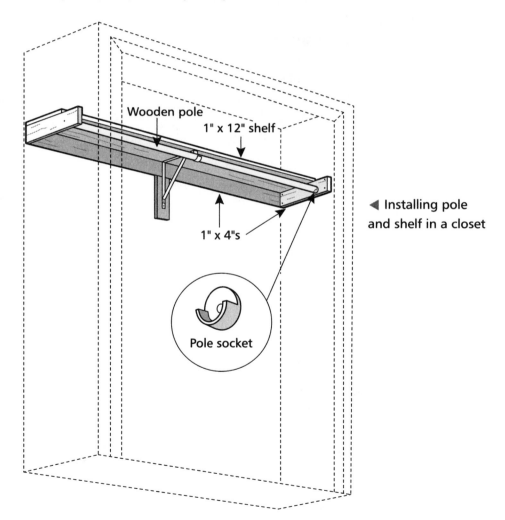

Wooden pole

1" x 12" shelf

1" x 4"s

Pole socket

◀ Installing pole and shelf in a closet

At the very least, you'll want to install a pole from which to hang your clothes and one shelf running the length of the pole for upper closet storage. To install a pole, measure up the closet walls 66 inches (or however high you want the pole to be placed), and mark the wall. Cut 1×4s to fit on either side and along the back of the wall. Nail them into the studs, making sure to position the top of the board on the line you marked. Screw in pole sockets on each side's 1×4, making them an equal distance from the back wall. The pole will rest in these sockets. Use a 1×12 for the shelf. Secure each end of the shelf by nailing it into the side 1×4s. Of course, if you have a large closet, both the pole and shelf will need additional support.

It's fun to get creative and design your own closet space. You can get several ideas for organization from magazines and at your local home center. You can always stick with the standard one-pole, one-shelf idea, but you can better use the closet's space by adding more shelves and even more poles set at different heights.

Chapter 18
Flooring

Your house is almost done. One major project remains: installing the finish flooring. While this can be a time-consuming project, many people get a lot of pleasure from its progress. Working on the floors means your homebuilding project is coming to a close, and the move-in date is just around the corner.

Finish Flooring

Your house already has a floor of sorts, the subflooring. However, this isn't very appealing. That's why you install finish flooring. Finish flooring is the flooring that will be laid on top of the subflooring. The most common types of finish flooring are vinyl, wood, ceramic tile, and carpeting.

Carefully consider your options before making a final decision on finish flooring. Of course, cost will be a major factor. Typically, vinyl flooring is the least expensive option. Because it comes in a huge array of colors, patterns, and styles, vinyl is a popular choice for many homebuilders. On the other hand, many people don't find the thought of putting vinyl flooring throughout the entire house very appealing. They'd prefer to use more attractive materials, such as carpet or wood flooring in common living areas, even though they may be a little more expensive. Because there are so many flooring companies and styles available, doing a little comparison shopping should help you find the flooring you want that's still within your budget.

You'll probably use a combination of finish floorings throughout the house. For instance, many people choose vinyl flooring for high-traffic areas because it is durable and easy to clean and carpet for living and bedrooms because it is comfortable and inviting.

You should also consider the function of flooring in each room. For instance, you may have children who like to play on the floor in the living room in front of the television. In this case, you'll want to install flooring, such as carpet, that is comfortable to lie down on. Or maybe you have dogs that come into the house through a mudroom. In that case, you'll want to install something that is easy to clean, like vinyl flooring. The flooring in the bathroom is inevitably going to get wet, so the floor you install must stand up to moisture—ceramic tile or vinyl are good choices here. Carefully consider how the flooring in each room will be used (or abused), and use this information to help you decide on a type of flooring.

Once you've decided on the type of finish flooring to use for each room, you'll need to make the tough decision of the style, color, and pattern to use. Each type of flooring has a wide array of options with their own sets of pros and cons. For instance, plush is more appealing and feels better than Berber carpet, but it doesn't withstand wear as well. Lighter colors make a room seem lighter and more open, but they also show dirt more easily than darker colors. Whatever you choose, make sure it is aesthetically pleasing and the best fit for its function.

Vinyl Floors

Vinyl flooring has become a popular choice for areas such as the kitchen, bathroom, and entranceways. It can be very beautiful. In addition, it is durable, waterproof, and easy to maintain and clean. Vinyl is also less expensive than some other types of flooring. However, you are better off spending a little more to go with a higher grade of vinyl— some of the lower grades don't withstand wear and tear as well. There are two types of vinyl flooring: sheet vinyl, which comes in rolls, and tile vinyl which comes in individual tiles. Installing vinyl flooring isn't all that difficult, and there are plenty of kits available that are designed specifically for the do-it-yourselfer.

Preparing the Area

Before you can install the vinyl flooring, you must install an underlayment of ¼-inch-thick plywood, which ensures a firm base for the flooring. You cannot install vinyl flooring over the subfloor itself. A vinyl flooring manufacturer's approved underlayment must always be used.

ALERT!

Be sure to check for protruding nail heads. Nail heads should be driven slightly below the surface of the underlayment so they won't impair the installation of the vinyl.

Lay the underlayment so that the joints aren't positioned over the joints of the subflooring. To allow room for expansion, leave a gap of approximately ½ inch between the underlayment and the wall and $1/16$ inch between the panels of underlayment. Underlayment staples work better than nails because, over time, the staples are less likely to work loose and protrude into the vinyl, as nails tend to do. Staple the underlayment to the subflooring, spacing the staples approximately 4 inches apart. Sweep and vacuum the underlayment, making sure there are no splinters along the surface. Once the surface is smooth, clean, and level, you can begin installing the finish flooring.

Installing Tile Vinyl

Tile vinyl is just as it sounds—individual vinyl tiles. While somewhat time consuming, installing tile vinyl isn't difficult. Most tile vinyl comes with a self-adhesive on the back to make installation that much easier. The hardest part of installing vinyl tile is figuring out the installation pattern. You will be starting at the center of the room and working your way out to the edges within quadrants.

To divide the room into the four quadrants, first measure the length (or the width) of your room. Find the midpoint of this measure, and snap a chalkline at that point from this wall to the wall opposite. Next, find the midpoint of the two other walls. Lay out a line between these two, and make a small mark where the two lines intersect. This mark represents the middle of the room. Before you snap the second chalkline, use a square to make sure the two lines intersect at a 90-degree angle. If they don't, adjust your lines as needed. It's imperative that these lines create a nice, square 90-degree angle. This center point marks the place where you begin installing the tiles. Its alignment will affect the rest of the installation.

Once your lines are square, lay out loose tile along one line from the center point to the wall. If the distance between the last tile and the wall is less than half a tile length, shift your intersecting line a half-tile length away, toward the opposite wall. Repeat this process along the other line. By taking the time to do this, you ensure that your border tiles are no smaller than a half tile. This consistency creates an even look.

FACT

You will have to cut vinyl tiles to create your even borders and to fit around obstacles. Vinyl tile is easy to cut, and you can use a standard utility knife to do the job. Create a pattern for the cut by using butcher paper and then transfer that pattern to the tile to be cut.

The backs of the tiles are printed with an arrow indicating the direction in which they should be laid and a piece of paper that you remove to expose the adhesive. Pick a quadrant, and lay your first tile at the center of the room, edges aligned with the 90-degree angle at the intersection. Remove the paper backing, and press down on the tile to secure the adhesive. Work your way out towards the walls within that first quadrant. You will complete one quadrant before moving on to the next.

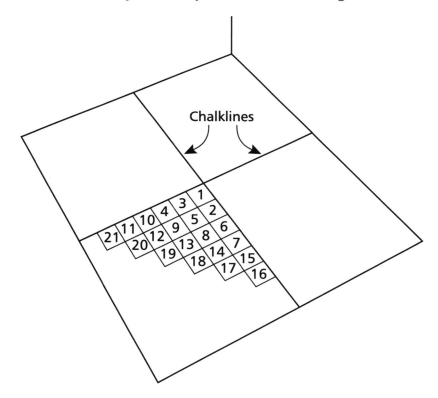

▲ Vinyl tiles laid in quadrants

Installing Sheet Vinyl

Sheet vinyl comes in large rolls that are cut to fit the floor. Once cut, you simply unroll the vinyl and secure it to the underlayment. While this may seem easier than installing tile vinyl, it requires more prep work. Before you can begin cutting the vinyl to size, you have to create a paper template of the room's floor. If you have purchased a do-it-yourself vinyl flooring installation kit, the paper will be included. If not, you can use either butcher paper or craft paper for the template.

Lay out the paper over the floor of the room you plan to cover in vinyl. To make sure the paper doesn't shift while you are creating the template, cut small triangles out from several areas of the paper. Place a piece of tape over these triangles, securing the paper to the underlayment. Make sure the paper is flat and smooth before making any marks in the template. The paper should cover every area where the vinyl flooring will be installed.

Join two sheets of paper by overlapping their edges and securing them with tape in several places along the edges. Again, make sure the paper lays flat and smooth. Make a crease in the paper for where it needs to be cut to fit up against a wall or other obstacles. Cut the template to size, and double-check to be sure it covers the entire floor.

Unroll the sheet vinyl on a clean, smooth surface. If you will need to use more than one sheet to cover the floor, overlap the sheets and make sure to match the pattern. Tape them together, and then cut through the overlap so you end up with two sheets that fit together perfectly at the seam. Tape the two sheets together.

Unroll your template on top of the sheet vinyl. After you have positioned it properly, use the triangles you cut earlier to tape the template to the flooring. Using a utility knife, cut the flooring to match the template. Once this is done, roll up the vinyl, and move it into the room where it will be installed.

ESSENTIAL

If at all possible, position the template over the flooring so that any seams created by the joining of two vinyl sheets will be in an out-of-the-way area of the room. Dirt from high-traffic areas has a tendency to collect in the seam, making it more visible.

Unroll the sheet vinyl, and make sure it fits the floor properly. The seam, if applicable, will need to be secured first. Remove the tape holding the two sheets together. Pull one sheet back and mark the seam line by running your pencil along the edge of the other sheet. Pull the other sheet back and out of the way and apply a band of adhesive 3 to 6 inches wide. Lay one sheet down on the adhesive and press firmly. Then do the same with the other sheet. Make sure the two sheets fit together tightly and then seal the seam with a solvent specially made for vinyl flooring.

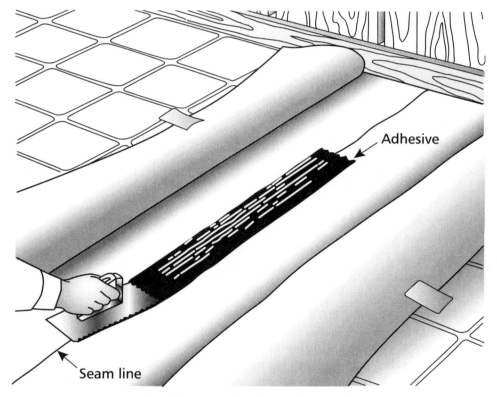

Adhesive

Seam line

▲ Applying an adhesive to the seam line

The perimeter of the vinyl flooring is either stapled or secured with adhesive. Use a staple gun to secure the edges that will be covered by baseboard trim. Use the adhesive for those edges that cannot be reached by the staple gun or that won't be covered with trim.

Wood Floors

Many people consider wood floors to be the most beautiful of the finish flooring types. As they are also very durable and now easy to install, they have recently gained a lot of popularity. Older tongue-and-groove solid-wood floors took a lot of time and were more difficult to install compared to other types of finish flooring. These days, however, prefinished wood floors are available in tile, strip, or plank form. They are just as easy to install as vinyl flooring but still maintain the beauty and charm of older wood floors.

Prepare the Area

Before you begin installing your wood floor, you'll need to make sure that the subflooring is clean, level, and smooth. Fill in any holes, cracks, or dips. Also install an underlayment of plywood to create an even, firm, and smooth surface on which to work. As stated before, you'll need to lay the underlayment so that the joints aren't positioned over the joints of the subflooring. Leave approximately ½ inch between the underlayment and the wall and ¹⁄₁₆ inch between the panels of underlayment to allow room for expansion. Staples should be placed approximately 4 inches apart along all edges and in the middle. Most hardwood floor manufacturers require a subfloor and underlayment combined thickness of at least 1¼ inches. Once the surface is smooth, clean, and level, you can begin installing the finish flooring.

Installing Parquet Tiles

Parquet tiles are made of thin strips of wood. They are installed using the same basic method used for vinyl tile with a few differences. You first divide the room into four quadrants. To do this, find the midpoint of two opposite walls. Snap a chalkline connecting these two points. Next, find the midpoint of the two other walls. Lay out a line between these two and make a small mark where the two lines intersect in the middle. Before marking the second chalkline, use a square to make sure the two lines intersect at a precise 90-degree angle. If they don't, adjust the second line.

Because you will be working with an adhesive, make sure the room is well ventilated. The fumes from the adhesive can be toxic. They are also combustible, so don't have any open flames or gas appliances turned on nearby.

Once the lines are square, lay out loose parquet tile along one line from the center to the wall. If the last tile is less than half a tile away from the wall, move the intersecting line toward the opposite wall the equivalent of a half tile. Repeat this process for the other line. This ensures that the border tiles are no smaller than a half tile and creates an even, smooth look.

Unlike the vinyl flooring process, in which you lay tile quadrant by quadrant, with parquet you work first with one half of the room and then the other. Starting at your center point, you work out from one of your chalklines toward a wall, laying tiles on either side of your center point. Work toward the wall in a pyramid fashion, using fewer tiles for each row. As you work out toward the wall, you will find yourself having to kneel on tiles you've just laid. Put a piece of plywood over these fresh tiles to distribute your weight and keep from popping them out of place.

You will only spread enough adhesive for the number of tiles you can place in a couple of hours. The manufacturer's instructions will specify the amount of adhesive you should spread at one time. The easiest way to spread the adhesive is with a toothed trowel held at a 45-degree angle. Spread it along one of your chalklines, being careful not to cover the chalk. Allow the adhesive to set until it becomes tacky and a bit thicker. The label on the adhesive will tell you about how long it takes to set up.

Once the adhesive has had time to set up, start laying the tile by aligning the first tile with the 90-degree angle created by the intersection of the two lines. Lay your second tile on the other side of the center point. Your third tile goes beside the first one. Work your way out to the sides and down towards the wall, creating a pyramid. Your second row of tile will be shorter than the first, and third shorter still, so the rows stack upon each other pyramid-style. The reason for working in this pattern is the natural variation in sizes of parquet tile. Whereas vinyl tile is cut to one standard measure, parquet can vary by as much a $\frac{1}{32}$ inch. Laying the tiles in a pyramid means you fit most tiles into an angle created by its neighbors. This method helps even out that variation and lets you lay a consistent, smooth pattern.

Once you have built your pyramid, work out on that half of the room toward the walls. With each section you complete, you'll need to roll over it to secure the tiles in place. You can rent floor rollers at most building supply companies. When you reach the wall, cut the tile to fit with a fine-tooth handsaw, leaving a $\frac{1}{4}$ inch gap between the tile and wall to allow room for expansion. Complete the other half of the room in the same fashion as the first.

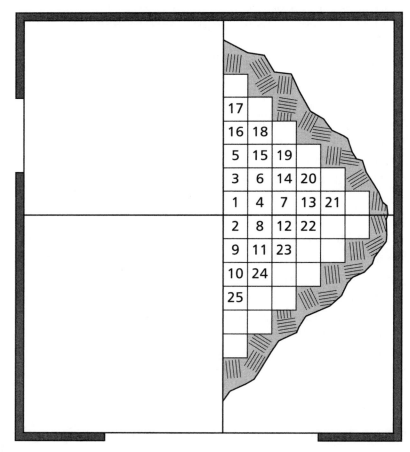

▲ Installing parquet tiles

▲ Use a floor roller to secure the tiles

Installing Wood Strips or Planks

You'll need to plan your layout before you begin installing strips or planks. The boards should run parallel to the longer and most visible wall of the room. If you are using boards of differing widths, you'll want to make sure a wide board is installed against the long wall. To ensure that the boards are laid out straight, temporarily nail down a 2×4 approximately 30¼ inches from the long wall. The exact distance will depend on the width of the boards you are using. For instance, if you are using boards of two different widths, say, one 3 inches and the other 5 inches wide, then you'll need to measure out 32¼ inches from the wall. (Four 3-inch boards equal 12 inches, plus four 5-inch boards that equal 20 inches; the extra ¼ inch allows for a gap between the wall and flooring.) If you are using boards of all the same width, the measurement is easy. Ten 3-inch boards give you a measurement of 30¼ inches from the wall; six 5-inch boards will give you a measurement of 30¼ inches from the wall.

FACT

The information given here is for prefinished wood floors. If you purchase unfinished wood flooring, you will need to sand and then stain or finish the floor yourself.

Snap a chalkline at the correct measurement from the wall, and temporarily nail a 2×4 exactly along this line. Next, spread your adhesive in the area between the 2×4 and the long wall. Use a toothed trowel held at a 45-degree angle. Allow the adhesive to set up and become tacky. If you are using differing widths, your first board should be the smaller to ensure that the wide board is set up against the long wall. Install the tongue-side of the board tight up against the 2×4. Work your way along the 2×4 making sure the boards are fitted tightly together.

Use a mallet to fit the next row into the grooves of the first. Make sure the end joints of adjacent rows are staggered by at least 5 inches. Keep working in this fashion until you reach the long wall. Use a piece of plywood to distribute your weight over the boards you've already laid. Don't forget to leave a ¼-inch gap between the wall and flooring to allow for expansion. Once you've finished this section, go over it with a floor roller.

Remove the temporary 2×4 and begin working on the other side of the room by setting the next row tightly against the first. The last row may not fit perfectly. Simply cut it to fit, being sure to leave the ¼-inch gap. Finish by going over the floor with the floor roller.

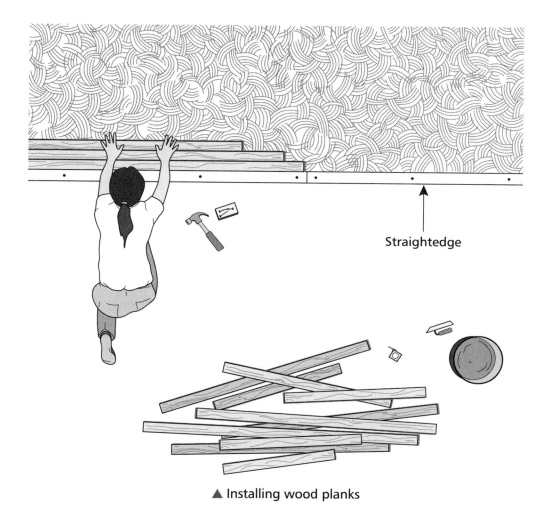

Straightedge

▲ Installing wood planks

Ceramic Tile

There are many different beautiful styles and designs of ceramic tiles, in a variety that gives you plenty of creative license. They also come in many shapes and sizes, including strips, rectangles, squares, and hexagons. Because glazed ceramic tiles are waterproof, they are most often used in bathrooms and kitchens. You should always purchase glazed tiles for flooring as unglazed tile will absorb water. Installing ceramic tile is another good do-it-yourself project, but you need to work slowly and carefully to make sure the finished product looks professionally installed.

Ceramic tiled floors require an underlayment installed over the subflooring. Laying ceramic tile requires a subfloor and underlayment combined thickness of 1¼ inches; this helps prevent floor deflection, which can contribute to the cracking of grout. Install the underlayment (as described in the section on vinyl flooring titled Preparing the Area, on page 229). Drive the nails so that their heads are slightly below surface level. Once the underlayment is smooth, level, and clean, you can begin installing the ceramic tile.

Installing the Tile

Starting at the most visible corner of the room, lay out dry tiles to find the best working pattern. This may take a little trial and error, but is better done now before the adhesive is applied. Make sure all borders are at least a half-tile wide. If they aren't, move the row to the left or right a half-tile's width.

If the corner is square, you can start right there. If not, you'll need to temporarily nail down two 1×2s at a right angle a tile's width plus the width of two grout lines away from the walls. This will be your starting point. Spread the adhesive using a toothed trowel held at a 45-degree angle over an area you can cover in approximately thirty minutes. You want to be sure the adhesive doesn't set up before you have time to lay down the tile.

When laying out the tile, you can either align the joints of the tiles or stagger them. By staggering the joints, you are adding a little decorative value to the flooring. Aligning the joints makes the floor look nice and neat, but in order to achieve this effect, they must be perfectly aligned.

Working from the corner, lay the tile down in rows. Place a plastic spacer in between each tile. This spacer keeps the tiles aligned properly and allows room in between the tiles for the grout. When you reach the end of a row, you may need to cut the tile to fit. The best way to do this is to use a tile cutter. This tool ensures a straight cut with ease.

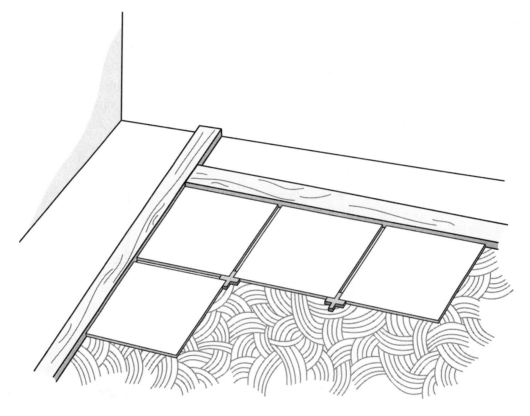

▲ Installing ceramic tile

Grouting

Grout is placed between the tiles to act as a sealant and to ensure that water is not able to seep in behind the tile. When shopping for grout, look for a color that complements the color and design of your tile. You will find that grout comes in many colors. If your tile has a very narrow grout line, it's best to use nonsanded grout. If the grout lines are wide, it's best to use sanded grout. If you are unsure, consult a professional at your local building supply company.

Using a grout trowel, spread the grout across a small area, making sure each grout line is completely filled. After you have covered the small area, go back over it with your grout trowel to remove any excess grout, and then wipe it down with a damp sponge. Make sure the area is clean of excess grout before moving on to the next small area. Once you have grouted the floor, allow it to dry for approximately thirty minutes. Then wipe it with a clean cloth. Run a margin trowel along the grout lines to push the grout in one last time. It's a good idea to put a grout sealer over the finished grout to prevent staining and to make it easier to clean.

▲ Spread grout with grout trowel

Carpeting

Carpet is another favorite choice of finish flooring for homebuilders. It is most often used in living areas, like bedrooms and family rooms. However, it's a good idea to use a different type of flooring for high-traffic areas or rooms where the flooring is likely to get wet. You have a wide selection of carpeting available to you. Visit your local supplier and browse through the many different colors and materials. The price varies depending upon the quality, durability, and strength. It's best to go for the best quality you can afford. Inexpensive carpets do not hold up well, and you will just end up having to replace it anyway before long.

ALERT!

If a member of your family has allergies, consider this before purchasing carpeting. Carpets are known to collect dirt and shelter dust mites. They also aren't as easy to clean as other types of finish flooring.

If you have experience installing carpet, by all means take this project upon yourself to save a little money. However, if you do not have experience, it is highly recommended that you not try this yourself. Laying carpet requires special tools, strength, and a skilled hand. Stretching the carpet properly and creating a seamless look is a job for professionals. Do yourself a favor. Spend a little extra money on installation and save yourself the frustration, time, and energy of trying to do this job yourself. (E)

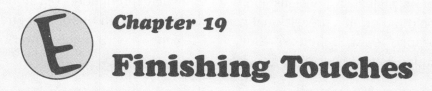

Chapter 19

Finishing Touches

Your house is complete. Now it's time to turn that house into your home. It's time to decide on the finishing touches and little things to express yourself and truly make your home unique. This chapter helps you explore and think about those important finishing touches.

Hiring an Interior Designer

Decorating a brand-new house can seem like an overwhelming project. There are so many decisions to make and so many choices for each decision! That's why many people hire an interior designer for part or all of the decorating challenge. An interior designer will help you select the colors, styles, and designs you want to display throughout your home. If you'd rather, this professional can also come up with the design and surprise you with the end result. The designer has as much power of choice as you choose to give.

Finding a Designer

When hiring an interior designer, make sure you find one with experience who comes with good recommendations. The best source is word of mouth. Ask around among your friends, family, and coworkers. Visit decorating stores, and ask the workers for recommendations. You can also always skim through the Yellow Pages. Regardless of how you get these names, it's important that you interview your candidates to find the best match for your budget and project.

QUESTION?

What's the difference between an interior designer and an interior decorator?
An interior designer has a formal degree in the field. An interior decorator doesn't have to have a formal degree in designing.

When interviewing interior designers, you'll need to ask several questions to get a feel for the person you may be working with as well as a good overview of the designer's experience. If a license is required in your state, get the designer's license number. Find out where he obtained formal training. Ask to look at the designer's portfolio. Ask for references, and check up on them. Find out if the designer belongs to any associations. Typically, designers belong to associations such as the American Society of Interior Designers (ASID), the Institute of Business Designers (IBD), or the International Society of Interior Designers (ISID).

Of course, you will also need to discuss money. You should have a budget set up for your decorating expenses. Show your budget to the designer. Find out whether your candidate can work within that budget and whether he has any ideas to help save money. Find out how the designer charges and how much. Some designers charge an hourly rate; others charge a percentage of how much they purchase. Some simply set a flat fee per project or per day.

Working with the Designer

Working with a designer can be a little intimidating. It's easy to think that you have to give complete control to the designer, who is after all the pro on the job. This isn't at all true. The interior designer wants to please you and thus will ask for your input. The designer should be someone you are comfortable speaking and brainstorming with. He will offer suggestions, but you should never feel as though you are under pressure to go with those ideas. Keep in mind that this is your home. You have to live in it, not the designer.

Look at decorating magazines and visit showcases to get an idea of what you like. Collect as many pictures as you can—from magazines, the Internet, and so on—so you can show the designer what you have in mind. Discuss the colors and patterns you would like to use. Talk about how each room will be used and what kind of feeling you want for the rooms. Also, let the designer know what pieces of your current furniture you intend to keep. The more information you can provide to the designer, the happier you are likely to be with the final result.

Buying Furniture

The furniture in your home has a tremendous impact on the style, overall look, and function of each room. You will probably buy at least one new piece of furniture for your new home. Even if you decide to get a few more good years out of your current furniture, you should look to the future. Consider styles and designs you like that will complement the finishing touches you are adding to your home. Whether you will be buying furniture tomorrow or years from now, it's a good idea to plan ahead.

Design Decisions

Make several trips to furniture showcases and decorating retail outlets to get an idea of the different styles, colors, and patterns available. Take notes on any ideas that pop into your head and those pieces or styles that jump out at you. Also invest in several decorating, furniture, and home enhancement magazines. Clip out those pictures that strike you and any articles that pertain to your design ideas. Keep all your ideas and references in a folder to go through later, when your research is done and you're ready to make some decisions.

FACT

Furniture typically falls within five broad style categories: contemporary, country, casual, traditional, and eclectic. A good way to narrow down your search is to decide which category best suits your taste and complements the house.

Typically, people purchase furniture that fits a particular style they like. For instance, if you like the elegance of Victorian style, you'll likely be looking for pieces and patterns that were common in that era. Or perhaps you like the charm of country-style living. In that case, you'll want to go with wooden furniture with floral or checkered patterns. Maybe you like the contemporary look of bold colors and metal frames. If you are unsure which style appeals to you, figure out the best fit for the home you've built. For example, a log cabin calls for the more rustic look of a country style, and a modern home will be complemented with contemporary style furniture.

Buy Smart

Create a budget for your furniture purchases. This will make you more selective and help you stay in control. Unless you fall completely in love with a piece and simply can't leave the store without it, don't buy anything the first time you see it. It's best to make note of it and do a little more shopping before making any final decisions. Keep in mind that you'll want your furniture to last for years. You should be sure that you'll be happy with its style and design for a long time. Comparison shopping is a must. Consider cost, quality, durability, and function as you look at each piece.

Make a list of priorities. For instance, let's say your bedroom suite is in good shape and still stylish, but you don't have a table for the dining room. Obviously, you'll want to shop for the dining room suite before looking at new bedroom suites. Keep control of your spending, and get those pieces you need the most right now. If you can't afford all you need or want right now, make up a budget for future purchases.

Painting the Walls and Ceilings

Another decorating decision you'll need to make is whether to paint the walls and/or ceilings. Adding color to a room can really make a significant difference in its overall look and feel. You'll want to select a color that complements the function and personality of the room and the style of furnishings in it. Painting isn't a difficult job, and most people find that they enjoy doing the work themselves.

Types of Paint

Visit any building supply store or home center, and you'll see that there are a variety of paints to choose from. Which is best? Oil-based paints are more resistant to wear, but cleanup from the job is more difficult and requires a solvent. They are typically used on walls or ceilings that will need frequent washing. Latex paints are the most popular for walls and ceilings. They are easy to apply and clean up easily with soap and water.

ALERT!

If you will be using several gallons of one color, combine them all into one large container. By doing this, you will ensure that the pigments are all mixed and you will end up with one uniform color.

You'll also have to choose between finishes. Paints come as primers, gloss, flat, and semi-gloss. Primers are used as the base coat. They seal the surface and ensure that the finish coats are absorbed evenly. Gloss paints are water-repellent and thus are often used in kitchens and bathrooms. Flat paints have more pigment than gloss paints and therefore aren't as resistant to wear. They cover better than the other paints, and they are often used on ceilings and walls in rooms that do not require the water-repellent properties of gloss paints.

Prep the Area

Prep work is extremely important. You can't just grab a brush and a bucket of paint and expect the outcome to look professional. First, you must remove everything from the ceiling and walls, including switch and outlet plates and light fixtures. Next, clean the walls and ceilings. Using a vacuum cleaner or a cotton cloth, make sure there is no debris or dust on the area to be painted. Put a dropcloth down to protect the floor, and use masking tape to cover the windows, woodwork, and trim. Finally, apply a primer coat. This will seal the area and keep the drywall from absorbing the paint.

Applying the Paint

Paint application is done in two steps: cutting in and rolling. Cutting in is done first. In this step, you will use a 3- or 4-inch brush to paint all edges where a roller cannot reach—where the ceiling and walls intersect, next to trim, and next to baseboards. Paint a band along these edges, being careful to not get paint on any woodwork.

Your brushes will last a long time if you take good care of them. Always wash them well after use. If you are using oil-based paints, clean the brush with paint thinner. If using latex paints, you can wash the brush in soapy water. Allow it to dry completely, and then store it back in its wrapper.

Once you have finished cutting in, use a roller to paint the open spaces. Always paint the ceiling before you start on the walls so that any drips that fall on the walls can be covered later. To paint the ceiling, use a roller with an extension pole. Saturate the roller with the paint from the paint pan, and then roll it along the washboard to get rid of the excess paint that could drip. Roll the paint along the ceiling or wall in a slow, methodical fashion. Be careful to not roll too fast or haphazardly, or the paint will splatter. Try to paint in 3-foot squares at a time. Use V-shaped strokes first, and then go back over the unpainted areas, overlapping each V-shaped stroke slightly. Be sure to cover the area evenly.

▲ Painting with V-shaped strokes

When you need to reload with paint, start a new section. Using the V-shaped strokes, bring it in to the border of the area you just covered and then back out, covering the entire area completely and evenly.

Overlap the cut-in areas, but be careful not to hit the edges. If you have used a primer, one coat of quality paint should be sufficient, but if it looks thin, apply a second coat in the same manner as the first.

Wallpapering

Wallpapering is another good do-it-yourself project. There is a huge variety of color and patterns available. Plan to spend a lot of time looking through wallpapering books to find the pattern and color that best complements the room and your style preferences. Once you find the paper you like best, be sure to order more than enough to cover the entire room at once. Also make sure that all the rolls have the same run number. This ensures that the rolls were all made at the same time and the colors are exactly the same. If you have to go back later to order more paper from a different stock, the pattern may be the same, but the colors may be slightly off. Also be sure to order the prepasted type of paper. This has an adhesive on the back and will make the application process much easier and cleaner.

Prep Work

Remove all outlet and switch plates from the walls. Clean the walls with a vacuum or a cotton cloth. It's important that there isn't any debris or dirt on the wall—if there is, you run the risk that it will show through the wallpaper. You may need to apply a primer or sizing (a paint-like substance that dries tacky) to the wall before applying the wallpaper. Talk to your supplier to find out if this is needed.

You'll want to make sure the wallpaper is hung plumb. Even the slightest variance will show up drastically. To ensure this, measure out from a corner 1 inch less than the width of the wallpaper and draw a line from top to bottom that is plumb. This will be your guideline.

Next you'll need to cut the paper. To ensure a tight fit, allow for at least 2 inches extra at the top and bottom of the paper (this will be trimmed away later). Decide where you want to cut the pattern on the paper at the top where it will fit up against the ceiling. Use a straightedge and a utility knife with a sharp blade to cut the paper.

FACT

If you have not purchased prepasted paper, you have to apply a wallpaper paste before applying the wallpaper. Consult your supplier about the proper procedure for applying the paste.

If you have purchased prepasted wallpaper as recommended, you'll need to soak the wallpaper in water before applying it. Roll up the paper with the pattern on the inside, and place it in a tray of lukewarm water. Follow the manufacturer's instructions for the amount of time it needs to soak. When you remove the paper, unroll it and then fold the ends in towards the middle with the pasted sides touching. Allow the paper to cure for the amount of time as specified by the manufacturer.

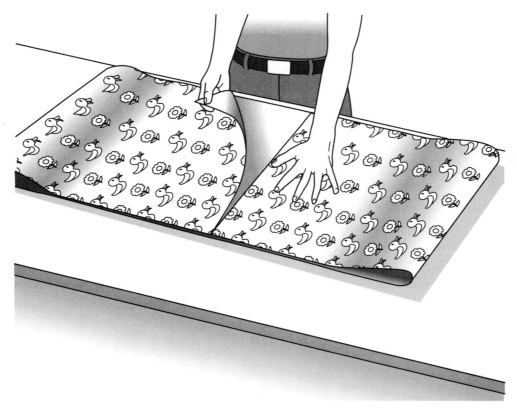

▲ Fold the wallpaper after soaking

Applying the Wallpaper

Unfold the top portion of the paper and align it with the plumb mark on the wall. Lap the excess inch into the corner; this will be cut away later. Using a wallpaper brush, stroke the paper from the corner out to the outside edge of the paper. Smooth the paper, and get rid of all air bubbles. Work your way down the wall, using the wallpaper brush to secure the paper and get rid of all bubbles. Keep an eye on your plumb mark to make sure the paper remains aligned. Once the upper portion is finished, unfold the bottom portion and position it on the wall using your hands. Secure it to the wall with the wallpaper brush, just as you did for the upper portion.

The following sheets will butt up tightly against the first, but the two will not overlap. Make sure you cut the paper to allow for pattern matching. Apply the second sheet just as you did the first, making sure you leave no gaps in the seam. After the second sheet has been applied, wait about a half hour and then go over the seam with a seam roller to secure the seams in place. You can now go back to the first sheet and trim the excess off the top and bottom with a sharp utility knife. Continue in this manner all along the wall.

Always allow for an excess of 1 inch to overlap into the corners. When the sheets are set up, you can go back and use a utility knife to cut down along the corner and remove the excess strips. This way you make sure that the paper butts up tightly at the corner seams.

To wallpaper around windows and doors, press the paper up loosely against the trim. Cut the paper to allow for a 2-inch excess. Once the paper has set up, you can go back and cut the excess away from the trim. Cover outlets and switches completely with the paper. Again, once the paper has set up, go back and make diagonal cuts to remove the excess paper.

Paneling

Many people choose to install wood-faced paneling in one or more rooms of the house to add a touch of elegance and variety. There are many patterns, styles, and wood types of paneling to choose from. Usually darker wood paneling is installed in rooms that are already bright and sunny. The lighter wood paneling is installed in rooms that are on the darker side. Use your best judgment, and choose a style of paneling to suit the room and your tastes.

Installing wood-faced paneling isn't all too difficult. The panels typically come in 4×8 sheets, though you can also find them in 4×10 and 4×12 sizes. Paneling is almost always installed vertically and covers drywall. Make sure the floor and ceiling are marked to show the location of the wall studs.

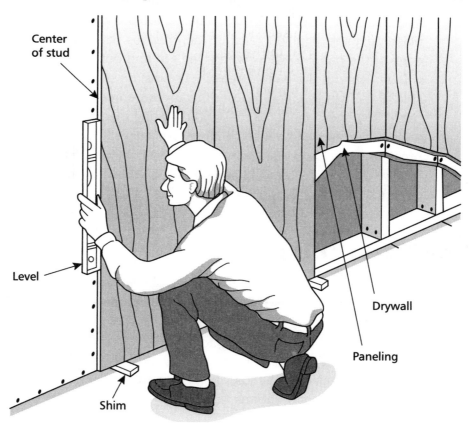

▲ Make sure the panels are plumb

The first panel should be installed in the most visible corner. The edge of the panel must fall on a stud, so figure out if you need to cut the panel before installing it. Fit the panel flush against the ceiling, and use shims to leave a small gap between the bottom of the panel and the floor. This gap will later be covered by the baseboard trim. Drive nails every 6 inches along the perimeter of the panel and every 8 inches in the middle. Always check to make sure the paneling is plumb. Because most wood-faced panels have recessed lines, you'll be able to notice very easily if the panels aren't plumb. Fit the next panel up against the first and nail it in place. Follow this in sequence all along the wall. You will probably need to cut the last panel to fit.

You'll need to cut the paneling to fit around windows, doors, switches, and outlets. To install paneling around windows and doors, place the panel tightly up against the previous panel, and mark the edge of the panel to show where the top and bottom of the opening will be. Remove the panel. Measure the distance from the mark to the side of the window, and transfer this measurement to the back of the panel. Use these marks to make your cutting marks. To install paneling around switches and outlets, outline their edges with colored chalk and press the panel into place, covering the switch or outlet. When you remove the panel, you will have a colored outline of the opening you need to cut.

The Little Things

In addition to those projects mentioned above, several other small projects will add the final finishing touches to make your house your home.

Here's a list to start with:

- Curtains, valances, blinds, and decorative curtain rods
- Book and display shelves
- Mirrors
- Lamps and other lighting

- Wall decorations (pictures, paintings, sconces, and so on)
- Area rugs
- Plants (along with hangers and stands)
- Framed pictures
- Statues, sculptures, and other decorative pieces of art
- Candles, vases, and other decorative items

These little things come together and give your home its individual style, so don't neglect or underestimate them.

Chapter 20
Decks

Building a deck is a very satisfying do-it-yourself project that can be completed on weekends—even in one weekend, for that matter. After building a house, building a deck will seem like child's play. However, you need to know a little of what you are doing to create a beautiful outdoor living space that will last for years.

Planning for a Deck

You can build a deck now to enhance the beauty of your newly built home, or you can add one on later. Either way, you'll need to plan carefully. Take a drive, and look at other decks in the area. Look through books and magazines about decks. Watch a couple of videos on how to build a deck. Are there any designs that appeal to you? What is it that you like about those that catch your eye? What don't you like? Get a general idea of what type of deck you think would be both aesthetically pleasing and complement your house.

Consider Function

The way the deck will be used is an important consideration and will determine its size and location. What do you plan to do with the deck? Do you want it to be an area where you can entertain guests? Do you plan to put a grill and tables and chairs on it? Perhaps you want a place to sit with a cup of coffee where you can enjoy the peaceful mornings before the chaos of the day sets in. Maybe you want just an area large enough to hold a couple of plants and a place to kick off your shoes before stepping inside.

ALERT!

Always check your local building codes before constructing a deck. You may need to obtain a permit before you can begin building. If so, ask the clerk at the permit office what your deck plans need to detail in order to obtain the permit.

Once you figure out how you want to use the deck, you'll next need to think about how large the deck should be to accommodate its function. Keep in mind that the larger the deck, the smaller the yard space. Location is another important consideration in regard to function. If you want to use the deck as a place to kick back and enjoy the view, then the deck needs to be positioned to get the best view possible. Do you want the deck to come off the side, back, or front door? Do you want the deck to wrap around some or all of the house? If you plan to entertain on the deck, where should you position it to get the most privacy possible?

Design Elements

When you've figured out function, size, and location, it's time to get down to the details. What kind of railings do you want on the deck? Do you want built-in benches along the railings? Should the deck be partially or completely covered, or remain open? Where do you want the stairs to be located? What kind of decorative elements would you like to add to the deck, if any? What type of material do you want to use for the decking? Make a list of those design elements you want to include, and then start pricing them. If you aren't able to afford all you want now, don't despair; you can always add more later.

Ledger and Foundation

When attaching a deck to the house, you'll need to first install a ledger. The ledger is a joist that is attached to the house to serve as the header joist for the deck framing. The deck needs to be 1 inch lower than the finished floors of the house. This ensures that water from the deck doesn't spill into the house. Plus, it's more pleasing to step down onto the deck from the house. The deck boards that will be nailed on top of the ledger will be 1½ inches thick. Therefore, you need to position the ledger 2½ inches lower than the finished floors. The easiest way to find the location of the ledger is to measure down from a window to the finished floor inside the house and then transfer that measurement to the outside of the house, measuring down from the same window. Add another 2½ inches from that mark, and you have the height of the ledger.

Use the straightest, most perfect board you can find to use as the ledger. Any bows or curves in the ledger will result in bows or curves in the deck. If you cannot find a straight board long enough to extend the entire length, you can use two boards, but it's best if each measure at least 6 feet.

The length of the ledger will be the width of the deck minus 3 inches. This allows 1½ inches on either side of the ledger for the end joists, which are 1½ inches thick each. Make a mark on the exterior of the house where the ledger will be attached. Make sure this line is straight and level.

Installing the Ledger

Attach the ledger to the house using lag screws. Predrill holes in the ledger every 16 inches. Temporarily nail the ledger to the house. Once you've made sure it is level, mark the wall where each of the lag screw holes were drilled. Remove the ledger, and predrill holes in the wall. You'll need to leave a gap of ½ to ¾ inch between the ledger and the wall to allow water to run down to the ground. The easiest way to do this is to stack an appropriate number of washers on the lag screws between the wall and the ledger. Squirt a little bit of caulking into each hole, and then install the ledger with the lag screws, making sure the washers are tight up against the wall and the screws go into solid wood. As the ledger will most likely be at the same level as floor joists of the house, this shouldn't be a problem.

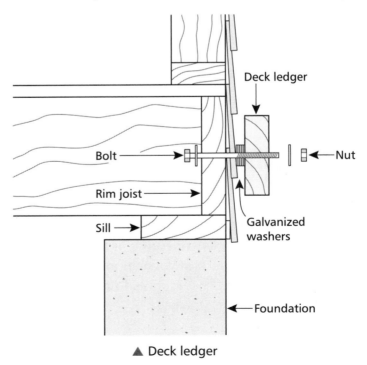

▲ Deck ledger

Installing the Outer Joists

Once the ledger is secured, you can attach the two outer joists to it. It's best if these two joists are the straightest of the remaining joists. If they do have a bow, make sure it points up. The weight of the deck and gravity will help it to straighten out. Have someone hold the loose end of the joist and drive three or four nails into the joist through the end of the ledger. Set up a temporary stake to hold the end of the joist at a right angle to the ledger. Secure the other joist in the same manner. Make sure the joists are level and at exactly a 90-degree angle from the ledger. Nail temporary braces at a diagonal from the ledger to the joists to make sure they do not move from position.

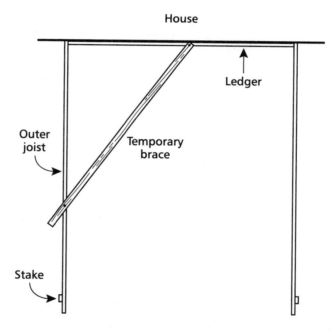

▲ Outer joists attached

Setting the Pier Blocks

Your deck plans and building codes will specify how many and where the pier blocks need to be placed for the foundation. Most deck plans allow for an overhang, which means the piers won't be located right at the end of the deck. Also, the piers are typically hidden beneath the deck, so they will be placed a couple of feet in from the outer joists. Refer to your plans for these exact measurements. Measure out from the wall along the outer joists to the measurement specified, and drive a nail at the mark. Run a piece of string attaching each end to the nails. Then measure in along the string from the outer joists, according to the measurements on your plan and mark the string. Use a plumb bob to make sure the center of the pier blocks are plumb to the marks on the string.

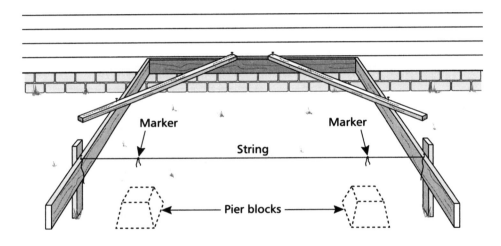

▲ String markers for location of pier blocks

QUESTION?

What is a plumb bob?
A plumb bob is a weighted object that is suspended from a string to find the true vertical. The weighted object typically comes down to a point that must be aligned with the center of the pier block.

Dig a hole for the pier blocks according to local code (typically 16 inches in diameter). Pour concrete into the hole and set the pier block in the concrete, making sure the base goes down at least 3 inches into the concrete. Use a plumb bob from the string to make sure the center of the pier block is plumb with the mark you made. You'll also need to make sure the pier block is level. Allow the concrete to harden according to the manufacturer's instructions.

Constructing the Deck

It's now time to actually build the deck itself. You need a frame to lay the deck boards on. This frame is built much like the frame for your house—with joists and girders. The girder will be set upon the pier block posts parallel with the ledger, and the joists will run perpendicular to the ledger and girder. The deck boards will run perpendicular to the joists. And then you have a deck! Sounds easy enough, right?

Cut the Posts to Height

The first thing you'll need to do is cut the posts for the pier blocks to the correct height. The posts will be at the same level as the bottom of the joists. Therefore, you can use the two outer joists you've already installed as a measurement guide. Remove the nails from the outer joists that held the string you used to find the location of the pier blocks. Move the string to the bottom of the joists and nail it in place. Now, simply measure from the top of the pier block to the string; this is the measurement you will use to cut the posts. If you'd like the deck to slope away a bit to ensure proper drainage, subtract ½ inch from the measurement. Cut the posts, and secure them to the pier blocks with post anchors.

Installing the Girder and Joists

The girder is a 4x6 that will be attached to the posts parallel with the ledger. Cut this board to be the length of the ledger plus 3 inches. Try to find as straight a board as you can. If the board has a bow (most do), make sure the bow is pointing up. Gravity and the weight of the deck will straighten it out over time. Toenail the girder to the tops of the posts, and reinforce it using metal fasteners with bolts.

The joists will run from the ledger to the girder. Mark the girder and the ledger to show where each joist will be attached. Joists are usually spaced 24 inches apart; refer to your deck plans for the proper measurements. You will attach the joists to the ledger with joist hangers. Nail one side of the joist hanger into the ledger. Then, once the joist has been positioned in the joist hanger, nail the other side into both the joist and the ledger. The other end of the joists will be toenailed into the girder. Make sure you position each joist so that the bow points up.

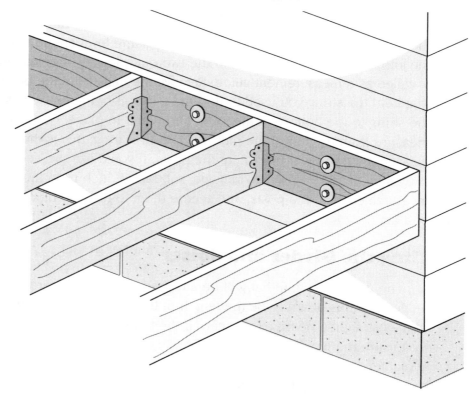

▲ Joist hangers for installing joists

Laying the Decking

You are now ready to lay the deck boards. This is a pretty easy task and doesn't take much time. Starting at the wall, lay the boards perpendicular to the joists. Try to find the straightest boards for this first row, as it will affect the straightness of the rest of the rows. Leave a small gap (approximately ¼ inch) between the first row and the wall and between each row of deck boards so that water can drain through. To ensure that the gaps are all evenly spaced, use a pencil or nail between the boards as your guide. You can allow the ends to go over one of the outer joists if you wish and then cut them off evenly later. Make sure you stagger the joints of the boards over different joists for adjacent rows. Nail the deck boards to the joists, using two nails at each end of the board.

Building the Stairs

Unless you want to jump from the deck to the ground, you'll need to install stairs. Building stairs can be a complicated task for the novice builder, so you may want to consult or hire an expert. However, if you are careful in your planning and execution, you can build the stairs yourself successfully.

Planning for Stairs

It's best if you sketch out your plan for the stairs including dimensions before beginning work. First figure out the total rise, or height, of the stairs. To do this, measure from the deck straight down to the ground. If the ground slopes down to where the bottom of the stairs will be located, you'll need to add in the number of inches of the slope. Once you have the total rise, you can figure out how many risers (the vertical part of the steps) you will need. Typically, risers measure about 7 inches. So, take the total rise and divide that by seven. Round that number off to the closest whole number. This is the number of risers you will need. Now, take the total rise again and divide it by the number of risers. This will give you the exact height of each riser. Sketch out your stairs according to these dimensions.

The construction of stairs is regulated by local building codes. While most codes are uniform, some have their own regulations and stipulations. Always be sure to check with your local codes before building.

Stairs typically have a tread (the horizontal part of the steps) of 11 inches. Use this and your sketch to find out what the total run, or distance from the front edge of the first tread to the back edge of the last tread, is for the stairs. If the tread width is 11 inches, multiply eleven by the number of treads. Check with your local building codes to see if there are restrictions on the stair width.

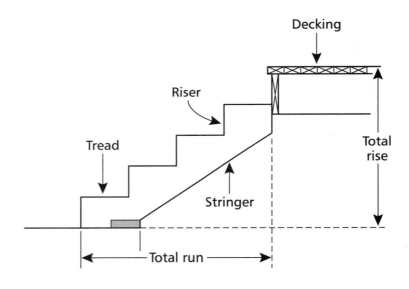

▲ Anatomy of stairs

Cut the Stringers

The stringers are the diagonal framing members that support the risers and tread on each side. You can usually cut 2×12s to be your stringers. Using the dimensions as outlined on your sketch, transfer the measurements of the risers and treads to the 2×12. The easiest way to do this is to use a square. Starting at the top, set one side of the square to equal the tread and the other to equal the riser. Mark this using pencil.

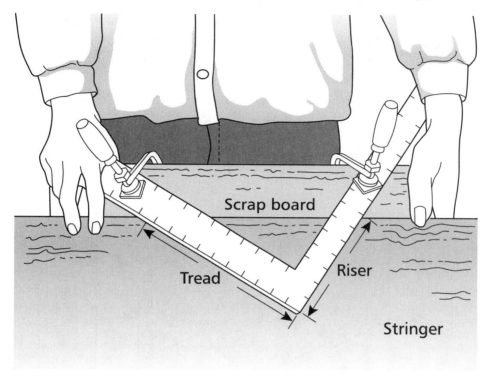

▲ Measuring and marking the stringer

Move the square so that the mark for the tread of the next stair intersects the mark for the riser of the first at the edge of the board. Repeat this until you have marked the 2×12 for the correct number of treads and risers. Use the square to make a level mark at the bottom of the stringer and a plumb mark at the top. Remember that the treads you will be installing are 1½ inches thick, and you have to account for this extra height on the first tread. Simply cut 1½ inches off the bottom of the stringer; this will ensure that each riser will be the same height.

Cut along your marks. Use this stringer as a template for the other. If the stairs are 36 inches wide, then you'll need to use three stringers. If the width is less than that, you can use just the two. Mark the second stringer along the cuts of the first, and then cut it out.

Install the Stringers and Tread

Install the top of the stringers to the deck using joist hangers. Make sure that the stringers are level both on their own and with each other. Cut a 2×4 the width of the stairs, and attach the bottom of the stringers to this. If you have a concrete landing, this board can be attached to the landing with concrete anchors.

Use two 2×6s for the tread. Hold the first flush against the riser cut, and nail it into place. Allow a ¼-inch gap between the two boards for water to drain through. Nail the second 2×6 into place. Complete the rest of the treads in the same manner.

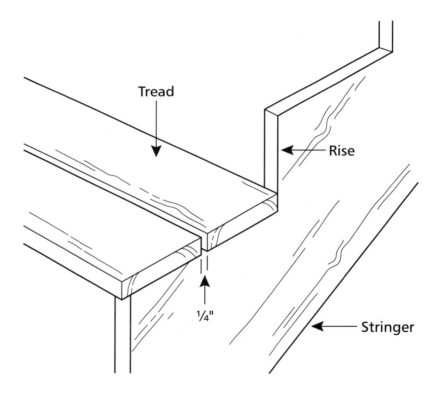

▲ Stair tread installed

Railings

There are several different styles and designs of railings to choose from. If you have a covered deck, the railings may extend all the way up to the roof framing. If the deck is uncovered, then the railing may only be 36 inches tall. You can allow the balusters to extend all the way down to the deck or fall short of the deck a few inches. You can opt to have both top and bottom rails or just top rails. Whatever railing design you choose, make sure it is installed for stability above all else. You certainly don't want anyone to lean up against the railing only to fall through to the yard.

If you would like (or are required by local codes) to install a handrail for your stairs, make sure it matches the railings on the deck. Installing a handrail is basically the same process as installing the deck railings, except each baluster needs to be individually measured.

Most building codes regulate the installation of railings. For instance, if your deck is a certain distance off the ground (distances vary by codes), then a railing is required. Some codes regulate the gap between balusters (typically, between 4 and 8 inches) so that children cannot slip through them. Sometimes, codes require that the balusters run horizontally. Most codes stipulate that the height of the railing, if required, is between 36 and 42 inches. Be sure to check your local building codes before installing the railing.

Weatherproofing

Because decks are left exposed to the elements, untreated wood doesn't last as long as it could. It's a good idea to treat your deck with a transparent water repellent. This not only seals your deck, protecting it from the elements, but it also helps the wood keep its natural coloring. Water repellent is applied like paint, and you can use a brush or roller. It goes on easily and is absorbed quickly. However, you'll need to make sure that the wood is completely dry before applying the water repellent. If the wood is already saturated with moisture, the repellent won't be absorbed. Apply two coats for maximum protection. Allow the first coat to penetrate the wood, but don't let it dry completely before applying the second coat. Visit your local building supply store or home center, and consult a professional for the proper type of water repellent to use on your deck. E

Appendices

Appendix A
Homebuilding Resources

Appendix B
Glossary

Appendix A

Homebuilding Resources

Books

Be Your Own House Contractor, by Carl Heldmann

The Brand-New House Book, by Katherine Salant

Builder's Guide to Foundations and Floor Framing, by Dan Ramsey

Building Your Own House, by Robert Roskind

Carpentry and Building Construction, 5th Edition, by John Louis Feirer, Gilbert R. Hutchings, and Mark D. Feirer

Code Check: A Field Guide to Building a Safe House, by Redwood Kardon, Michael Casey, and Douglas Hanson

The Complete Guide to Contracting Your Home, by Dave McGuerty and Kent Lester

The Complete Guide to Designing Your Own Home, by Scott T. Ballard

Do-It-Yourself Housebuilding: The Complete Handbook, by George Nash

Habitat for Humanity: How to Build a House, by Larry Haun, et al.

Housebuilding: A Do-It-Yourself Guide, by Mary DeCristoforo and R. J. DeCristoforo

How to Design & Build Your Own House, by Lupe DiDonno and Phyllis Sperling

How to Plan, Contract and Build Your Own Home, by Richard M. Scutella and David Heberle

How to Plan, Subcontract and Build Your Dream House, by Warren V. Jaeger

The Owner-Builder Book, by Mark A. Smith and Elaine M. Smith

Association Web Sites

American Concrete Institute: www.aci-int.org

American Hardware Manufacturers Association: www.ahma.org

American Institute of Building Design: www.aibd.org

American Society of Heating, Refrigerating, and Air Conditioning Engineers: www.ashrae.org

American Society of Interior Designers: www.asid.org

Associated Builders and Contractors: www.abc.org

Associated General Contractors of America: www.agc.org

Contractor License Reference Site: www.contractors-license.org

Energy and Environmental Building Association: www.eeba.org

Home Builders Institute: www.hbi.org

International Code Council: www.bocai.org

Manufactured Housing Institute: www.manufacturedhousing.org

National Association of Home Builders: www.nahb.com

National Electrical Contractors Association: www.necanet.org

National Fire Protection Association: www.nfpa.org

National Roofing Contractors Association: www.nrca.net

National Tile Contractors Association: www.tile-assn.com

National Wood Flooring Association: www.woodfloors.org

Plumbing-Heating-Cooling Contractors Association: www.phccweb.org

Vinyl Siding Institute: www.vinylsiding.org

Glossary

adjustable-rate mortgage:
A loan in which the interest rate and monthly payments change periodically according to a standardized index.

air return:
Ducts that carry old air back to the heating and air conditioning system to be cleaned and conditioned.

air supply:
Ducts that transport conditioned air to the rooms of the house.

anchor bolt:
A bolt that is used to secure the sill to the foundation.

apron:
Trim that is placed against the wall directly beneath the window's sill.

awning window:
Windows that are hinged at the top and that typically open outwards, though some models do open inwards.

backfill:
Excavated soil that is replaced into the trench around and against the house's foundation.

backsplash:
A small strip attached to the back of a countertop that rests against the wall to protect the wall against stains and water.

baluster:
The vertical member of a railing.

band:
The perimeter of the joist system, made up of the header joists and the first and last joists.

base cabinet:
A cabinet that is secured to the floor and that typically supports a countertop or appliance.

baseboard:
A board that is placed at the base of the wall to cover the intersection of the wall and flooring.

batt insulation:
Type of insulation that comes in precut sheets of insulation, typically with a paper backing.

batter boards:
Three wooden stakes (usually 2×4s) connected with horizontal cross members (usually 1×4s), creating a right angle used to mark a corner of the foundation outline.

bay window:
A type of window that projects outward from the wall.

blanket insulation:
Type of insulation that comes in large rolls. Must be cut to size; typically has a paper backing.

blown-in insulation:
Type of insulation that is loose and comes in bags. It must be poured or blown into spaces.

bridging:
Wood or metal placed between the joists either perpendicularly or diagonally to add rigidity to the frame and brace the joists.

builder's risk insurance:
Insurance that protects your homebuilding project from natural events that damage your property, such as tornadoes, hailstorms, or hurricanes. It also often covers the losses from theft, fire, and injury on your property.

building code:
Legal requirements for the construction of a building or structure.

cable:
A conductor that consists of two or more wires wrapped in an outer covering of insulation.

cable stripper:
An electrician's tool that cuts cable but ensures that wire coatings are not cut.

casement window:
A type of window that is hinged on the side and that typically opens outwards, though some models do open inwards.

caulk:
A material used to seal a joint to keep it water-tight and airtight.

change order:
A legal document that details the change to the building plans that is to be made and will be signed by both the owner and the contractor making the change.

circuit:
A path of electricity flowing from the breaker box to the fixture and back to the breaker box.

circuit breaker:
A safety mechanism designed to shut off the flow of electricity in the event of an overload or short.

closed overhang:
An overhang that has its underside restricted from view by a soffit material.

compressor:
On an air conditioner, the pump that moves the refrigerant between the evaporator and condenser, aiding the transfer of the heated air outdoors.

concrete:
A substance made up of cement, sand, and gravel that when mixed with water, poured, and allowed to set, becomes a strong, durable, and long-lasting material that holds up well to wear and weather.

condenser:
On an air conditioner, the hot outdoor coil that releases the captured heat into the outside air.

construction loan:
A short-term loan that is used to finance the building of a house.

continuous wall foundation:
A type of foundation that consists of a continuous wall along all sides of the house. The most common type of foundation.

contract:
A legally binding document that secures a promise made from one party to the other.

convertible loan:
A loan that includes both the construction loan and the home mortgage. The construction loan is given first, and then, when the project is finished the construction loan is rolled over into a permanent loan, or home mortgage. Also known as a construction permanent loan.

coped joint:
The type of joint often used on pieces of trim that have shaped profiles. This type of joint ensures that the two pieces of trim fit together to create a tight fit.

cornice:
The section between the edge of the roof and the exterior of the house, made up of the soffit and fascia board. Also called overhang or eave.

cost estimate:
A document that details the estimated costs for all phases of construction, including materials and labor.

cripple stud:
Shortened studs used for support between the plates above the headers and below the rough sills.

dehumidifier:
A device that pulls the excess moisture out of the air in your home.

direct heat system:
A heating system in which a furnace heats the heat exchanger and then blows the resulting warm air through the ductwork into the living areas.

double-hung window:
A type of window in which both sashes can slide open vertically—the bottom half slides up and the top half slides down.

drain/waste/vent (DWV) system:
Part of the plumbing system responsible for removing the used water and waste from the house.

draw:
An amount of money that is paid to you from the construction account. The amount of the draw will vary according to the amount of work that has been done.

drip edge:
A piece of metal attached to the edge of the roof that directs water to the outer edge instead of allowing it to find its way into the roofing material and/or into the house.

drywall:
Gypsum core sandwiched between two pieces of heavy-gauge paper. Often used to finish walls and ceilings.

ductwork:
The transportation system for your HVAC system. It is comprised of ducts that circulate the conditioned air in the house.

eave:
The section between the edge of the roof and the exterior of the house, made up of the soffit and fascia board. Also called overhang or cornice.

electrical box:
Boxes, typically made of metal, that hold the electrical wires coming from/to receptacles and switches.

evaporator:
On an air conditioner, the cold indoor coil that pulls heat out of the house, using the refrigerant.

excavation:
Removing soil from the building site to prepare for the building of the foundation.

fascia board:
A board that is nailed to the edge of the overhang.

finish flooring:
The flooring that will be laid on top of the subflooring. The most common types of finish flooring are vinyl, wood, ceramic tile, and carpeting.

fixed window:
A type of window that is permanently fixed in its frame and does not open.

fixed-rate mortgage:
A loan with an interest rate that doesn't change throughout the life of the loan.

flashing:
A material (usually metal or roofing felt) used at the joints of surfaces to keep water from entering.

foam insulation:
Type of insulation that comes as foam boards and is often applied as exterior sheathing. Also called rigid insulation.

footings:
A concrete base that supports the walls of the foundation.

forms:
A temporary device typically made of wood that is used to form concrete into a particular shape until it dries.

foundation:
The part of the house responsible for supporting and stabilizing the rest of the structure.

fuse:
Small piece of metal that is found in an encasement where a current passes into a circuit. It is designed to interrupt the flow of electricity if a circuit is carrying too much electricity for too long of a time.

gable:
The vertical, triangular part of the exterior wall extending from the overhang to the peak of the roof.

gable vent:
Louvered vents that are installed in the gable end of the roof.

gauge:
A unit of measurement that indicates a wire's size and electrical capacity.

girder:
A large beam of wood or steel that provides midspan support for the joists in the house's frame.

graduated-payment mortgage:
A loan that starts out with a low interest rate and monthly payments and then increases gradually.

greenboard:
Water-resistant drywall, named for its green paper facing.

gussets:
Steel plates that are attached at the joints to hold the components of a truss together.

gutter:
A channel attached to the overhang that collects the runoff from the roof and carries it along to downspouts that direct it away from the house.

H-clip:
A metal clip used to attach two rows of roof sheathing.

header joist:
One component of the band. A joist that runs perpendicular to the joists of the frame.

heat pump:
Both a heating and cooling system combined into one unit. It is essentially just a regular air conditioner; however, it has a valve that can be switched to reverse the flow of the refrigerant.

home mortgage:
A long-term loan that pays off the construction loan using the real property as security.

horizontal sliding window:
A type of window that is typically made up of two sashes (though some styles will have more) that slide open horizontally on a track. Often, only one sash is able to open and the other is fixed.

housewrap:
Slick, lightweight material that keeps water and air from coming into the house, but allows water vapor to escape from inside.

humidifier:
A device that replenishes moisture to the air in your home.

HVAC system:
The system that controls the temperature and quality of the air in your home by providing heat, air conditioning, and ventilation as needed.

jalousie window:
A type of window made up of several horizontal slats of glass that are fitted together like the slats on Venetian blinds. The slats are tilted open to allow for ventilation.

J-channel:
Trim that goes around the tops and sides of doors and windows to hide the ends of the siding panels.

joist:
Parallel beams that provide the support for the floor.

king stud:
A stud that offers support to window and door frames. It is secured between the top and bottom plates and to the outside edges of the headers.

ledger:
A joist that is attached to the house and serves as the header joist for the deck framing.

lien:
A legal document that gives contractors and subcontractors the right to a portion of your property until their services have been paid for.

lien release:
A document that waives the contractor's rights to the lien once he has been paid.

loan-to-value ratio (LV):
A formula lenders typically use to determine an applicant's risk level. This is the ratio of the total value of the house and land to the loan amount. Most loans will not go higher than 90 percent of appraised value of the house.

main service panel:
The service panel from which the electricity is sent to various parts of the house. It houses the circuit breakers and fuses. Also called a breaker box.

mortgage payment-to-income ratio (MR):
A formula lenders typically use to determine an applicant's risk level. The principal, interest, taxes, and insurance of your monthly mortgage payment should be between 28 and 30 percent of your gross monthly income.

nailguard:
A metal plate that is placed over wires and pipes to protect them from being punctured by nails or screws.

open overhang:
An overhang that leaves the underside of the roof exposed.

overhang:
The section between the edge of the roof and the exterior of the house, made up of the soffit and fascia board. Also called eave or cornice.

pier foundation:
A type of foundation in which the house is supported by piers.

pigtailing:
A method of connecting two or more wires together to reduce the number of wires that need to be connected at the receptacle.

plate:
A horizontal member that will either be the top or bottom of a framed wall.

plywood:
A common construction material made up of layers of wood veneer joined with glue.

receptacle:
An outlet you plug your electrical devices into.

register:
A device through which the conditioned air enters a room from the ducts.

reveal:
The exposed part of a jamb, typically ¼ inch.

ridge vent:
Vents that span the length of the roof and are installed along the peak.

riser:
The vertical part of stairs.

roof louver:
Small, covered opening that serves as a vent in the roof.

roofing felt:
A material often used to sheathe the roof. Also called tar paper or builder's felt.

rotating window:
A type of window that pivots open from a central point in the window.

R-value:
A unit of measurement that indicates a material's level of resistance to heat flow. The higher the number given to the R-value, the more resistance of heat transfer it will offer.

sheathing:
Material used to cover the studs or rafters of a house.

sill:
The lowest wooden member of your house's frame. It sits on the foundation and gives support to the floor joists. Also called sill plate or mudsill.

slab foundation:
A type of foundation in which a concrete slab that serves as the house's foundation sits directly on the soil.

soffit:
The underside of the overhang of the roof.

soffit vent:
A louvered vent installed in the soffit of the roof. Soffit vents are designed to allow fresh air inside the roof but don't allow for proper elimination of hot air and moisture.

starter strips:
A long strip of metal with several precut slots to which the first course of vinyl siding is attached.

step flashing:
A type of flashing that is composed of several long, L-shaped pieces of metal that are overlapped to create a trough.

stringer:
The diagonal framing member of the stairs that supports the risers and tread on each side.

stucco:
An exterior covering made of sand, lime, and Portland cement.

subfloor:
A material, typically plywood, that is laid on top

of the joists to act as a platform while building. This will be covered by finished flooring.

supply system:
Part of the plumbing system responsible for bringing fresh water into your home.

switch:
Device that allows you to control the flow of electricity by turning it on or off.

T1-11:
Exterior plywood siding.

termite shield:
Metal shield installed between the foundation and sill that prevents termites from gaining access to the sill and framing.

toenailing:
A process of driving a nail in at a 60-degree angle to penetrate two pieces of wood that cannot otherwise be nailed directly.

total debt-to-income ratio (DR):
A formula lenders typically use to determine an applicant's risk level. The total of your monthly debt payments should be between 36 and 41 percent of your gross monthly income.

tread:
The horizontal part of the steps.

trim:
Finish material installed around openings, along the base of the wall, or to cover any other joints.

trimmer stud:
Studs placed on the inside of openings to support the headers.

truss:
A structure that consists of a pair of rafters attached to a bottom joist chord by webbing (short pieces of wood).

underlayment:
A material, typically plywood, that is placed beneath the finish flooring to provide a smooth, even, and firm base.

undersill trim:
Trim that fits beneath the windowsill and serves to both cover and lock the siding panel in place.

valley flashing:
A type of flashing composed of long strips of metal with a center crimp.

vapor barrier:
A material, typically polyethylene sheeting, installed to prevent moisture buildup in the attic and exterior walls where trapped moisture could cause the wood to rot.

wind turbine:
Sphere-shaped projections that are installed near the peak of the roof. They are designed with specially shaped vanes that will catch the wind, causing the turbine to spin and pull air out of the attic.

worker's compensation insurance:
A type of insurance that covers workers who might be hurt on the building site.

zoning laws:
Laws that restrict the use of particular areas of land. These laws also regulate the types of buildings that can be built there.

Index

THE EVERYTHING SERIES!

BUSINESS

Everything® Business Planning Book
Everything® Coaching and Mentoring Book
Everything® Fundraising Book
Everything® Home-Based Business Book
Everything® Landlording Book
Everything® Leadership Book
Everything® Managing People Book
Everything® Negotiating Book
Everything® Online Business Book
Everything® Project Management Book
Everything® Robert's Rules Book, $7.95
Everything® Selling Book
Everything® Start Your Own Business Book
Everything® Time Management Book

COMPUTERS

Everything® Computer Book

COOKBOOKS

Everything® Barbecue Cookbook
Everything® Bartender's Book, $9.95
Everything® Chinese Cookbook
Everything® Chocolate Cookbook
Everything® Cookbook
Everything® Dessert Cookbook
Everything® Diabetes Cookbook
Everything® Fondue Cookbook
Everything® Grilling Cookbook
Everything® Holiday Cookbook
Everything® Indian Cookbook
Everything® Low-Carb Cookbook
Everything® Low-Fat High-Flavor Cookbook
Everything® Low-Salt Cookbook
Everything® Mediterranean Cookbook
Everything® Mexican Cookbook
Everything® One-Pot Cookbook
Everything® Pasta Cookbook
Everything® Quick Meals Cookbook
Everything® Slow Cooker Cookbook
Everything® Soup Cookbook

Everything® Thai Cookbook
Everything® Vegetarian Cookbook
Everything® Wine Book

HEALTH

Everything® Alzheimer's Book
Everything® Anti-Aging Book
Everything® Diabetes Book
Everything® Dieting Book
Everything® Hypnosis Book
Everything® Low Cholesterol Book
Everything® Massage Book
Everything® Menopause Book
Everything® Nutrition Book
Everything® Reflexology Book
Everything® Reiki Book
Everything® Stress Management Book
Everything® Vitamins, Minerals, and
    Nutritional Supplements Book

HISTORY

Everything® American Government Book
Everything® American History Book
Everything® Civil War Book
Everything® Irish History & Heritage Book
Everything® Mafia Book
Everything® Middle East Book

HOBBIES & GAMES

Everything® Bridge Book
Everything® Candlemaking Book
Everything® Card Games Book
Everything® Cartooning Book
Everything® Casino Gambling Book, 2nd Ed.
Everything® Chess Basics Book
Everything® Crossword and Puzzle Book
Everything® Crossword Challenge Book
Everything® Drawing Book
Everything® Digital Photography Book
Everything® Easy Crosswords Book
Everything® Family Tree Book

Everything® Games Book
Everything® Knitting Book
Everything® Magic Book
Everything® Motorcycle Book
Everything® Online Genealogy Book
Everything® Photography Book
Everything® Poker Strategy Book
Everything® Pool & Billiards Book
Everything® Quilting Book
Everything® Scrapbooking Book
Everything® Sewing Book
Everything® Soapmaking Book

HOME IMPROVEMENT

Everything® Feng Shui Book
Everything® Feng Shui Decluttering Book, $9.95
Everything® Fix-It Book
Everything® Homebuilding Book
Everything® Home Decorating Book
Everything® Landscaping Book
Everything® Lawn Care Book
Everything® Organize Your Home Book

EVERYTHING® KIDS' BOOKS

All titles are $6.95

Everything® Kids' Baseball Book, 3rd Ed.
Everything® Kids' Bible Trivia Book
Everything® Kids' Bugs Book
Everything® Kids' Christmas Puzzle
    & Activity Book
Everything® Kids' Cookbook
Everything® Kids' Halloween Puzzle
    & Activity Book
Everything® Kids' Hidden Pictures Book
    Everything® Kids' Joke Book
Everything® Kids' Knock Knock Book
Everything® Kids' Math Puzzles Book
Everything® Kids' Mazes Book
Everything® Kids' Money Book

All Everything® books are priced at $12.95 or $14.95, unless otherwise stated. Prices subject to change without notice.

Everything® Kids' Monsters Book
Everything® Kids' Nature Book
Everything® Kids' Puzzle Book
Everything® Kids' Riddles & Brain Teasers Book
Everything® Kids' Science Experiments Book
Everything® Kids' Soccer Book
Everything® Kids' Travel Activity Book

KIDS' STORY BOOKS

Everything® Bedtime Story Book
Everything® Bible Stories Book
Everything® Fairy Tales Book

LANGUAGE

Everything® Conversational Japanese Book
(with CD), $19.95
Everything® Inglés Book
Everything® French Phrase Book, $9.95
Everything® Learning French Book
Everything® Learning German Book
Everything® Learning Italian Book
Everything® Learning Latin Book
Everything® Learning Spanish Book
Everything® Sign Language Book
Everything® Spanish Phrase Book, $9.95
Everything® Spanish Verb Book, $9.95

MUSIC

Everything® Drums Book (with CD), $19.95
Everything® Guitar Book
Everything® Home Recording Book
Everything® Playing Piano and Keyboards Book
Everything® Rock & Blues Guitar Book
(with CD), $19.95
Everything® Songwriting Book

NEW AGE

Everything® Astrology Book
Everything® Dreams Book
Everything® Ghost Book
Everything® Love Signs Book, $9.95
Everything® Meditation Book
Everything® Numerology Book
Everything® Paganism Book
Everything® Palmistry Book
Everything® Psychic Book
Everything® Spells & Charms Book
Everything® Tarot Book
Everything® Wicca and Witchcraft Book

PARENTING

Everything® Baby Names Book
Everything® Baby Shower Book
Everything® Baby's First Food Book
Everything® Baby's First Year Book
Everything® Birthing Book
Everything® Breastfeeding Book
Everything® Father-to-Be Book
Everything® Get Ready for Baby Book
Everything® Getting Pregnant Book
Everything® Homeschooling Book
Everything® Parent's Guide to Children
with Asperger's Syndrome
Everything® Parent's Guide to Children
with Autism
Everything® Parent's Guide to Children
with Dyslexia
Everything® Parent's Guide to Positive Discipline
Everything® Parent's Guide to Raising a
Successful Child
Everything® Parenting a Teenager Book
Everything® Potty Training Book, $9.95
Everything® Pregnancy Book, 2nd Ed.
Everything® Pregnancy Fitness Book
Everything® Pregnancy Nutrition Book
Everything® Pregnancy Organizer, $15.00
Everything® Toddler Book
Everything® Tween Book

PERSONAL FINANCE

Everything® Budgeting Book
Everything® Get Out of Debt Book
Everything® Homebuying Book, 2nd Ed.
Everything® Homeselling Book
Everything® Investing Book
Everything® Online Business Book
Everything® Personal Finance Book
Everything® Personal Finance in Your
20s & 30s Book
Everything® Real Estate Investing Book
Everything® Wills & Estate Planning Book

PETS

Everything® Cat Book
Everything® Dog Book
Everything® Dog Training and Tricks Book
Everything® Golden Retriever Book
Everything® Horse Book
Everything® Labrador Retriever Book
Everything® Poodle Book

Everything® Puppy Book
Everything® Rottweiler Book
Everything® Tropical Fish Book

REFERENCE

Everything® Car Care Book
Everything® Classical Mythology Book
Everything® Einstein Book
Everything® Etiquette Book
Everything® Great Thinkers Book
Everything® Philosophy Book
Everything® Psychology Book
Everything® Shakespeare Book
Everything® Toasts Book

RELIGION

Everything® Angels Book
Everything® Bible Book
Everything® Buddhism Book
Everything® Catholicism Book
Everything® Christianity Book
Everything® Jewish History & Heritage Book
Everything® Judaism Book
Everything® Koran Book
Everything® Prayer Book
Everything® Saints Book
Everything® Understanding Islam Book
Everything® World's Religions Book
Everything® Zen Book

SCHOOL & CAREERS

Everything® After College Book
Everything® Alternative Careers Book
Everything® College Survival Book
Everything® Cover Letter Book
Everything® Get-a-Job Book
Everything® Job Interview Book
Everything® New Teacher Book
Everything® Online Job Search Book
Everything® Personal Finance Book
Everything® Practice Interview Book
Everything® Resume Book, 2nd Ed.
Everything® Study Book

SELF-HELP/ RELATIONSHIPS

Everything® Dating Book
Everything® Divorce Book
Everything® Great Sex Book

All Everything® books are priced at $12.95 or $14.95, unless otherwise stated. Prices subject to change without notice.